SECM in Brooklyn 2010

Selected Papers from the

Fourth Biennial Conference of the

Society for Eighteenth-Century Music

at St. Francis College in

Brooklyn, NY, 8–11 April 2010

SECM in Brooklyn 2010

Topics in Eighteenth-Century Music I

Edited by Margaret R. Butler

and Janet K. Page

Steglein Publishing, Inc.
Ann Arbor

Steglein Publishing, Inc., Ann Arbor 48105

© 2014 by Steglein Publishing, Inc.
All rights reserved
Printed in the United States of America

Library of Congress Cataloging-in-Publication Data

Society for Eighteenth-Century Music biennial conference, (4th ; 2010 ; Brooklyn)
  SECM in Brooklyn, 2010 : topics in eighteenth-century music I / edited by Margaret R. Butler and Janet K. Page.
    pages cm
  Includes bibliographical references.
  ISBN 978-0-9819850-5-3 (alk. paper)
  1. Music--18th century--Congresses. I. Butler, Margaret Ruth, 1966-, editor of compilation. II. Page, Janet Kathleen, 1957-, editor of compilation. III. Society for Eighteenth-Century Music. IV. Title. V. Title: Society for Eighteenth-Century Music in Brooklyn, 2010.
  ML195.S75 2010
  780.9'033--dc23
                            2014004714

Cover Illustration

Henri-Horace Roland de la Porte (1724–1793): *Vase de Lapis, sphère et musette* (1763, Paris, musée du Louvre), used by permission

∞ This paper meets the requirements of ANSI/NISO
Z39.48-1992 (Permanence of Paper).

Contents

Preface	vii
Contributors	xi
Travels with *Hésione:* The *tragédie en musique* outside Paris, Anita Hardeman	1
A Missing Link? The Suite-Symphony in Mid-Eighteenth-Century North Germany, Joanna Cobb Biermann	22
"Ein Musikdirector hat an einem Instrumente Mangel": Obbligato Organ in the Bach Cantatas, Evan Philip Cortens	52
A Tale of Two Brothers: Friedemann and Emanuel Bach, David Schulenberg	78
Haydn's "Irregularities": Ambiguous Openings in the B-minor String Quartets, op. 33/1 and op. 64/2, Mathieu Langlois	103
Issues of Authenticity and Chronology in the Sacred Music of Leopold Hofmann, Allan Badley	131
Courting the Amorous Muse: The Instrumental Romance in the Music of Antonio Rosetti, Sterling E. Murray	159
Mozart's Quintet for Horn and Strings in E-flat Major, K. 407 (386c), in Two Arrangements for *Harmoniemusik* by Joseph Heidenreich, Peter Heckl	188

Musical Landskips: Scottish Songbooks in English Drawing Rooms,
Paul F. Moulton 211

Censoring the Censor: Karl Glossy's Selective Transcription (1897) of
Karl Hägelin's Directive on Viennese Theatrical Censorship (1795),
Lisa de Alwis 232

Preface

The fourth biennial conference of the Society for Eighteenth-Century Music was held at St. Francis College in Brooklyn Heights, New York, April 8–11, 2010. The conference was dedicated to the memory of H. C. Robbins Landon (1926–2009), eminent scholar of the music of Haydn and Mozart and an honorary member of SECM.[1] This volume contains a selection of papers read at the conference.

Anita Hardeman's "Travels with *Hésione*: The *tragédie en musique* outside Paris," is a case study of a single *tragédie en musique*, *Hésione* (1700), with text by Antoine Danchet and music by André Campra. Hardeman discusses the dissemination of *Hésione*, highlighting the challenges of producing the piece outside the Académie Royale de Musique and describing how the work was adapted to local tastes and circumstances.

Joanna Cobb Biermann posits the "suite-symphony," a North-German form centered on the court of Hessen-Darmstadt, as a "missing link" between the Italian sinfonia and the later four-movement symphony. The Darmstadt *Kapellmeister* Christoph Graupner and Johann Samuel Endler composed many such works in the mid-eighteenth century. These mix abstract and dance types, feature rich orchestration and *concertante* writing, make use of sonata form, and contain four or more movements.

Evan Cortens, in "'Ein Musikdirector hat an einem Instrumente Mangel': Obbligato Organ in the Bach Cantatas," discusses the ways in which Bach used the organ as an obbligato instrument, and his practices of substitution and rewriting. Working from autograph sources and other contemporary material, Cortens suggests that for Bach, the organ "served as an extension of himself, filling in where necessary" to bring the cantata to "perfect whole," a practice inextricably linked with the composer's own performance at the instrument.

"A Tale of Two Brothers: Friedemann and Emanuel Bach" by David Schulenberg explores the lives and the very different careers and music of two

---

1. Stephen C. Fisher reviews the conference in "2010 SECM Conference in Brooklyn Heights," *Newsletter of the Society for Eighteenth-Century Music* 16 (April 2010): 1, 11–12. This issue of the Newsletter also includes tributes to Landon by SECM members Charles Sherman and Paul Bryan.

brothers born within four years of each other and brought up in the same musical environment. Comparison of the two brothers' music reveals something of J. S. Bach's methods of musical instruction.

Mathieu Langlois, in "Haydn's 'Irregularities': Ambiguous Openings in the B Minor String Quartets, op. 33/1 and op. 64/2," examines the ambiguous opening as an aesthetic idea and as a compositional device. He explores how the opening gestures of the two quartets define the rest of each opening movement, and how Haydn creatively produces layers of meaning from these "focal points of invention."

Allan Badley addresses the difficult problems of authenticating and dating Leopold Hofmann's sacred works, which are preserved mostly in parts in the hands of copyists and show a complexity of variants. Working from musical manuscripts, catalogs, and other documents, Badley fills out Hofmann's biography and reconstructs his working repertory.

Sterling E. Murray's "Courting the Amorous Muse: The Instrumental Romance in the Music of Antonio Rosetti" examines Rosetti's commitment to the slow-movement Romance. Murray defines the Romance as a type, describes its appearance as a fad in Paris and its popularity at the Oettingen-Wallerstein court, and links Rosetti's continuing interest in the genre to his "special gift for pleasing melody" and the Romance's mingling of naïveté and sophistication.

Peter Heckl, in "W. A. Mozart's Quintet for Horn and Strings in E-flat Major, K. 407 (386c), in Two Arrangements for *Harmoniemusik* by Joseph Heidenreich," focuses on Heidenreich's transcriptions of ca. 1794, which must be considered the oldest surviving sources for the work, probably deriving from early copies. He explores Heidenreich's career, especially as composer and arranger, concluding that he was a solid musician active in Viennese musical circles, and that his arrangements thus provide useful evidence for reconstructing Mozart's version.

Paul F. Moulton examines Scottish songbooks published in the eighteenth century and explores the English attraction to Scottish songs in social and historical context. The books provided songs tamed to domestic music for drawing rooms, creating a sonic representation of Scotland like a framed "musical landskip" (landscape painting).

Lisa de Alwis's paper "Censoring the Censor: Karl Glossy's Selective Transcription (1897) of Karl Hägelin's Directive on Viennese Censorship (1795)" was awarded the 2010 SECM prize for the best student paper. De Alwis discusses a nineteenth-century manuscript transcription of Karl Hägelin's guidelines for censors of 1795. The manuscript reveals that Glossy, in his well-known published version of Hägelin's Directive, omitted discussion of many sensitive topics.

With thanks to Margaret Butler for chairing the program committee, to Suzanne Forsberg, local arrangements chair for the conference, and to Mark Knoll for all his work on the volume.

Janet K. Page, President
Society for Eighteenth-Century Music
January 2014

The conference included the following sessions and papers:

1. Genres and Developments: Narrative, Connections, Topoi
Neal Zaslaw, chair
Pierpaolo Polzonetti, "Haydn and Ovid's *Metamorphoses*"
Joanne Cobb Biermann, "A 'Missing Link'"?
Sterling E. Murray, "Courting an Amorous Muse: The Romance in the Instrumental Music of Antonio Rosetti (c. 1750–1792)"

2. Handel Revisited
David Schulenberg, chair
Andrew Shryock, "Scene Unseen: The Sublime Role of the Messenger in the mid 1740s"
Joseph Darby, "Revisiting the Early Performance History of Handel's Twelve Grand Concertos"

3. Contrasts and Transformations
Paul Corneilson, chair
David Schulenberg, "A Tale of Two Brothers: Friedemann and Emanuel Bach"
Charles Gower Price, "A Popular Source of Notated Embellishments and Cadenzas: The Handel Keyboard Transcriptions of William Babell"
Peter Heckl, "W. A. Mozart's Quintet for Horn and Strings in E-flat Major, K. 407 (386c) in Two Arrangements for *Harmoniemusik* by Joseph Heidenreich"

4. Neapolitan Developments
Bertil van Boer, chair

Keith Johnston, "A Newly Discovered Scene from Molière in the Intermezzo Repertory"

Anthony R. DelDonna "Opera, Antiquity and the Neapolitan Enlightenment in Paisiello's *Socrate immaginario* (1775)"

5. Venue and Context in French and Italian Opera
John A. Rice, chair

Anita Hardeman, "Travels with *Hésione*: The *tragédie en musique* outside Paris"

Erin Jerome, "Putting a Comic Work into *Seria* Context: Haydn's *La canterina*"

Roland Pfeiffer, "Two Important Private Collections of Manuscripts in Rome and Their Impact on Research in Late Eighteenth-Century Italian Opera"

6. Compositional Process and Form
Steven Zohn, chair

Evan Cortens, " 'Ein Musikdirector hat an einem Instrumente Mangel, und schreibt solche Melodie in den Continuo': Obbligato Organ in J. S. Bach's Cantatas"

Mathieu Langlois, "Haydn's 'Irregularities': Ambiguous Openings in the Quartets"

Edward Green, "A New Look at the Ployer/Attwood Notebooks—Or, Mozart: Teacher of Chromatic Completion"

7. Perspectives on Landscape
Therese Ellsworth, chair

Estelle Joubert, "Landscape and Time in Mozart's *Die Zauberflöte*"

Paul F. Moulton, "Musical Landskips: Scottish Songbooks in English Drawing Rooms"

8. Sacred and Secular in Late Eighteenth-Century Vienna and Beyond
Jane S. Hettrick, chair

Lisa de Alwis, "Censoring the Censor: Karl Glossy's Selective Transcription (1896) of Karl Hägelin's Directive on Viennese Theatrical Censorship (1795)"

Allan Badley, "Issue of Authenticity and Chronology in the Sacred Works of
    Leopold Hofmann"
Edgardo Raul Salinas, "Romantic Irony and the 'Neue Manier': Beethoven's
    Undoing of Form in the Piano Sonatas Opus 3"

Contributors

Allan Badley is a specialist in late eighteenth-century Viennese music whose publications include several hundred scholarly editions of works by major contemporaries of Haydn, Mozart, and Beethoven. Among the most significant of these are his editions of the complete works for piano and orchestra by Ferdinand Ries, mass settings by Wanhal, Hofmann and Hummel, and an extensive series of symphonies and concertos. He has published articles on Leopold Hofmann, Ignaz Pleyel and Haydn, and more recently, contributed analytical essays on the symphonies of Wagenseil and Pleyel for *The Symphonic Repertoire – The Eighteenth-Century Symphony* edited by Bathia Churgin and Mary Sue Morrow (Bloomington: Indiana University Press, 2012). Badley co-founded the now Hong-Kong based publishing house Artaria Editions in 1995, which is regarded as one of the leading specialist publishers in its field. His own editions have featured in over fifty critically-acclaimed recordings on the Naxos label. A graduate of the University of Auckland (PhD 1986), Badley is a Distinguished Alumni Award winner (2003) and in 2007 was awarded the Goldene-Pleyel-Medaille of the Internationale Ignaz Joseph Pleyel Gesellschaft (Austria). He is a member of the editorial boards of *Eighteenth-Century Music* and *Haydn*, and was recently elected Executive President of the Swiss-based Johann Baptist Wanhal Society. Badley has held academic appointments at Massey University (Wellington, New Zealand) and at the University of Auckland where he is currently Senior Lecturer in Musicology and Deputy Head of School.

Joanna Cobb Biermann is currently Associate Professor of Musicology at the University of Alabama, having previously taught at Indiana University and worked as a scholar at the Beethoven-Archiv in Bonn, Germany. She received her degrees from Barnard College (BA), Columbia University (MA), and the

Friedrich-Wilhelms-Universität, Bonn Germany (PhD). Her research interests include Beethoven, the eighteenth-century symphony, and music in Nazi Germany. Recently she finished two chapters for *The Symphonic Repertoire – The Eighteenth-Century Symphony* edited by Bathia Churgin and Mary Sue Morrow (Bloomington: Indiana University Press, 2012): an overview of the North German Symphony in that century, and a chapter on the early Darmstadt symphonist Johann Samuel Endler. Currently she is completing an edition of Beethoven's small piano pieces for the *Neue Gesamtausgabe* of the works of Beethoven (Series VII, Vol. 6). Work on this edition has been supported by a University of Alabama research grant (2008–2009) and a generous grant from the Thyssen Foundation of Cologne, Germany (2011).

Evan Cortens is a doctoral candidate in musicology at Cornell University, with a focus on eighteenth-century German music, and is currently completing a dissertation on the sacred cantatas of Christoph Graupner. He holds degrees in musicology from the University of Calgary (2006) and Boston University (2008) and his research interests include the computer-aided analysis of musical manuscripts. He has published in *Eighteenth-Century Music*, *Notes: Quarterly Journal of the Music Library Association*, *Keyboard Perspectives* and the *Newsletter of the Society for Eighteenth-Century Music* and his edition of Johann Samuel Schroeter's *Six Keyboard Concertos, op. 3* was recently published by A-R Editions.

Lisa de Alwis completed her PhD at the University of Southern California in 2012 with a dissertation on censorship and magical opera in early nineteenth-century Vienna. She has published several articles on music in eighteenth- and nineteenth-century Vienna, including, most recently, "Censoring *Don Juan*: Theater Censor Franz Karl Hägelin's Treatment of a Singspiel by Mozart," *Mozart Jahrbuch* 2012. In 2010 she received the award for the best student paper given at the SECM conference (which appears in this volume). She presented an invited talk at the Mozart Colloquium at Harvard University in 2012. She has received visiting-scholar grants from the Don Juan Archiv, Vienna and the Internationale Nestroy-Gesellschaft and fellowships from the Philanthropic Educational Organization and from the Graduate School of the University of Southern California. De Alwis has worked as the Editorial Assistant for the *Journal of the American Musicological Society* and has taught music history at the University of Nevada, Las Vegas, and the University of Colorado, Boulder.

Anita Hardeman completed her doctoral studies at the University of Western Ontario. Her area of specialization is French stage works of the *grand siècle*, specifically those of André Campra, with particular interest in intersections of music, text, movement, and staging. She has presented her research nationally and internationally and is currently researching depictions of Venus in French opera and ballet in the seventeenth and eighteenth centuries and preparing an edition of Campra's *Hésione*. She in on the faculty at Western Illinois University and has held teaching positions at the University of Western Ontario and Kenyon College in Ohio.

Peter Heckl completed his PhD dissertation, "Instrumental Compositions by Wolfgang Amadé Mozart in *Harmoniemusik* Arrangements from 1780 to 1840," at the University of Music and Dramatic Arts in Graz in 2011. A performer on both the natural and French horns, Heckl studied with Friedrich Gabler at the University of Music and Dramatic Arts in Vienna. Heckl is a member of the Graz Philharmonic Orchestra and also performs with the Concilium Musicum Wien, the Ensemble Harmonia Antiqua, and other ensembles. He is a teacher of French horn and directs several wind ensembles at the Johann-Joseph-Fux-State-Conservatory in Graz.

Mathieu Langlois is currently a PhD candidate at Cornell University, director of Cornell's early music ensemble, Les Petits Violons, and a part-time instructor at Syracuse University. An active performer on historical flutes, he holds degrees from the University of Western Ontario and The Royal Conservatory of The Hague. His research interests include eighteenth-century performance practices and aesthetics, music of the Berlin court under Frederick the Great, and musical pictorialism in French and German galant repertoire.

Paul Moulton is Associate Professor of Music and Assistant Dean of Faculty at The College of Idaho. He earned degrees from Brigham Young University (BA) and Florida State University (MM, PhD), completing his doctorate in 2008. Teaching a wide range of historical and education courses, Moulton is especially interested in music of the eighteenth and nineteenth centuries and the way it functioned in the lives of participants. His research projects concern representations of place in Scottish music and the way music informs personal and community identities.

Sterling E. Murray holds the PhD in musicology from the University of Michigan. Until his retirement in 2007 he was Chair and Professor of Music History in the School of Music at West Chester University. Murray was the founding president of the Society for Eighteenth-Century Music and recipient in 2005 of the society's Leadership Award. He is the editor of *Haydn and His Contemporaries* (Steglein Publishing, 2011), a collection of selected papers from the joint meeting of SECM and the Haydn Society of North America in Claremont, California in 2008. Murray is also author of *The Music of Antonio Rosetti (Anton Rösler) ca. 1750–1792: A Thematic Catalog*, and co-editor with Sonja Gerlach of *Sinfonien, 1782–1784* (Cologne, Germany: G. Henle Verlag, 2003), published as volume 11 in the *Joseph Haydn Werke* by the Joseph Haydn Institute. In 2006 Murray was a fellow of the John D. Rockefeller, Jr. Library in Williamsburg. He is a member of the boards of both the Mozart Society of America and SECM and has published and lectured widely on various aspects of eighteenth-century music in both Europe and this country. The fruits of his research have appeared in the *Journal of the American Musicological Society*, *Mozart Jahrbuch*, *Notes*, *Musik in Bayern*, *Music and Letters*, *The Journal of Musicology*, and *The Musical Quarterly*.

David Schulenberg performs on early keyboard instruments and teaches and publishes on European music of the seventeenth and eighteenth centuries, with particular emphasis on works of the Bach family. Professor and chair in the music department at Wagner College in New York City, he also teaches in the Historical Performance program at The Juilliard School. His books include *The Keyboard Music of J. S. Bach* and the textbook and anthology *Music of the Baroque*, and he has recorded CDs of chamber music by Quantz and King Frederick II of Prussia with baroque flutist Mary Oleskiewicz. His most recent book, *The Music of Wilhelm Friedemann Bach*, was published in 2010 by University of Rochester Press. He has also edited several volumes of keyboard sonatas and concertos by Carl Philipp Emanuel Bach and is a contributor to the new edition of the collected organ works of J. S. Bach currently being issued by Breitkopf und Härtel. Born in New York City, Schulenberg grew up in upstate New York near Albany and attended Harvard College, Stanford University, and the State University at Stony Brook, where he received his PhD in 1982. He previously taught at Columbia University, the University of North Carolina at Chapel Hill, and the University of Notre Dame, and was for several years a Research Associate at the

Shrine to Music Museum at the University of South Dakota. He is the recipient of grants from the National Endowment for the Humanities, the American Council of Learned Societies, and the Japan Society for the Promotion of Science, and he serves on the editorial board of *Early Keyboard Journal*; he also is vice-president of the Boston Clavichord society.

Travels with *Hésione:* The *tragédie en musique* outside Paris

ANITA HARDEMAN

Previous studies of the *tragédie en musique* have concentrated on the development of the genre in Paris, assuming that the capital set the fashion in opera as it did in so much else.[1] Indeed, the contracts between the Académie Royale de Musique in Paris and its provincial counterparts presumed that the provinces would draw the bulk of their repertoire from Parisian productions, with the occasional performance of works of local provenance.[2] Even the royal court, which had itself set the standard in the 1670s and 1680s under Jean-Baptiste Lully, was relegated to the status of follower by the 1730s. Yet an examination of the production history of one specific *tragédie en musique* both confirms and denies this general impression of the period. *Hésione*, with text by Antoine Danchet and music by André Campra, was performed in Paris, Lyon, at the royal court, and in Brussels throughout the early decades of the eighteenth century (see Appendix). This study examines the changes made to *Hésione* for each set of performances, changes that often reflect a mix of Parisian practices and local tastes, undermining the idea that Paris dominated all decisions. Indeed, while some revisions were made only locally, the adaptation of certain changes in multiple venues other than Paris, particularly Lyon and the royal court, implies an alternate model of dissemination in which opera houses communicated with one another without

---

1. Studies of the genre include James R. Anthony, *French Baroque Music from Beaujoyeulx to Rameau*, revised edition (Portland, OR: Amadeus Press, 1997), 93–164, and Cuthbert Girdlestone, *La Tragédie en musique (1673–1750) considérée comme genre littéraire* (Geneva: Librairie Droz, 1972), which considers only the librettos. Several French scholars have examined the history and repertoire of the Académie Royale de Musique, founded in 1671, including general histories of the institution by Jean Gourret, *Ces hommes qui ont fait l'opéra* (Paris: Éditions Albatros, 1984) and Jerôme de La Gorce, *L'Opéra à Paris au temps de Louis XIV: Histoire d'un théâtre* (Paris: Éditions Desjonquères, 1992), and repertoire studies by Ariane Ducrot, "Les représentations de l'Académie Royale de Musique à Paris au temps de Louis XIV (1671–1715)," *Recherches sur la musique française classique* 10 (1970): 19–55, and Robert Fajon, "Les incertitudes du succès: Etude du repertoire de l'Académie Royale de Musique des origins à 1750," in *L'Opéra au XVIIIe siècle: Actes du Colloque organisé à Aix-en-Provence par les Centre Aixois d'Études et de Recherches sur le XVIIIe siècle les 29, 30 avril et 1er mai 1977* (Aix-en-Provence: Université de Provence, 1982), 287–344. The major study of the *tragédie* outside France is Herbert Schneider, *Die Rezeption der Opern Lullys im Frankreich des Ancien regime* (Tutzing: Hans Schneider, 1982).
2. See, for example, the discussion of the terms for the opera privilege for Lyon below.

reference to Paris, perhaps through the performers and producers who circulated between these locations. Nonetheless, Parisian productions continued to be the primary motivation for personnel at these venues to consider mounting *Hésione*. Therefore a summary of the opera's production history in Paris provides a useful backdrop against which those in other locations can be examined.

Hésione at the Académie Royale de Musique

Hésione had its premiere on 21 December 1700 and was revised shortly thereafter. On 16 January, only three weeks after the opera opened, Danchet and Campra reworked the fifth act, eliminating the *divertissement* that had closed the opera and inserting a new one between the second and third scenes, as shown in Table 1.

Table 1. The 1700 and 1701 versions of Act 5 of *Hésione*

	1700 version		1701 version
Scene	Description	Scene	Description
1	Vénus reflects on her actions	1	Vénus reflects on her actions
2	Anchise confronts Vénus	2	Anchise confronts Vénus
3	Anchise is informed that Hésione has left Troy with Télamon; he falls into a prophetic trance, predicts the fall of Troy, then collapses.	3	The people of Troy arrive to celebrate the return of peace and Télamon's victory over the monster that threatened them.
4	Mercure (Mercury) descends to proclaim that Anchise will now love Vénus. The god's followers perform a *divertissement* that depicts the magnanimous generosity of Rome.	4	Anchise interrupts the celebration and is informed that Hésione has left Troy with Télamon; he falls into a prophetic trance, predicts the fall of Troy, then collapses.
	Vénus orders the Zephyrs to carry Anchise to her court.		
		5	Mercure descends to proclaim that Anchise will now love Vénus.
			Vénus orders the Zephyrs to carry Anchise to her court.

Travels with *Hésione*

In his libretto, Danchet reinterpreted the mythological story of Venus and Anchises, adding an obstacle to the seduction in the form of Anchises's betrothal to the Trojan princess Hesione.[3] After a series of failed attempts, the goddess Vénus succeeds in her quest to win Anchise, and in its original version, the opera ended with a *divertissement* in which the god Mercury orders his followers to show Anchise the magnificent Roman Empire to be founded by his descendants through his son Aeneas. The revised *divertissement*, now located in the middle of the act as the third scene, eliminates the supernatural and prophetic components of the original, instead celebrating the deliverance of the Trojan people from a terrible monster by Anchise's rival for Hésione's hand, the Greek prince Télamon. In all other respects the fifth act remained the same, so that the opera ended with the triumphant Vénus asking the Zephyrs to carry the unconscious Anchise to her court. Danchet and Campra also tightened the ending to the third act, shortening Vénus's final speech in the last scene.[4] In this form, the opera continued a successful run until the end of May 1701.

Revivals of *Hésione* occurred in 1709, 1729, and 1743, and as was customary, changes were made to the work. In 1709, Campra composed three airs in the fashionable Italian style to be inserted into the *divertissements* of acts 2, 3,

---

3. The opera begins with the Greek prince Télamon lamenting his choice to remain in Troy and woo Hésione now that she has chosen Anchise as her future husband. Vénus descends and vows to assist Télamon in winning Hésione for his own. When Anchise, Hésione, and her father Laomedon arrive to celebrate the marriage, the temple is destroyed and an oracle proclaims that Anchise must travel to the foot of Mount Ida. Anchise complies, only to discover Vénus, who declares herself in love with the Trojan prince. Anchise refuses her and Vénus creates supernatural jealousy in Hésione in an attempt to separate the lovers. Despite her jealousy, Hésione remains constant to Anchise, prompting Vénus to place an enchantment on Télamon that will render him irresistible to Hésione. This gambit apparently succeeds, until Anchise confronts Hésione over her unfaithfulness and the lovers are reunited. An enraged Vénus calls upon Neptune to attack the city of Troy with a monster that only Télamon will be able to slay. Télamon's success earns him Hésione's hand in marriage, while Anchise is unable to even wound the monster. Anchise confronts both Vénus and Laomedon and, in the midst of the argument, passes out. Vénus claims him, and Mercury descends to inform the goddess that her claim is supported by the rest of the Olympian gods.

4. In the original version of this scene, Vénus, who has just finished enchanting Télamon, instructs the prince in the limitations of the spell. Télamon objects to the use of magic to win his beloved in the revision: Vénus retorts that he should at least rejoice in Anchise's pending misfortune. Vénus's instructions are cut in the revision.

and 5 respectively.[5] At least one new dance may also have been composed, although no music for such a piece survives.[6] This production was seen as less successful by later commentators, including the *Mercure de France*, which blamed the performers for the failure in the review of the much more successful 1729 production of *Hésione*.[7] Under the direction of André Cardinal Destouches, this production opened on 13 September 1729 and ran until early November, with a reprise in January 1730 on Tuesdays. *Hésione* was lightly revised—two of the three airs from 1709 were dropped—and in this form the *Mercure* declared that this production demonstrated that the opera should always have been highly regarded.[8]

These positive associations were certainly part of the equation when *Hésione* was chosen as the vehicle to bring the lauded soprano Cathérine-Nicole Le Maure back to the opera stage in September 1730, in her first performance

---

5. All three airs share extensive *fioratura* for the soprano voice. Two of them were performed in 1709 by Mlle Dun, who was a frequent performer of Italianate airs in French operas between 1708 and 1710. See Barbara Nestola, "Italian Music, French Singers, Reception and Performance Practice on the Parisian Stage at the Beginning of the Eighteenth Century," in *D'une scène à l'autre: L'opéra italien en Europe*, vol. 1, *Les peregrinations d'une genre*, ed. Alessandro di Profio and Damien Colas (Wavre: Mardaga, 2009), 259.

6. A 1712 volume of choreographies created by Louis-Guillaume Pécour, choreographer at the Opéra, contains two dances from *Hésione*. The dancers are Mr. Dumoulin l'aîné and Mlle. Chaillou/Challion. The music for one of the dances is from the prologue, in which both performers appeared according to the libretto. I have not found a full score for the second piece, although its placement in the prologue seems likely, considering the performers and the key of the dance, which matches that of the prologue. See Michel Gadreau and Louis Guillaume Pécour, *Nouveau recueil de dance de bal et celle de ballet, contenant un très grand nombres des meilleures entrées de ballet de la composition de Mr. Pécour . . .* (Paris: Gaudrau, [1712?]), 36–42.

7. In the *Extrait* that appeared for the 1729 revival of *Hésione*, the anonymous reviewer wrote: "Les plus beaux Ouvrages sont exposez à perdre leur éclat par les circonstance dans lesquelles ils sont donnez; le choix des Acteurs est une des premieres causes du succès." (The most beautiful works may lose their brilliance by the circumstances in which they are given; the choice of actors is one of the leading causes of success.) *Mercure de France*, October 1729, 2477.

8. Only the act 5 air was retained. According to the *Mercure*, "tout le monde convient que cet Opera n'a jamais mieux été executé qu'il l'est aujourd'hui." (All the world knows that this opera has never been better executed than it is today.) *Mercure de France*, October 1729, 2477.

Travels with *Hésione*

since 1727. The return was not the success Le Maure or the opera administration anticipated, and the production ran for only one month before closing.[9] *Hésione*'s final performances at the Académie took place in 1743 for a month in March and two weeks in October. The work, insofar as the extant scores and libretto indicate, remained essentially unchanged from the 1729 performance—indeed, it even featured Le Maure as Hésione for at least some of the March performances.[10] She was replaced by Mlle Romainville in October, a name that was to reappear in reference to court performances of *Hésione*.

Hésione enjoyed moderate success in Paris with a triumphant initial run of performances that included a significant revision in 1701, and a less successful revival in 1709. Twenty years later, the opera was remounted, this time to some acclaim. The positive reaction was likely responsible for *Hésione*'s brief return in 1730, after which the opera was not produced until 1743.

Opera in the Provinces: Lyon

One method by which the holders of the royal opera privilege in Paris were able to increase the return on their investment was through the franchising of opera in the provinces. The city of Lyon was among the first locations to re-

---

9. Destouches, who had been director of the Opéra until July 1730, had feared just such an outcome. In a letter to the prince of Monaco, Destouches noted that while *Hésione* had at least two opportunities for Le Maure to shine vocally, the singer would need to excel in all aspects of the work. See André Tessier, "Correspondance d'André Cardinal des Touches et du Prince Antoine 1er de Monaco," *La Revue musicale* 8/7 (1927): 152, translated in Caroline Wood and Graham Sadler, *French Baroque Opera: A Reader* (Aldershot: Ashgate, 2000), 136.

10. Le Maure's tenure as the Trojan princess may have been intermittent: in 1775, J. M. B. Clément and J. de Laporte claimed that the role of Hésione was reassigned to Mlle Claire de la Tude, better known as Mlle Clairon, who in 1743 accepted a position with the Comédie Française, where she became one of the company's leading actresses. The Parfaict brothers agree with this statement in their entry on *Hésione*, but in their article on the actress, they list her role as Vénus, as does the *Mercure*. See Joseph de La Porte and Sébastien R. N. Chamfort, "Hésione," in *Anecdotes dramatique* 1 (Paris: Veuve Duchesne, 1775; reprint Oxford Brookes University, UK: The CESAR Project, 2002), 425 (accessed 10 May 2010) www.cesar.org.uk/cesar2/books/anecdotes; Claude and François Parfaict, "Hésione," in *Dictionnaire des Théâtres de Paris* (Paris: Librarie Chez Rozet, 1767; reprint Oxford Brookes University, UK: The CESAR Project, 2002), III, 73 (accessed 10 May 2010) www.cesar.org.uk/cesar2/books/parfaict1767; Parfaict, "Clairon," in *Dictionnaire des Théâtres de Paris* 2, 92 (accessed 10 May 2010) www.cesar.org.uk/cesar2/books/parfaict1767; *Mercure de France*, May 1743, 1009.

ceive a privilege for an Académie de Musique, issued to Jean-Pierre Leguay on 17 September 1687.[11] The contract allowed Leguay to issue librettos for his performances but not scores, and prohibited him from producing in Lyon operas that were still being performed in Paris.[12] A bankrupt Leguay stepped down as director in 1690, but when his successors also ran into financial difficulties, Leguay returned to the position in 1695. During this second term he faced additional obstacles, including the closure of the opera house in June 1699, after flooding caused the collapse of the building's walls.[13] In response, Leguay transformed his troupe into a touring company. In late March 1701 the company was in Marseille, performing Lully's *Isis* and *Armide* before the grandsons of Louis XIV, the Dukes of Burgundy and Berry. By the beginning of April, the two young princes had travelled to Lyon, where they heard the company perform Lully's *Phaëton* and Campra's *L'Europe galante*.[14]

Two surviving librettos indicate that *Hésione* also entered the company's repertory sometime in 1701.[15] Despite the privilege's implication that the provincial theater occupied a subservient position with regard to Paris, these two librettos indicate some independence from the Parisian version of *Hésione*. The most striking difference is the use of the original act 5 *divertissement*, the one situated in Rome. Certainly by June 1701, the earliest date that Leguay could have mounted a production of *Hésione*, the revised version of the opera was well known and scores were readily available. Indeed, the revision was known to the administration in Lyon, as the second alteration made in Paris, the shorten-

---

11. Léon Vallas, *Un Siècle de Musique et de Théâtre à Lyon, 1688–1789* (Lyon: n.p., 1932; reprint Geneva: Minkoff, 1971), 15. The privilege included the cities of Toulouse and Bordeaux within its limits.

12. Ibid., 16. As a result of this limitation on publication, librettos form the main body of evidence regarding the content of opera productions in Lyon.

13. Ibid., 36–37, 43–46, 49, 58.

14. The April performances are discussed in the *Mercure galant*, April 1701, Tome 1, 230–231, 253, 276, and in Vallas, *Théâtre*, 59. In May the princes viewed the operas at the Lyon Académie de Musique, suggesting Leguay had either reconstructed the original theater or found another space suitable for performances. *Mercure galant*, May 1701, Tome 2, 144.

15. The two librettos are: [Antoine Danchet], *Hésione, tragédie représentée par l'Académie Royale de Musique le vingt-unième jour de Decembre 1700* (Lyon: n.p., 1701), and [Danchet], *Hésione, tragédie représentée par l'Académie Royale de Musique le vingt-unième jour de Decembre 1700* (Lyon: A. Molin, 1701). The December 1700 dates cited here refer to the Parisian premiere; the date of the Lyon premiere is unknown.

ing of text at the end of the third act, is used in these librettos.[16] Why then might Leguay have preferred the original *divertissement* that had been rejected so quickly in Paris? One possible reason might be the importance of Rome to the area of France in which Lyon is located, which contains some of the best-preserved Roman ruins in the Rhône-Alpes region.[17] By keeping the Roman *divertissement*, Leguay could make the opera more relevant to his local audience.

Changes of management and additional floods and fires plagued the company in the years following 1701.[18] Madeleine Desmarais, a former actress who held the Lyon privilege from 1722 to 1739, was only marginally more successful than her predecessors. In 1729, after first reducing the size of the ensemble, she was forced to apply to the city of Lyon for additional funding in order to keep the theater open.[19] The series of librettos in Table 2 gives an idea of the repertory at this time.

Each of these works had been produced in Paris within the decade; indeed, the productions of *Hésione* and Destouches's *Le Carnaval et la Folie* occurred quite soon after their Paris revivals. The version of *Hésione* performed in 1730 appears to have been a revival in the truest sense of the word, matching the libretto of the 1701 Lyon premiere exactly. Thus, nearly three decades after

---

16. A third change made in Lyon was the omission of a stage direction for a troupe of Cupids present at the beginning of act 3, scene 5. The Parisian libretto states that "Les Amours se placent sur les costez du Theatre." (The Cupids are placed at the sides of the stage.) Possibly the machinery or the cast for such a group was not available in Lyon. See [Danchet], *Hésione, tragédie représentée par l'Académie Royale de Musique le vingt-unième jour de Decembre 1700* (Paris: Christophe Ballard, 1700), 3/5.

17. Jacob Spon documented a great deal of the remaining Roman structures in his *Recherche des antiquités et curiostiés de la ville de Lyon, Ancienne Colonie des Romains et Capitale de la Gaule Celtique. Avec un Mémoir des Principaux Antiquaires et Curieux de l'Europe* (Lyon: Antoine Cellier fils, 1675), including drawings of the amphitheater and the aqueducts near the Porte de Sainte Irenée, which at that time were outside the city limits. See Spon, 44 and 79 for the illustrations.

18. After Leguay stepped down as director in 1703, the new management was no more successful than his had been, and he returned to the position for two additional terms, 1705–1714 and 1716–1722. During the same period, the theater in which the company performed was damaged again by flooding (1711) and a fire (1722).

19. Vallas, *Théâtre*, 210. According to Vallas, the company dwindled from twenty-five to seventeen choristers, and from seventeen to thirteen dancers. The directors of the Lyon Académie were constrained not only by production costs but also by the necessity of paying pensions, including one to Leguay. In 1729 the city agreed to fund the theater directly with an annual subvention of 6000 livres. Ibid., 212.

Table 2. Librettos published by Antoine Olyer in Lyon for
Académie de Musique productions

1729   *Pirame et Thisbé* (*tragédie en musique*; libretto by de La Serre, music by Rebel and Francoeur; Paris, 1726)

   Les âges (*opéra-ballet*; libretto by Fuzelier, music by Campra; Paris, 1718, revived 1724)

1730   *Hésione* (Paris, 1700; revived 1709 and 1729)

   Le Carnaval et la Folie (*comédie-ballet*; libretto by Lamotte, music by Destouches; Paris, 1703, revived 1719 and 1730)

   Les amours déguisés (*opéra-ballet*; libretto by Fuzelier, music by Bourgeois; Paris, 1713, revived 1726)

Campra and Danchet originally revised the ending to the opera, their first version was still being performed in Lyon.[20] The principal roles were, as might be expected, assigned to the principal actors of the company, among them Justin Destouches Dubourg, who portrayed Anchise. Dubourg was listed as a well-established member of the company who deserved an increased pension based on his years of service in the appeal that Desmarais made to the city council.[21] He supplemented his Lyon Académie income by participating in other musical events, including the city's annual municipal celebrations in 1729; he was employed outside of Lyon as well, joining the royal chapel in Versailles in 1720.[22]

The years following the first revival of *Hésione* were again difficult for the Lyon Académie. Indeed, as the Prince de Carignan commented in 1736, "In order to give such a spectacle in Lyon with regularity, it will be necessary to

---

20. The shortened version of the act 3 ending was substituted for the original. Unfortunately, as in 1701, no score associated with this production has been discovered, and thus we do not know if any new music was composed for the opera.

21. Vallas, *Théâtre*, 211.

22. Dubourg's participation in the municipal celebrations is recorded in the Archives Municipales de Lyon, where records exist for the years 1727 (CC 3115, no. 101), 1728 (CC 3119, no. 147), 1729 (CC 3124, no. 136), 1732 (CC 3139, no. 151), and 1735 (CC 3162, no. 151), of which I consulted the first four. Of the soloists, only Dubourg participated in the municipal events (1729). Mme Desmarais also supplemented her income as opera director by singing at this event. Dubourg's date of appointment to the royal chapel is found in Raphaelle Legrand, "Dubourg, Justin Destouches," *Dictionnaire de la musique de France aux XVIIe et XVIIIe siècles*, ed. Marcelle Benoit (Paris: Fayard, 1992), 248.

make it free of charge, or failing that, increase the number of Sundays."[23] But a change in management in 1739 led to what Léon Vallas characterized as "one of the most brilliant periods in the history of the Lyon Opéra."[24] The new management, a syndicate composed of men of good families, included Nicolas-Antoine Bergiron, co-founder of the Lyon Académie des Beaux-Arts. This society, formed in 1713 and consisting of local professional and amateur musicians, produced regular concerts including complete operas. One of these may have been *Hésione*, as the society owned a copy of the opera as early as 1713.[25] Certainly, the possibility that Bergiron was familiar with the work may account for its revival in Lyon in 1742, where *Hésione* was one of at least ten different productions mounted by the Lyon company that year, as shown in Table 3.

Table 3. 1742 productions at the Lyon Académie de Musique[26]

Ajax (*tragédie en musique*; libretto by Mennesson, music by Bertin de la Doué; Paris, 1716; revived 1726, 1742)

Amadis de Grèce (*tragédie en musique*; libretto by Lamotte, music by Destouches; Paris, 1699; revived 1711, 1724)

Armide (*tragédie en musique*; libretto by Quinault, music by Lully; Paris, 1686; revived 1703, 1713, 1714, 1724)

---

23. "Pour que l'on pût entretenir un pareil spectacle à Lyon, il faudrait l'établier gratis ou, tout au moins, multiplier les dimanches." *Nouvelles à la main*, fol. 108, quoted in Vallas, *Théâtre*, 223.

24. Ibid., 223.

25. This score is one of two of the opera in the collection of the Bibliothèque Municipale de Lyon, Rés. FM 133638. According to the catalog at the Bibliothèque, the signature on the flyleaf is that of Jean-Baptiste Christin, the other founder of the Académie des Beaux-Arts. This score is Ballard's first edition of *Hésione*. Indeed, a familiarity with the work seems even more likely considering that Christin resided in Paris from 1702 to 1712, where he could easily have attended the 1709 revival. Vallas, *Théâtre*, 98–99. *Hésione* appears to have enjoyed continued popularity in Lyon, as Michel Hild lists a 1764 performance of "Oh ciel! Il me trahit," *Hésione*'s act 3 monologue, in his online catalog "Concert de l'Académie des Beaux-Arts de Lyon, 1759–1772," Centre de Musique Baroque de Versailles, (accessed 31 October 2009, <http://philidor.cmbv.fr/listeCorpus>).

26. Some of the librettos from this season are bound together in a collection held in the Bibliothèque Nationale de France (Arts du Spectacles) (RO-1032), and the order in which they are bound suggests that *Hésione* was the final production of that group. *Hésione* is the eighth work in the volume, which begins with two of the 1741 productions, *Pirame et Thisbé* and *Thesée*.

Table 3 continued

Atys (*tragédie en musique*; libretto by Quinault, music by Lully; Paris, 1676; revived 1678, 1682, 1689, 1690, 1699, 1708, 1709, 1725, 1738, 1740)

Hésione (Paris, 1700; revived 1709, 1729)

Hypermnestre (*tragédie en musique*; libretto by de La Font, music by Gervais; Paris, 1704; revived 1717, 1728)

Les amours de Protée (ballet; libretto by de La Font, music by Gervais; Paris, 1720; revived 1728)

Les amours de Ragonde (ballet; libretto by Néricault Destouches, music by Mouret; Paris, 1742)

Les romans (*ballet-heroïque*; libretto by de Bonneval, music by Niel; Paris, 1736)

Philomèle (*tragédie en musique*; libretto by Roy, music by La Coste; Paris, 1705; revived 1709, 1723, 1734)

With the exception of *Les Amours de Ragonde*, *Atys*, and *Ajax*, most of these works were not revivals of recent Parisian productions—indeed, several had not been seen in that city since the 1720s. The most interesting aspect of this season is the timing of the Lyon revival of *Hésione*. Whereas both the 1701 and 1730 Lyon productions of *Hésione* came after successful Parisian performances, this 1742 revival actually anticipates the 1743 Paris production—the first of two significant differences between this revival and previous Lyon productions of *Hésione*.[27]

For this revival, the fifth act of *Hésione* was modernized for the first time, eliminating the concluding *divertissement* set in Rome used in 1701 and 1730 and substituting instead the one celebrating Télamon's victory. But the most important change was the creation of a new ending for the *tragédie*. The 1742 Lyon version of *Hésione* ends with a *coup de théâtre*, with the deletion of the final two scenes of act 5 of the 1701 version. Thus the opera concludes just after Anchise faints in a climactic moment that caps the delivery of his speech foretelling the fall of Troy. Whether this change was made by the Académie based on critical response to the original ending or the administration's artistic taste is unknown; surprisingly, however, Lyon was not the only venue in which *Hésione* was per-

---

27. Of the other works in the list, only *Hypermnestre* had a Parisian performance subsequent to its Lyon performance, with a revival in 1746.

formed with this abrupt conclusion. This ending is also found in productions mounted for the royal court.

Opera at Court: The Concerts de la Reine

When Louis XV married the Polish princess Maria Leczinska, one of the many changes made at court for the new queen was the establishment of the Concerts de la Reine. Singers and instrumentalists employed by the various musical departments of the royal household, as well as soloists drawn from the Académie Royale de Musique in Paris, performed concert versions of operas both old and new, with each work usually taking three concerts to be performed in full.[28] Official responsibility for the repertory of the concerts rested with the two *surintendants de la musique de la chambre*, who each held the position for a six-month period. Through most of the 1730s and into the 1740s, these duties were shared by André Cardinal Destouches, responsible for the first semester (1 January to 30 June) and François Colin de Blamont, responsible for the second semester (1 July to 31 December). While Destouches supervised the suc-

---

28. The Concerts de la Reine have been neglected by scholars in comparison to the more famous productions mounted by Louis XV's mistress Mme de Pompadour. The repertoire of the Concerts is discussed in relation to *Armide* in Lois Rosow, "Lully's *Armide* at the Paris Opéra: A Performance History, 1686–1766" (PhD diss., Brandeis University, 1981), 134–136, and in relation to *Tancrède* in Antonia L. Banducci, "*Tancrède* by Antoine Danchet and André Campra: Performance History and Reception (1702–1764)" (PhD diss., Washington University, 1990), 96–100. Both Rosow and Banducci reconstruct performance schedules for their respective operas based on reports in the *Mercure de France*. Paul F. Rice relates the history and repertory of the Concerts as they pertain to a specific venue in *The Performing Arts at Fontainebleau from Louis XIV to Louis XVI* (Ann Arbor, MI: UMI Research Press, 1989). In contrast, several studies have been published on the repertory of Mme de Pompadour's troupe, beginning with a report from one of Pompadour's authors, Pierre Laujon, "Spectacles des petits cabinets de Louis XV," in *Oeuvres choisies de P. Laujon* (Paris: L. Collin, 1811). More recent works include Emile Campardon, *Mme de Pompadour et la Cour de Louis XV au milieu de XVIIIe siècle* (Paris: H. Plon, 1867), 78–125; Adolphe Julien, *Histoire du Théâtre de Madame de Pompadour* (Paris: J. Baur, 1874; reprint Geneva: Slatkine, 1978); and Winston Haverland Kaehler, "The Operatic Repertoire of Madame de Pompadour's Théâtre des Petits Cabinets (1747–1753)" (PhD diss., University of Michigan, 1971). Campra's *Tancrède* was the only *tragédie en musique* performed by Pompadour's troupe; Banducci determined that a score from the Bibliothèque Municipale de Versailles served as a promptbook for the 1748 performance. See Banducci, "Staging a *tragédie en musique*: A 1748 Promptbook of Campra's *Tancrède*," *Early Music* 21 (1993): 180–190.

cessful 1729 revival of the opera in Paris, *Hésione* was not mounted at court until the end of 1730, when it was given initially under the direction of Blamont. This performance included only the prologue and first act of the opera, leaving Destouches to oversee the production of the remainder of the work in February 1731. The performers listed in the *Mercure*'s summary of events at court were a mix of Parisian and court singers: Mlle Antier, who had been applauded in the role of Vénus in Paris, appeared again in that role, but that of Hésione, played most recently in the fall of 1730 by Mlle Le Maure, was taken instead by Mlle Lenner, a court singer.[29]

Further performances of *Hésione* occurred in 1736, as given in Table 4. Although the assignment of performers to roles is not specified, among the cast is Dubourg, who played Anchise in Lyon in 1730. A series of five productions followed between 1740 and 1743, most of which featured Mlle Romainville. The *Mercure* records that she sang the role of Hésione at court in 1743, as she likely did during the Académie revival of that year, and it seems probable that her previous court engagements were for this role as well. Joining Mlle Romainville in the 1740 concerts of Hésione was Mlle Huguenot who sang in the early 1730s with the Lyon Académie de Musique and the Académie des Beaux-Arts.[30]

Table 4. Court productions of *Hésione* [31]

Year	Performance Dates	Location	Performers
1730/31	end Dec, 8, 10 Feb	Marly	Anchise: M. d'Angerville; Vénus: Mlle Antier; Hésione: Mlle Lenner
1736	19, 21, 26 Nov	Versailles	including: (W) Mathieu, Lenner, d'Aigremont, Eermans, Minier, Deschamps, Duhamel; (M) d'Angerville, Petillot, Dubourg

---

29. *Mercure de France*, February 1731, 395–396.

30. Vallas, *Théâtre*, 253–254. Although Mlle Huguenot is listed in the group of performers that were part of the annual civic celebrations in 1727–1729, she does not appear on the cast list for the 1730 production of *Hésione*. Vallas, *Théâtre*, 202. The *Mercure* remarks on Huguenot's first appearance at court in June of 1738 (June 1738, 2, 1434). She kept her Lyon pension during this time, as her compatriot Dubourg likely did as well.

31. This list is based on performances reported by the *Mercure de France* (November 1736, 2562; October 1740, 2320; May 1741, 1045; November 1741, 2521; August 1742, 1887; March 1743, 587).

Travels with *Hésione*

Table 4 continued

Year	Performance Dates	Location	Performers
1740	26, 28 Sep	Fontainebleau	including: (W) Romainville, Huguenot; (M) d'Angerville, Ducros, Godonesche, le Begue, Poirier
1741	29 Apr, 3, 6 May	Marly	including: (W) d'Aigremont, Deschamps, Lenner; (M) le Begue, Benoît, le Cler, Godeneche, Jelyotte
1741	13, 18, 20 Nov	[Versailles][a]	Anchise: de la Garde; also: (W) Romainville, Lalande, Saint Marc
1742	28, 30 Jul, 1 Aug	Versailles	including: (W) Deschamps, Romainville; (M) d'Angerville, Poirier, Benoît, de la Garde
1743	23, 30 Mar	Versailles[b]	Vénus: Mlle La Lande; Hésione: Mlle Romainville; Anchise: Benoît; Télamon: Poirier
1746	19, 24, 26 Oct	Fontainebleau	including: (W) Lalande, Mathieu, Selle, Godeneche; (M) Poirer, Lagarde, Dubourg, Godoneche
1750	28 May; ?? Jun	Versailles/Compiegne[c]	including: (W) Lalande, Mathieu, Canavas, Guerdon; (M) Joguet, Godoneche, Bazire, Benoît, Poirier
1752	20, 22, 27 Nov	unknown[d]	including: (W) Lalande, Mathieu, Canavas; (M) Dubourg, Joguet, Poirier

[a]Nov 1741 performances most likely took place at Versailles based on other performances at the same time; however, the *Mercure* does not give a specific location for these performances.

[b]1743 performances at Versailles: prologue and first three acts only.

[c]A single production with the first part of the opera given at Versailles on 28 May and the remainder given at Compiegne sometime the following month.

[d]1752 peformances: no location given in the *Mercure*.

13

This cluster of performances at court and performers linked to both Paris and Lyon is intriguing because it suggests an inversion of the usually supposed method of dissemination. The model, demonstrated by the early Lyon performances, is that a success in Paris triggers productions in the provincial opera houses. Yet considering the links between the performers and producers of opera at court, in Paris, and in Lyon, the relative frequency of court performances in the early 1740s suggests that these productions may have prompted the Parisian and Lyon revivals. Evidence in support of this hypothesis appears in scores for *Hésione* found in the Bibliothèque Municipale de Versailles.[32]

Amidst several layers of cuts and changes, both Versailles scores give the same ending for the opera seen in Lyon. The new ending derives from the middle of the fourth scene of the fifth act of the 1701 version, just after Anchise tumbles unconscious to the ground, overcome by the strain of foretelling the fall of Troy. As in Lyon, this change creates a tragic ending to the opera, as the union of Anchise and Vénus is eliminated, leaving only an unwilling Hésione on her way to Greece with Télamon and Anchise overcome by her loss. Unfortunately there is no indication in the score, nor has other evidence surfaced, of when this alteration was first made to *Hésione* or for how long it was maintained. One possibility is September 1740, when the opera was performed in two nights as opposed to the usual three, according to the report in the *Mercure*. While the truncation of the work is in line with other changes made in the scores that have the effect of streamlining the performance, I do not believe enough of the opera would

---

32. The two scores are MSD45 and MSD46. Both are of the 1701 edition of *Hésione* and are stamped "Musique du Roy." Since both contain the 1729 print of "L'amour s'envole au bruit des armes," they were probably part of five copies of the opera purchased by the king's Menus Plaisirs in 1729, for which Ballard received a total of 76 livres, 10 sols. The accounts are part of the Comptes de la Maison du Roi (Menus Plaisirs) held in the Archives Nationales, O1 2858, fo. 394, as recorded in Marcelle Benoit, *Musiques du Cour, Chapelle, Chambre, Écurie: 1661–1733* (Paris: Éditions A. & J. Picard, 1971), 411. The Menus Plaisirs also purchased parts for *Hésione*: thirty chorus parts (six each for first and second dessus, haute-contre, and taille, and eight bass) and eight orchestral parts (two second dessus, one premier dessus de hautbois, one second dessus, and six basses continues); Benoit, *Musiques du Cour*, 410. The thirty chorus parts for the Menus Plaisirs matches the size of the chorus for the 1729 production of *Hésione* at the Opéra. Both scores have extensive cuts, marked in both red and lead pencils, some of which have been retracted at a later date, and MSD46 contains an additional layer of ink markings providing ornamentation for the solo vocal lines.

Travels with *Hésione*

have been eliminated by this change to firmly establish 1740 as a reliable date.[33] Indeed, when I examined the scores at the library in Versailles, the pages of the cut were still pinned together, so perhaps the last documented performance of the opera in 1752 featured this ending.

However, conditions at court during the early 1740s certainly suggest that rewriting *Hésione* to eliminate the triumph of the goddess of love over her mortal rival might have been a wise choice. The early years of the marriage of Louis XV and his queen were reasonably amicable, but beginning in 1738, after the birth of their last child, the king declared a series of royal mistresses, leading ultimately to the appointment of Madame de Pompadour in 1745.[34] These actions offended the queen and divided the court. Regardless of whether the fifth act's alteration happened first in Lyon or Versailles, perhaps presenting an opera in which the royally sanctioned engagement between Hésione and Anchise was destroyed by the interference of Vénus, goddess of love, could be perceived as unwise at best and disrespectful to the queen at worst.

Conversely, the cut may have been made only as an attempt to streamline the dramatic and musical presentation of the work, but the similarities between the versions presented in Lyon and Versailles certainly support a model of dissemination in which non-Parisian opera centers share production ideas.

---

33. Although none of the changes suggested in the Versailles scores are dated, they are generally consistent with cuts observed by Paul Rice in librettos and scores for productions at Fontainebleau of *Atys* in 1753 and *Thésée* and *Alceste* in 1754. The main focus of editorial attention seems to have been the prologues and *divertissements:* all three prologues were suppressed, while *divertissements* were also cut or restructured. Similarly, the prologue to *Hésione*, as well as some of the *divertissements*, was revised through the elimination of repeated numbers. The concluding scenes of both *Atys* and *Thésée* were cut in the Fontainebleau productions, but unlike the revised conclusion to *Hésione*, these changes did not materially affect the integrity of the drama. See Rice, *Performing Arts at Fontainebleau*, 125–127.

34. The first of these was Louise-Julie, Comtesse de Mailly, officially mistress from 1738 to 1742, when she was succeeded by her younger sister, Marie-Anne. Two other sisters, Pauline-Felicité and Diane-Adélaïde, were secondary mistresses during this time, with Diane-Adélaïde serving as *dame d'honneur* to the queen. Two of the sisters died during their time with Louis (Pauline in 1741, in childbirth, and Marie-Anne in 1744) and the two remaining sisters passed out of favor by 1745. Olivier Bernier suggests the king may have taken Louise-Julie as his mistress as early as 1733, based on a letter written by the queen to her father, which Bernier does not cite. In 1736, the Marquis d'Argenson stated that Louise-Julie had been Louis's mistress since early that year. Marquis d'Argenson, *Journals et memoires* (Paris: n.p., 1856), 1, 220, cited in Bernier, *Louis The Beloved: The Life of Louis XV* (Garden City, NY: Doubleday, 1984), 87.

Furthermore, while the original contracts for the Lyon opera house and other provincial theaters imply that these venues drew their repertory primarily from Paris, the cluster of performances of *Hésione* in the early 1740s that predate the Parisian revival of 1743 certainly suggests that by the 1740s the Académie Royale de Musique could as easily draw inspiration for its revivals from successful productions taking place outside the city.

French Opera outside France: Brussels

The modifications to the original model for dissemination of the *tragédie en musique* within France, where Paris dominates, raises questions about the production of French opera outside France, such as in the Low Countries. Although a frequent target of Louis XIV's armies, the area that became modern-day Belgium shared close cultural ties with France. Thus it is unsurprising to discover that French opera was an important musical and dramatic genre in Brussels, at that time the seat of the elector of Bavaria as governor of the Spanish Netherlands. While the Opéra du Quai au Foin, the city's first opera house, initially presented Italian operas, Lully's works soon came to dominate the theatrical scene.[35] The Quai au Foin productions were sporadic and unprofitable, and the privilege changed hands several times before being awarded to Pierre-Antoine Fiocco and Gio-Paolo Bombarda in 1694.[36] Fiocco became

---

35. The theater opened in 1682 with Antonio Zanettini's *Medea in Atene*, but later that year produced *Persée* (1682). In addition, costumes for *Phaëton, Proserpine, Cadmus et Hermione, Alceste,* and *Isis* were listed as part of a lawsuit filed against an actress at the theater in 1684. Notariat général de Brabant, Liasse 500, act of 8 March 1684, minutes of the notary J. Mailletz, cited in Henri Liebrecht, *Histoire du Théâtre Français à Bruxelles au XVIIe et au XVIIIe siècle* (Paris: Librairie Ancienne Édouard Champion, 1923; reprint Geneva: Slatkine, 1977), 98–99.

36. Pierre-Antoine Fiocco (1653–1717) was an Italian-born composer who found work in northern Europe, beginning with the composition of a new prologue to Lully's *Alceste* for a production in Hanover in 1681. He first appears in Brussels in early 1682, where he remained for the rest of his life, eventually becoming *maître de musique de la chapelle royale de la cour* in 1703. See Lewis Reece Baratz, "Fiocco," in *Grove Music Online*, http://www.oxfordmusiconline.com (accessed 26 May 2010). Gio-Paolo Bombarda (?1650–1712) came to Brussels with the elector, after having first been employed as a musician at the Bavarian court. He became the elector's treasurer in 1688. See Manuel Couvreur and Jean-Philippe Van Aelbrouck, "Gio Paolo Bombarda et la creation du Grand Théâtre de Bruxelles," in *Le Théâtre de la Monnaie au XVIII siècle* (Brussels: Université libre de Bruxelles, 1996), 8–11.

musical director of the company, conducting the orchestra and composing new prologues that flattered the elector.[37] Bombarda, who held an important role in the elector's court as his chief financial advisor, kept the Quai au Foin open only until the extravagantly finished Théâtre de la Monnaie was completed in 1700.

The new theater opened on 19 November 1700 with a gala performance of Lully's *Atys* in honor of the succession of Philip Duke of Anjou to the Spanish throne. Opera was not as lucrative a business as Bombarda had anticipated, and by 1702 he had leased his operatic performance rights to Domenico Lorenzoni and Giuseppe Contri for the sum of 3000 florins.[38] When these gentlemen also ran into financial difficulty, Bombarda reasserted his control in 1704. Hoping to build a superlative group of actors, Bombarda then contracted the services of Pierre Guyenet to recruit French singers.[39] The War of the Spanish Succession prevented Bombarda from reaping the rewards of his efforts: in 1706 Brussels fell to the Allied armies (England, Holland, and the Austrian Habsburgs) and Bombarda left the city. Despite the hostilities taking place between the occupying armies and France, French opera remained popular, and several works were performed during the years of occupation, as Table 5 shows.

Evidence for many of these productions survives in the form of librettos issued for special performances, as is the case with Collasse's *Ballet des saisons*, which entertained the newly arrived Prince Eugene of Savoy and the Duke of Marlborough on 21 November 1710. Another gala performance of an unknown work followed on 25 November, and Destouches's *Amadis de Grèce* was mounted on 2 January 1711.[40] This emphasis on special occasion performances, as well

---

37. Liebrecht, *Histoire du Théâtre Français*, 104. Fiocco composed replacement prologues for Lully's *Armide* (Paris, 1686; Brussels, 1695), *Acis et Galatée* (Paris, 1686; Brussels, 1695), and *Thésée* (Paris, 1676; Brussels, 1697).

38. Liebrecht, *Histoire du Théâtre Français*, 129.

39. Ibid., 130. Pierre Guyenet became the director of the Paris Académie in the same year, purchasing the privilege for the sum of 100,000 livres and assuming responsibility for all the Académie's outstanding debts. By the time of his death in 1712, the Académie was nearly bankrupt and Guyenet's personal debts to the Opéra's creditors, including Bombarda, were rumoured to be nearly 1,500,000 livres. See Gourret, *Ces hommes qui ont fait l'opéra*, 33–34 and La Gorce, *L'Opéra à Paris*, 155.

40. Liebrecht, *Histoire du Théâtre Français*, 137. Since the 25 November production is unnamed, it is tempting to assign that date to *Hésione*; however the extant libretto conveys only the year of the production. [Danchet], *Hésione, tragédie representée par l'Academie de Musique* (Brussels: n.p., 1710), Bibliothèque royale de Belgique, Faber 1.946.

Table 5. Productions at the Théâtre de la Monnaie, 1707–1711[41]

1707 *Armide* (*tragédie en musique*, libretto by Quinault, music by Lully; Paris, 1686; revived 1688, 1692, 1697, 1703)

Bellérophon (*tragédie en musique*, libretto by Corneille, music by Lully; Paris, 1679; revived 1680, 1705)

Tancrède (*tragédie en musique*, libretto by Danchet, music by Campra; Paris, 1702; revived October 1707)

1709 *Amadis* (*tragédie en musique*, libretto by Quinault, music by Lully; Paris, 1684; revived 1685, 1686, 1687, 1701, 1707)

1710 *Ballet des saisons* (ballet, libretto by Pic, music by Collasse; Paris, 1695; revived 1700, 1707; Brussels 1698)

Hésione (Paris, 1700; revived 1709)

1711 *Amadis de Grèce* (*tragédie en musique*, libretto by Lamotte, music by Destouches; Paris 1699; revived November 1711)

as the significant gap in time between Parisian revivals and productions at the Monnaie, makes a direct link between the Académie Royale and its Brussels counterpart difficult to perceive during this time. Other factors, such as the consistent popularity of Lully's operas, may account for the repertory choices. Moreover, in the case of the four non-Lully operas, the productions of both *Tancrède* in 1707 and *Amadis de Grèce* in 1711 may have predated the Paris revivals, while the *Ballet des saisons* of 1710 could be regarded as a revival of the 1698 Brussels production rather than the 1707 Paris version. Even the 1710 production of *Hésione* was not of the most recent 1709 revival, as the libretto conforms almost exactly to the 1701 Paris production. Certainly, while the Paris Académie remained an important source of repertoire for Brussels, the administration at the Monnaie did not feel compelled to ensure their productions reflected current Parisian trends.

One significant change to *Hésione* further demonstrates the separation between Brussels and Paris. Although for the most part the work reproduces the 1701 Paris version, the Brussels production omits the opera's prologue. This type of change had been popular in Brussels since the 1690s, and considering that the city was occupied by forces massed in opposition to Louis XIV, a prologue that

---

41. Liebrecht, *Histoire du Théâtre Français*, 104, 134–137.

lauded the King of France would certainly have been out of place. Indeed, the production of *Armide* in 1707 also omitted the prologue.[42] The result in both cases was an opera that entertained but did not present material potentially offensive to the dignitaries who gathered for these gala entertainments.

Conclusions

This survey of opera productions of *Hésione* in Paris, Lyon, at the royal court, and in Brussels provides evidence for a different model of opera dissemination in France in the early eighteenth century. The original model, supported by the contracts between the provincial opera franchises and the Académie Royale de Musique in Paris, places the Académie at the center of opera production in France, such that successful performances of a work in Paris encourage imitations in the other opera houses. The productions of *Hésione* that occur in 1700–1701 in Paris and Lyon and in 1729–1730 in Paris, Lyon, and at the royal court provide a specific example of this type of distribution, but a more detailed examination of the contents of each production reveals that each venue felt free to alter the opera in order to suit local circumstances. Thus, the original fifth act to *Hésione* was performed in Lyon thirty years after a new version had been premiered in Paris, while the prologue to the opera was omitted in Brussels, where content praising Louis XIV would have been most unwelcome considering that the city was occupied by forces hostile to the French. The influence of Paris seems even weaker when the recomposition of the ending to the opera found in Lyon in 1742 and at court likely around the same time is considered. In this case, communication seems to have occurred between the opera houses

---

42. Bram van Oostveldt, in noting that the 1707 performance of *Armide* also lacked a prologue, states somewhat obviously that these omissions result in "a toning down of the ideological function of the prologue." Oostveldt, "The Théâtre de la Monnaie and Theatre Life in the Eighteenth-Century Austrian Netherlands: From a Courtly-Aristocratic to a Civil-Enlightened Discourse?," edited by Jaak van Schoor and translated by Johan Bonthuys, in *Studies in Performing Arts and Film* 2 (Ghent: Academia Press, 2000), 27. Scholars of the *tragédie en musique* agree that the prologue, in addition to having its dramaturgical function of introducing the *tragédie* and helping the audience make the transition from everyday life into theatrical space, also served to reinforce the power and imagery of Louis XIV. See in particular Buford Norman, *Touched by the Graces: The Librettos of Philippe Quinault in the Context of French Classicism* (Birmingham, AL: Summa, 2001), 45–68, and Downing A. Thomas, *Aesthetics of Opera in the Ancien Régime, 1647–1785* (Cambridge: Cambridge University Press, 2002), 53–99.

directly, without reference to Paris. A tantalizing hint at one method by which these changes may have been distributed can be found in the community of performers who circulated between multiple locations. Moreover, the frequency of performances in venues other than Paris in the early 1740s leads to the possibility that the 1743 Parisian revival of *Hésione* may have occurred in response to the Lyon and court productions, placing the capital in the position of follower rather than leader. Further research, whether centered on individual works or specific locations, would help to elucidate whether this circumstance was peculiar to *Hésione* or whether by the mid-eighteenth century a more equal status obtained between the Académie Royale de Musique and those venues which hitherto have been regarded as its imitators.

Travels with *Hésione*

Appendix. Productions of *Hésione* in Paris, Lyon, at court, and in Brussels, 1700–1752

Year	Location	Remarks
1700	Paris	21 Dec 1700 to 31 May 1701; revisions: acts 3 and 5 revised, 16 Jan 1701
1701	Lyon	dates unknown; using 1700 Paris for act 5 and 1701 Paris for act 3
1709	Paris	19 Jul 1709 to 3 Sep 1709; revisions: 3 new airs inserted into acts 2, 3, and 5; new dance for prologue?
1710	Brussels	dates unknown; using Paris 1701
1729	Paris	13 Sep 1729 to 11 Oct 1729; Tuesdays in Jan 1730; 31 Aug 1730 to 28 Sep 1730; revisions: 1709 airs for acts 2 and 3 cut and original airs reinstated; 1709 air for act 5 retained
1729	Lyon	dates unknown; using 1701 Lyon
1730	Court	end of Dec 1730; 8 & 10 Feb 1731
1736	Court	19, 21, 26 Nov 1736
1740	Court	26 & 28 Sep 1740
1741	Court	29 Apr, 3 & 6 May; 13, 18, 20 Nov 1741
1742	Lyon	dates unknown; using Paris 1729 with abbreviated act 5
1742	Court	28 & 30 Jul; 1 Aug 1742
1743	Paris	1–30 Mar 1743; 6–20 Oct 1743; no revisions
1743	Court	23 & 30 Mar 1743 (prologue and first 3 acts)
1746	Court	19, 24, 26 Oct 1746
1750	Court	28 May (until Jun?)
1752	Court	20, 22, 27 Nov 1752

A Missing Link?
The Suite-Symphony in Mid-Eighteenth-Century North Germany

JOANNA COBB BIERMANN

Modern scholarship of the eighteenth-century symphony, while making progress in shaking off the 100-year-old notion that this form descended solely from the three-movement Italian *sinfonia* model, is still struggling with subtle, Darwinian ideas about symphonic "evolution." This paper will discuss a largely overlooked mid-century formal type, the suite-symphony, which was composed primarily in North Germany, appearing very often in certain courts, and occasionally at others, and attempt to place it in the eighteenth-century, North German musical "landscape."[1] The court of Hessen-Darmstadt was the unequivocal center for this symphonic type at mid-century, and its two *Kapellmeister*, Christoph Graupner (1683–1760) and Johann Samuel Endler (1694–1762), were the most prolific composers of suite-symphonies. They (and especially Endler) will be the focus of this article, although mention will be made of two further composers working in nearby Kassel who also composed some suite-symphonies. The South German/Austro-Bohemian orchestral pieces that were variously titled divertimento, cassation, serenade, and so on, and which show some similarities to the North German suite-symphony in their larger number of movements and mixtures of dance and abstract movements, are not treated here. None of these titles, as ubiquitous and interchangeable as they were in the South, appears on a single autograph of an orchestral work by Endler or Graupner. (Endler was especially precise about his generic titles and it behooves us to take his designations seriously.) The lack of these typically South German and Austro-Bohemian titles in their works seems to indicate that Endler and Graupner were looking toward other models in their compositional efforts. This is also strongly suggested by the list of works copied by them for use in perfor-

---

This essay is dedicated with the profoundest gratitude to Professor Bathia Churgin, dear friend and mentor, in honor of her eightieth birthday, 9 October 2008.

1. *The Symphonic Repertoire*, vol. I, *The Eighteenth-Century Symphony*, ed. Mary Sue Morrow and Bathia Churgin (Bloomington: Indiana University Press, 2012) presents an overview of the genre of the symphony in the eighteenth century in all centers and single essays on many composers. Other literature specific to the composers treated in this essay will be cited here in further footnotes.

mances by the *Hofkapelle*.[2] Endler copied Telemann most commonly: Telemann is represented by ca. thirty-four works; symphonies ascribed to the Grauns are also numerous, with twenty-five orchestral pieces in Endler's hand; fourteen works of Johann Friedrich Fasch, Graupner's student and friend, were copied by Endler and are still in the Darmstadt collection. In contrast, works by South Germans and composers from both Austria/Bohemia and Italy are comparatively rare. One South German composer, Placidus von Camerloher, who had visited Darmstadt in 1742 together with Emperor Carl VII, "the Bavarian," is unusually well represented with eight symphonies copied by Endler; three symphonies by "Steinmetz" (Johann Stamitz) are also in Endler's hand. The Italian symphonist who is best represented is Antonio Brioschi, with six symphonies reproduced by Endler. The situation is similar with Graupner, indicating a strong bias toward North German models in the *Hofkapelle* library in general.

The signal characteristics of the suite-symphonies I will be treating here include having

> four or more movements (and here I must emphasize that I am comparing these cycles to the three-movement form of the symphonic cycle otherwise so dominant in North Germany, not to the Mannheim, four-movement type);
>
> a mixture of abstract and dance or character types.

Further typical characteristics are their

> elaborate orchestrations, including much wind and brass usage in addition to strings and basso continuo; as well as
>
> frequent *concertante* segments within movements.

To the degree that this formal type has been treated at all in the modern historical narrative of the development of the symphony, it has been relegated to the footnotes of music history as a dead branch on the evolutionary tree. I will explore here its roots, and suggest that it did bear fruit in less conspicuous ways,

---

2. These numbers are taken from Friedrich Noack's handwritten notes in the card catalog of the Darmstadt library—the former Hessische Landes- und Hochschulbibliothek (D-DS), since 2004 under the new name Universitäts- und Landesbibliothek Darmstadt—and are to be regarded only as approximate. Note that the numbers quoted here refer only to copies by Endler. Graupner, too, produced many manuscripts of works by other composers, as did anonymous copyists, so that the total number of works by the composers mentioned above in the collection is often much higher.

and that perhaps its seeds were viable. Two older genres that impacted these mid-century symphonies will be singled out first for our discussion.

The first is the overture-suite in its German Baroque variant, that is to say, one made up of a newly-composed French overture movement and suite of dances and airs, not the French model of overture and suite extracted from an opera or ballet. These German overture-suites were the *locus classicus* of that synthesis of French, Italian, German and other national styles dubbed *der vermischte deutsche Geschmack*, the mixed German taste of composers such as Telemann, J. S. Bach, Christoph Graupner, Johann Friedrich Fasch, Johann Georg Pisendel, the Grauns, and many more North-German composers. Contemporary commentators such as Quantz and Scheibe had proudly cited this style as creating something they considered superior to the achievements of any single land. The main centers for this style amalgam were Dresden, Darmstadt, Kassel, and anywhere that the hugely influential Telemann appeared on the scene, and we see in those centers also symphonies that include many French stylistic traits. Telemann and his model unquestionably had a powerful influence on the Darmstadt composers. His works were well known to them, and many copies in both Graupner's and Endler's hand are in the collection in Darmstadt to this day. Endler was a card-carrying fan: he owned a large private collection of copies of Telemann's works, including some that he had copied a decade or more before coming to Darmstadt in 1723.[3] Graupner had known Telemann in Leipzig at the beginning of the century, and Telemann had been a Darmstadt neighbor from 1712 until 1721, when he worked in nearby Frankfurt, maintaining a lively connection to the superb musicians of the *Hofkapelle* and "borrowing" them on numerous occasions for his own performances.[4]

The overture-suite genre has been portrayed in common musical historiography as a quintessentially Baroque genre, and one that disappeared along with that era. One important eighteenth-century author, Berlin's Johann Joachim Quantz, concurred. In 1752 he mourned the demise of the overture-suite (pre-

---

3. D-DS Mus. ms. 1033/80, an oboe concerto by Telemann in Endler's hand, was copied on Saxon paper, and signed and dated 1713 by Endler. Four further Endler copies dating from his time in Saxony are in the Darmstadt collection today. See Joanna Cobb Biermann, *Die Sinfonien des Darmstädter Kapellmeisters Johann Samuel Endler 1694–1762. Ein Beitrag zur Geschichte der Sinfonie* (Mainz: Schott, 1996), 46–47.

4. Elisabeth Noack, *Musikgeschichte Darmstadts vom Mittelalter bis zur Goethezeit* (Mainz: Schott, 1967), 190–191.

maturely, as we shall see): "Because of the good effect they make, it is to be regretted that they are no longer common in Germany."[5] Twenty-two years later, in 1774, another Berlin theorist, J. A. P. Schulz, linked them explicitly to the modern symphonic genre, surmising that the origins of the symphony lay in the orchestral suite ("Parthie"),[6] as Bathia Churgin reminded us thirty years ago.[7] I argue that the later suite-symphonies examined here testify to the continuing, post-Baroque influence of *der vermischte Geschmack*, and that they perhaps did play a unique role in the history of the eighteenth-century symphony.

Another seminal influence on the early symphony that has not always been adequately recognized was that of the concerto, specifically Antonio Vivaldi's concerti. His widely imitated ritornello form influenced not only concerto form and style, but also provided a formal model for both the cycle and the individual movements in many early symphonies.[8] The *concertante* episodes in North German symphonies that appear so abundantly in works composed for Darmstadt are examples of another legacy of the concerto: the creation of variety of instrumental sound, as well as clarification of structure through variations in the performance forces within a single movement, and within a

---

5. "Nur ist, wegen der guten Wirkung, welche die Ouvertüren thun, zu bedauern, daß sie in Deutschland nicht mehr üblich sind." See Johann Joachim Quantz, *Versuch einer Anweisung die Flöte traversiere zu spielen* (Berlin: Johann Friedrich Voß, 1752; reprint Kassel: Bärenreiter, 1983), chap. 18, para. 42, 301. This and all other translations in the text are mine.

6. Schulz's definition appeared in the article "Symphonie" in Sulzer's *Allgemeine Theorie der schönen Künste* 2 and reads (in the 1794 edition from which Bathia Churgin quotes in "The Symphony as Described by J. A. P. Schulz (1774): A Commentary and Translation," *Current Musicology* 29 (1980): 10–11): "Symphonie. Ein vielstimmiges Instrumentalstük, das anstatt der abgekommenen Ouvertüren gebraucht wird. Die Schwierigkeit eine Ouvertüre gut vorzutragen, und die noch grössere Schwierigkeit, eine gute Ouvertüre zu machen, hat zu der leichteren Form der Symphonie, die Anfangs aus ein oder etlichen fugirten Stüken, die mit Tanzstüken von verschiedener Art abwechselten, bestand, und insgemein *Partie* genennt wurde, Anlass gegeben."

7. Churgin, "The Symphony as Described by J. A. P. Schulz," 7–16.

8. Vivaldi's concerti were widely disseminated, in North Germany through centers such as Dresden (whose *Konzertmeister*, Pisendel, had studied with Vivaldi), Darmstadt, and also the southern court of Oettingen-Wallerstein. Darmstadt's Prince Philipp, a brother of Landgraf Ernst Ludwig, imperial *Feldmarschall* and Governor of Mantua, had hired Vivaldi in the early years of the eighteenth century as his *Kapellmeister*. See Noack, *Musikgeschichte Darmstadts*, 167. Numerous works by Vivaldi made their way subsequently into the Darmstadt collection, some of which were destroyed in World War II.

multi-movement work. Two German musicological terms clarify neatly the different spheres in which the concerto can exert its influence on other genres: as *Formprinzip* (formal principle) through the adoption of ritornello structure; and as *Klangprinzip* (sounding principle) through the use of differing instrumental groups for various purposes.

The Composers and Their Circumstances
Kassel composers

The situation of Johan Joachim Agrell (1701–1765) and Fortunato Chelleri (ca. 1690–1757) in Kassel is less clearly documented than that of the Darmstadt composers, and much of the music produced and performed there has been lost.[9] The discussion here will hence be short, by necessity. Agrell, a young Swedish composer, was the first of the two to be called to Kassel, in his case, seemingly in 1723, to serve in the small private *Kapelle* of Prince Maximilian of Hessen-Kassel (1689–1753), the third son of the ruling landgrave, Karl (r. 1677–1730).[10] Agrell remained in Kassel (occasionally also helping out in the landgrave's musical establishment) until 1746, when—successfully fleeing the financial chaos of Maximilian's household—he became *Kapellmeister* to the free city of Nuremberg. It seems certain that before 1746 he frequently visited Darmstadt, the home of Maximilian's wife, Friederike Charlotte, the daughter of Ernst Ludwig, landgrave there until his death in 1739. Agrell clearly knew the musical repertoires of Darmstadt and of Kassel well.[11] Less clear are the occasions for which Agrell composed his symphonies. Of his twenty-eight extant, authentic symphonies, nine were apparently composed during his tenure in Kassel, and the rest as part of his duties in Nuremberg.[12] According to Jeannette Morgenroth Sheerin's thematic index, twelve Agrell symphonies are suite-symphonies having four to six movements, and of these twelve, four have extant Darmstadt sources.

---

9. See Jeannette Morgenroth Sheerin's discussion of Agrell in *The Symphony, 1720–1840*, ed. Barry Brook and Barbara Heyman [hereafter *The Symphony*], Series C, Vol. 1, (New York and London: Garland, 1983), xxi.

10. See ibid., xvi-xvii for Sheerin's discussion of the documentary situation regarding Agrell in Kassel. Maximilian visited Sweden as an emissary of the court of Hessen-Kassel in 1723, at which time Agrell was a student there (xxi).

11. Ibid., xxiii.

12. Ibid., xxvii.

The Suite-Symphony

Chelleri—whose name has been spelled in many ways in contemporary sources: Kellery, Kelleri, Keller, Cheller—was an Italian composer born in Parma to a German father and an Italian mother of the Bassani/Bazzani family of musicians.[13] After many years as an opera composer for theaters in Italy, Germany, and Spain, and travels throughout Europe, he was hired in 1725 as *Kapellmeister* to Landgrave Karl at Kassel. Chronic financial problems after Karl's death in 1730 caused his successors to reduce the size of the *Hofkapelle* severely and to limit its musical activities to church and military music.[14] Chelleri was able to save his own position, but the orchestra, which had had twenty-eight members in 1730, and which Chelleri had led to a high degree of excellence, was disbanded.[15] The ensemble for which he composed his symphonies after the death of Landgrave Karl in 1730 is not completely clear. The composer apparently spent two years in Sweden at the royal court in the early 1730s and he may have composed some of his symphonies there.[16] They were popular there and are well represented in Swedish libraries, as are those of his Kassel colleague Agrell, a native Swede. After Chelleri returned to Kassel in 1734 he supposedly had a small ensemble at his disposal.[17]

Twenty-one symphonies are extant; one has been lost. Eighteen have three movements. Four of the eighteen end with a minuet in 3/4 meter. There are three suite-symphonies with four, six, or eight movements, in which the composer appends a mixture of abstract and dance movements to a fast first movement. (The four-movement symphony, for example, includes a giga-like third movement and a minuet finale.) All of Chelleri's symphonies are scored for *a 4*

---

13. See Bathia Churgin, "Fortunato Chelleri," in *The Symphony*, Series A, Vol. 3, (New York and London: Garland, 1985), xxv–xxvi for an overview of the biographical information known about the composer.

14. Horst Heussner, "Zur Musikpflege im Umkreis des Prinzen Maximilian von Hessen: Pietro Locatelli und Johann Sebastian Bach in Kassel," in *Bachiana et alia Musicologica: Festschrift Alfred Dürr zum 65. Geburtstag*, ed. Wolfgang Rehm (Kassel: Bärenreiter, 1983), 108–115. He states that the orchestra was dissolved in 1730.

15. Wilhelm Lynker, *Geschichte des Theaters und der Musik in Kassel*, ed. Th. Köhler, (Kassel: Key, 1865), 268, quoted in Churgin, "Chelleri," in *The Symphony*, Series A, Vol. 3, xxvi, fn. 3.

16. Ibid., xxvi, fn. 2; and Heussner, "Maximilian," 109 for a list of the conflicting information about this visit.

17. Dorothea Schröder, "Chelleri," in *Die Musik in Geschichte und Gegenwart*, 2nd ed., ed. Ludwig Finscher (Kassel: Bärenreiter; Stuttgart and Weimar: Metzler, 2000), [hereafter MGG2] Personenteil, Vol. 4, col. 823.

strings, with winds and/or brass instruments called for in seven works. Timpani are sometimes utilized, including in the two large and festive symphonies in six and eight movements.

Darmstadt composers

The source situation for both our knowledge of the activities and also the compositions of the Darmstadt composers is incomparably better than for the Kassel *Kapellmeister*. Despite the relatively small size and degree of poverty of the state of Hessen-Darmstadt, the court at Darmstadt was one of the greatest musical centers in Germany in the early to mid-eighteenth century, rivaling both its North German competitors Dresden and Berlin, and later its South German rival Mannheim in both size of its musical establishment and also in its importance.[18] Both Graupner and Endler spent most of their professional lives at the court of Hessen-Darmstadt, working with a splendid orchestra whose performances Telemann praised in 1731 as "incomparable."[19] They were the employees of two landgraves whose fondness for music helped ultimately to lead the small and poor state into bankruptcy. The musical enthusiasm exhibited by these two noble dilettante composers and performers led the first one, Ernst Ludwig, to involve himself in 1733–1734 in a scheme to mint inferior gold coins, called—after himself—Ernest-d'or, and to use the profits to pay his musicians.[20] His son and successor, Ludwig VIII, who also partook of the typical eighteenth-century princely vices of elaborate building schemes, hunting, mistresses, and, not the least, music-making, continued his father's profligate spending habits, so that at his death in 1768 the *Hofkapelle* was disbanded and his land finally put under the direct financial administration of the empire.[21]

Earlier, in happier times, after the end of the Palatine War of Succession (1689–1697) and the return of the court to its hereditary seat at Darmstadt,

---

18. For information on the size and makeup of the Darmstadt *Hofkapelle*, see Biermann, *Endler*, 11–41.

19. Telemann praised the "incomparable execution of the Darmstadt orchestra" (unvergleichlich Execution des Darmstädtischen Orchesters) in Johann Mattheson, *Grosse General-Bass-Schule: oder der exemplarischen Organisten-Probe*, zweite, verbesserte und vermehrte Auflage (Hamburg, 1731; reprint, Hildesheim: Olms, 1968), 178.

20. Jürgen Rainer Wolf, "Joseph Süß Oppenheimer ("Jud Süß") und die Darmstädter Goldmunzprägung unter Landgraf Ernst Ludwig," *Numismatisches Nachrichtenblatt* 30 (1981): 94.

21. See Biermann, *Endler*, 11–41.

The Suite-Symphony

the first music-loving landgrave, Ernst Ludwig, hired a young composer away from the Hamburg opera, Christoph Graupner, and gave him *carte blanche* to hire good new instrumentalists and singers. A second wave of hires of outside musicians, in 1723, brought Johann Samuel Endler from Leipzig, where he had been the director of music at the Neue Kirche,[22] and of the second *Collegium musicum*, founded by Johann Friedrich Fasch in 1708 in the wake of Telemann's successful first *Collegium*. Endler was hired first as a singer (falsetto alto) and violinist. About 1740, when Ludwig VIII became landgrave, Endler rose first to the rank of concertmaster, and then, to *Vice-Kapellmeister* under Graupner. This promotion was also linked to new duties which seemingly occasioned the composition of his first symphonic works.

Princely tastes, unsurprisingly, seem to have played a role in the new interest in the symphony. The first landgrave, Ernst Ludwig, had early on fancied French music, and then later Italian and German opera, but seemingly not the Italian (and increasingly, German) genre of the symphony. His successor, Ludwig VIII, did not attempt to support an opera, and most of the music composed at the court beyond Graupner's Sunday cantatas was instrumental, including numerous symphonies. Both landgraves apparently shared an abiding affection for the overture-suite, however, even as it went out of fashion elsewhere.

As far as we know, very few if any symphonies were composed at Darmstadt before 1740, when Ludwig VIII's reign began. Seemingly around 1746 or 1747, Graupner turned to the symphony and, in his typical fashion, created a large number of them within a short period, apparently about 113 from that time until total blindness overcame him in 1754.[23] (Graupner rivals Telemann as a *Vielschreiber*. His 1300 extant cantatas in the Darmstadt library today rival the 1400 cantatas by Telemann which, of his original ca. 1700, are still extant.) Graupner's *Vice-Kapellmeister*, Endler, was obviously not required to produce the same quantity of works that Graupner did. Twenty-nine authentic symphonies

---

22. Ibid., 10, fn. 7.
23. Peter Cahn, "Die Sinfonien Christoph Graupners," in *Christoph Graupner, Hofkapellmeister in Darmstadt 1709–1760*, ed. Oswald Bill (Mainz: Schott, 1987), 214. Although highly critical of the datings offered by Friedrich Noack in his notations in the Darmstadt Library catalog, Cahn does not attempt to replace them. These dates, which are wholly inadequate and in great need of a critical revision, have been the basis of every subsequent discussion of Graupner's symphonies in the literature since Noack first proposed them.

by Endler are extant,[24] and there is no evidence that any number of others have been destroyed. Two-thirds of them are dated and the place of first performance noted in the composer's own hand.[25] All were performed at festivities in the years between 1748 and 1761.[26]

Table 1 offers a quick overview of the number of movements in the symphonies composed by Endler and Graupner, as well as by the two composers working in neighboring Kassel.

As we can see, more than one-half of Graupner's symphonies contain four or more movements, but there is a substantial block of fifty-five more Italianate three-movement cycles. Endler, on the other hand, consistently preferred the possibility of creating greater variety within his cycle by utilizing the larger number of movements. They number between three and seven. The largest group, thirteen symphonies, has six movements. Agrell and Chelleri, the Kassel composers, wrote fewer suite-symphonies, but they make up a significant portion of their respective *oeuvres*.

The Cycle

The shaping of the cycle in Endler's and Graupner's symphonies was extraordinarily free, both in number and order of movements as well as their type. However, all four movement types characteristic of the cycle that later in the century became the most common model, are represented in their symphonies. In addition they include other dance types and almost always an expanded inner

---

24. D-DS lists thirty-one symphonic works under Endler's name. Two of them (Mus. ms. 1213/3 and 1213/26) show identical string parts, but reduced brass parts in one. A further work (Mus. ms. 1213/31) is fragmentary and of doubtful attribution and hence not counted among the twenty-nine under discussion here. He also composed other orchestral works entitled either *Ouverture* (orchestral suites with French overture opening movements), or *Pièce* (suites without a characteristic first movement). In 1900, Wilibald Nagel listed ten overtures by Endler with incipits in, "Zur Geschichte der Musik am Hofe von Darmstadt," *Monatshefte für Musikgeschichte* 32 (1900): 63–64. Of these, three are now lost. When they were lost is not known; they are not registered in the Darmstadt catalog of works burned during the Second World War.

25. See Joanna Cobb Biermann, "Johann Samuel Endler," in *The Symphony*, Series C, Vol. 2 (New York and London: Garland, 1984), 180 for a reproduction of an autograph title page, 142 for an autograph clarino part, and 212 for an autograph violin part.

26. Only three days of the year are named: 1 January; 16 April, the birthday of Ludwig VIII; and 25 August, *Ludwigstag*, his nameday. The performances took place at "Cranigstein" (today spelled Kranigstein) outside of Darmstadt, in the hunting palace that was Ludwig's favored residence.

Table 1. Symphonies by Darmstadt and Kassel composers

No. of Movements	Graupner[a]	Endler[b]	Agrell[c]	Chelleri[d]
3	55	2	13	18
4	28	7	9	1
5	20	6	2	0
6	7	13	1	1
7	2	1	0	0
8	1	0	0	1
Sum:	113	29	25	21

a. Cahn, "Graupner," 230.
b. See Biermann, *Endler*, 202–231, for the incipits of all the movements.
c. Jeannette Morgenroth Sheerin numbers twenty-eight authentic symphonies by Agrell. The discrepancy in numbers here is explained by the fact that three symphonies are known only through entries in the Breitkopf catalog, which does not reveal the number of movements. See Sheerin's thematic index in *The Symphony*, Series C, Vol. 1 (New York and London: Garland, 1983), xxxix–xliv.
d. Churgin, "Chelleri," in *The Symphony*, Series A, Vol. 3, xxvii.

movement of some kind, either a dance or an abstract movement.[27] In common with later practice, their symphonies utilized:

1) a quick first movement;
2) a slow movement as an inner movement;
3) a minuet and trio, either as an inner movement, or sometimes as a finale;
4) a further quick, dance-like or dance-titled finale.

First Movements

Endler's allegro first movements are consistently cast in a modern, energetic Italianate style that follows sonata practice.[28] They always demonstrate the

---

27. The exceptions to this rule can be found in those symphonies which in their movement series are closer to a suite of dances. See Symphony E-flat 4 in Biermann, "Endler" in *The Symphony*, Series C, Vol. 2, 179–210.

28. Extensive examples of Endler's first movements are given in Biermann, *Endler*, and in *The Symphonic Repertoire*, vol. 1, in addition to the three examples of full symphonies in Biermann, "Endler" in *The Symphony*, Series C, Vol. 2. For this reason, the non-initial movements are treated in greater detail in this essay.

"lebhafte brillierende Melodie" ("brilliant, lively melody") that Johann Adolph Scheibe had recommended a decade or more earlier in his *Compendium musices*. Endler's colleague Graupner knew this work well: his autograph copy of it, dated 1736, is now in the Yale University library.[29] But seemingly his strong penchant for creating lovely, dream-like moods conquered his better knowledge of the generic expectations which had already grown up around aspects of this relatively new genre. Peter Cahn describes Graupner's first movements as an alternation between energetic, rhythmically forward-moving tutti segments and gentle, harmonically stagnant areas of lingering, in which he creates "islands" of idyllic, pastoral or *galant* character.[30]

Endler's first movements could hardly have been more different. In terms of form we find among Endler's first movements:

Sonata forms with and without internal repeats;

Occasional binary forms without repeats;

A few examples showing ritornello-influenced forms in which, however, sonata principles clearly dominate.

Most of Endler's first movement forms are structured with the same type of divisions described by Koch later in the century in his *Anleitung*. Their harmonic movement is standard, too: they progress from the tonic to the dominant in the first section, then, in the first half of the second section, to the submediant, subsequently returning to the tonic in the second half of the second section. Perfect authentic cadences are heard in all three keys areas: the dominant, the submediant, and the tonic. Occasional first movements utilize the mediant in additional to the submediant key area.

Graupner, on the other hand, generally chooses ritornello forms for his first movements, with and without actual soli. Various binary forms, generally non-repeating, are the second most important structural principle seen at the beginning of Graupner's symphonies. Some of his first movements in works titled "symphony" show, oddly enough, even French overture form (twice) as well as a single da-capo form,[31] a kind of generic confusion that Endler did not show.

---

29. Shelf number Misc. Ms. 219.
30. Cahn, "Graupner," 244.
31. Ibid., 240.

The Suite-Symphony

Slow Movements

As a slow inner movement, Endler usually choses an *Andante*, though even slower tempi such as *Largo*, sometimes with additional character indications such as *Largo e cantabile*, or *Arietta-Largo* can be found.[32] Formally, Endler prefers binary forms in slow movements, often with no return of the primary material at the point of return of the tonic key.[33] This type of more continuous formal structure fits well to the leisurely flow of his spun-out motivic material, which is often found here. Graupner's expansive slow movements are some of his most impressive accomplishments, giving him ample room for his lyrical, tarrying bent.

Minuet and Trio

A minuet and trio movement as an inner or final movement is found in every symphony by Endler but one. (However, one work, his seven-movement Symphony in D (D 16), contains two minuets.) Graupner is not so consistent: while most of his symphonies with four or more movements have a minuet, numerous such cycles have no dance movement whatsoever, not even the minuet.[34]

Finales

A further dance-like or dance-titled finale most often completes the cycle. It is most commonly in 3/8 meter and, when titled, is called by Endler a passepied, or, in three cases, a passetemps (an even simpler passepied type). These, and many finales with only a tempo marking such as *Allegro* (1 and 2) or *Presto* (1 and 2), all show the typical passepied traits of 3/8 meter, use of an eighth-note upbeat, and four-measure phrase structure. Four further finales are of the passepied type, but have character titles, in the manner of Telemann in his overture-suites: Endler's "Schwab" 1 and 2 (D 10), a burlesque dance characterized by huge, awkward leaps in the melody, pokes fun at the Swabians of southwest Germany;

---

32. Further characterizing titles of slow movements are *Andante alla Pastorella*, *Dolce*, *Arioso*, *Air en Pastorelle*, *Affetuoso*, and *Contentement*. A slow dance form could also serve the purpose of variety of tempo, and Endler chose that solution in works that were closer in spirit to the French style, using a polonaise (or even a slow minuet) in some symphonies.

33. See the slow movement in Symphony D 6, in Biermann, "Endler" in *The Symphony*, Series C, Vol. 2, 157–159.

34. Cahn, "Graupner," 230.

another similarly comic piece is entitled "Passepied burlesque" 1 and 2 (D 12); a pair of dances called "Le bon vivant" 1 and 2 ends Symphony E-flat 4;[35] and finally, a passepied-type movement named "Les Postillons" utilizes, of course, horns (D 1). Minuet finales are found in six symphonies, and a pair of rigaudons in one. Only three finales are not passepied types, minuets, or rigaudons. All finales show relatively quick to very quick tempi, regardless of type.

Dance Types: An Overview

Endler's cycles include occasional movements with dance titles, and many with dance characteristics, but without the titles, some of which have already been mentioned. He uses eight different named dance types in toto (in order of frequency): Menuett (29), Passepied/Passetemps (7), Polonaise (6), Bourrée (4), Rigaudon and Marche (each twice), and Rondeau (1). Unnamed, but present in five cases is a gavotte type (in one instance without the characteristic half-measure pick-up). Graupner also used eight dance titles, sometimes prefaced by the little disclaimer "Tempo di" or "Air en," which indicates a greater degree of formal freedom for the movement. In common with Endler's cycles are the minuet, bourrée, rigaudon, and marche; additionally Graupner also named the fashionable gigue and gavotte, but also the older sarabande and loure. The goal of both composers was clearly to create an attractive variety of movement types, keys, meters, tempi, instrumentation, and styles within each of their multi-movement works—in other words, to transfer the overture-suite aesthetic to the newer symphonic genre.

An important and forward-looking aspect of both composers' sometime use of dance types, however, is the unusual expansion of some of these forms in movements without the dance titles. Endler developed many of these beyond the binary or rounded binary norm, instead giving them new breadth and weight through the use of sonata procedures and/or concerto texture. To support both expanded dance movements and fast, non-dance inner movements, Endler had recourse to the harmonic scheme he used for his sonata-type first movements, moving from the tonic to the dominant and then also to the submediant before returning to the tonic. Perfect authentic cadences occur in all three tonal areas. Graupner developed his final movements sometimes into mini-sonatas, with

---

35. See Biermann, "Endler" in *The Symphony*, Series C, Vol. 2, 179–210 for the whole symphony, 204–210 for the "Bon vivant" movements.

The Suite-Symphony

quasi-developmental second sections and clear marking of the "double return" (with hardly any regular recapitulations, however).[36] A comparison to what was happening in Mannheim, where the minuet became the standard addition to the three-movement symphony, is revealing: Eugene Wolf found as dance movements within Stamitz's symphonies thirty-three minuet/trio movements and two early polonaises, which, in comparison to the Darmstadt composers, represents a severe limiting of the type of dances included, and a self-limitation that would come to generally dominate the symphonic style in the next years. However, none of Stamitz's minuets and polonaises shows either an expansion involving any key beyond the tonic and dominant, or an increase in size: they retain their tiny dimensions, as in the old-fashioned suite: the most common type is made up of two eight-measure, repeated sections.[37]

The second movement of Symphony D 11 (1757), marked in 3/8 time, is entitled *Presto*, and is eighty-four measures long. It is a greatly expanded passepied-type movement, with the characteristic time signature, eighth-note upbeat and regular four-measure phrase structure we expect from this dance type. It is represented schematically in Table 2.

This movement is longer than a normal passepied movement, even somewhat longer than a normal pair of passepied movements with all repeats would be. The A section, heard three times, remains tonally stable and in the tonic, D-Major. The rondo structure is combined with the expanded harmonic scheme found in most of Endler's extended movements, especially his sonata-type movements, with the episodes venturing beyond tonic and dominant to the submediant. True perfect authentic cadences sound in all three key areas. In terms of instrumental color, Endler creates in the fourth segment (mm. 49–56) a charming contrast as a solo segment for two trumpets with timpani bass.

An earlier example, the fourth movement (*Vivace*) of Symphony D 6, dated 1 January 1751, shows the same expanded harmonic structure, and an alternation of orchestral groups that colors it strongly. Concerto texture contributes to the shape and the length of this movement. An extremely regular alternation of two groupings marks this movement: the trumpets and timpani in six-measure units versus the strings with oboe and horns in twelve-bar segments.

---

36. Cahn, "Graupner," 255.
37. Eugene K. Wolf, *The Symphonies of Johann Stamitz: A Study in the Formation of the Classic Style* (Utrecht: Bohn; The Hague: Nijhoff, 1981), 347–349.

Table 2. Endler's Symphony D 11, Presto (ii), structure

a + b	a + b	c + d + e + f	a + b	a + b	g + h	etc.	a + b	a + b
4+4 4+4	4+4 4+4	4+4 4+4	4+4 4+4	4+4	4+4	4+4+4	4+4 4+4	
I	I	I V/V V	I	I	I V	mod vi vi	I	I
I PAC		V HC PAC			V HC	→vi HC PAC		I PAC
m. 16	m. 32		m. 48		m. 56	m. 68	(the da capo)	
A	B		A		C		A	
Tutti	Str str tutti		Tutti		2 hr/timp	Str tutti str	Tutti	

The Suite-Symphony

The brass make up the tonally stable sections, and the string and wind segments modulate. Much of this is concerto-like, a tri-ritornello form, to be exact. But there are significant differences here: Endler overrides the normally through-composed concerto structure by turning this into a binary form with repeats of both sections. And although the alternation is regular, there is no thematically stable ritornello; instead, each group in turn varies the motivic material it played before. Both groups do retain their own typical characteristics in each segment, with the brass playing rhythmically regular, fanfare-like material. The strings answer with syncopated motives which instead stress the offbeats.

Large-Scale Inner Movements

The final movement type which Endler and Graupner included in their suite-symphonies, and which again supports the contention that these works are truly symphonies and not just orchestral suites under a false title, is the large-scale, abstract inner movement. Endler's movement entitled *Fanfaron*, Symphony D 2 (iv), reproduced in the appendix (pp. 52–57), shows one of his many ways of synthesizing elements of sonata principles with other generic types, such as the concerto, and even with reminders of ABA form. It has three instrumental groupings that play *concertante* segments: three trumpets with timpani bass; solo violin; solo violin plus solo oboe. The concerto texture here is subsumed under sonata principles, however, and is rather strictly periodic (four-measure units until the final one), perhaps because of the march-like character that the fanfares suggest. Each of the three sections, exposition, development, and recapitulation, begins with a fanfare; the first and the third are the same, and the middle one, which sounds after the double bar and repeat of the exposition, is different, although returning to the tonic key (for technical reasons with the natural trumpet). The sonata-like characteristics of this movement are not exhausted in its expanded binary form with internal repeats, nor with its harmonic scheme, which is the augmented one he uses for all his longer and weightier movements (tonic, dominant, [return to tonic here], submediant, tonic): the different instrumental blocks can also be understood as outlining—and underscoring—primary, transitional, secondary, and closing material in the exposition. As in many of Endler's first movements—and in those of numerous other contemporaries' sonata-type movements—the secondary material is the least clearly articulated functional area, out of concern for continuity. In this example, the solo violin episode, mm. 13–16, confirms the new key with a new motive and a new texture, and hence fulfills the function of a secondary area in this diminutive sonata movement. The retransition (mm. 43–50) utilizes a simple circle of fifths, with a motive tossed back and forth between solo oboe and solo violin. The accompaniment is thinned out, as it had been for the confirmation of the new key in the exposition, to simple eighth-notes, *piano*, in the second violin and viola parts, a fine preparation here, as in the exposition, for the return of the brilliant brass sound. The recapitulation is complete, and the motivic/thematic material presented in the original order.

These composers' cycles, made up of abstract, dance, dance-like, and character movements (titled sometimes in Italian, sometimes in French), are obviously connected to *der vermischte deutsche Geschmack*. These large-scale orchestral cycles are made up of many varied, contrasting, and colorful movements, full of unusual orchestral effects, a style that was especially suited to both composers' talents. Suites were obviously still admired and desired at court: Endler composed some of his own overture-suites in the 1750s, dating one 1753 and another 1755. Two further overture-suites without a French overture opening movement, which he titled simply *Pièces*, are also dated in the 1750s (1755 and 1759). Telemann stands as final witness to the love for this genre at Darmstadt: in the last year of his life, inspired in his own words by the announcement in a newspaper of planned festivities for the nameday of Landgrave Ludwig VIII of Hessen-Darmstadt, Telemann returned to the overture-suite genre that he had so influenced in his younger days in order to write a set of such pieces in Ludwig's honor.[38] The particular Darmstadt style as seen in the works of Endler especially, and Graupner to a somewhat lesser degree, extended the local taste for the overture-suite to the newer genre of the symphony.

Orchestration

Endler's and Graupner's striking—and especially attractive—use of instrumental color was made possible by the "incomparable" Darmstadt orchestra—to cite Telemann once again—with its rich contingent of wind and brass instruments. One of the main reasons for the production of such a number of suite-

---

38. *Georg Philipp Telemann: Briefwechsel*, ed. Hans Grosse and Hans Rudolf Jung (Leipzig: VEB Deutscher Verlag für Musik, 1972), 192–193, quoted in Steven Zohn, *Music for a Mixed Taste: Style, Genre, and Meaning in Telemann's Instrumental Works* (Oxford and New York: Oxford University Press, 2008), 57 (English translation) and 526, fn. 95 (German original).

The Suite-Symphony

symphonies at the court of Darmstadt was that this genre could demonstrate a broader spectrum of the orchestra's capabilities in a single work, more than any three-movement symphony ever could. In Endler's symphonies, *concertante* episodes were possible in any movement other than the first (Graupner sometimes had solo voices even there, a kind of generic confusion which Endler never fell prey to). Endler also always varied his *concertante* groups within a single work, so that many different colors would sound. (He composed no work which he titled "Concerto" as far as we know, and seemingly made the generic distinction between his *Sinfonia*-titled works and what might have been considered a concerto by avoiding ritornello form in his first movements and not maintaining a single soloist or consistent solo grouping throughout a work.)

Princely taste appreciated such works, as has been shown, and both composers, happily, were gifted as imaginative and virtuosic orchestrators. As two-thirds of Endler's symphonies were written for festive occasions, he could be assured of the services of a larger orchestra than would have been available for more normal *Tafelmusik*. Table 3 shows the orchestration of all of Endler's symphonies.[39]

The scores produced by Endler and Graupner bear witness to the extremely high level of skill of the orchestra. For instance, both trumpeters and horn players had mastered clarino technique, and both composers used this capability to create brilliant and festive pieces. Endler even occasionally—as a special effect at the beginning and end of a movement, especially in early symphonies—used the first trumpet sounding an octave above the first violin, with the first horn at the octave of the first violin, all of this creating a stunningly brilliant, festive brass sound.

Symphony D 11 can serve as an example of the kind of variety of instrumental color, formal types, and textural surprises that Endler would muster within a single work. Composed for Landgrave Ludwig's birthday festivities in 1757, the autograph parts seem to indicate a special effect not documented in any of his other works. Before the first notes of the exposition and again at the development/recapitulation of this sonata-form movement the words "Marche

---

39. The numbering of the symphonies, c 1, D 1, etc. follows my thematic index published in "Endler" in *The Symphony,* Series C, Vol. 2, lxxi-lxxiv. In the table, the shelf number of the manuscript D-DS Mus. ms. 1213/… follows; then the autograph date, if noted by Endler; the instrumentation is explained, if necessary, in the footnotes. The number of timpani is not noted.

Table 3. Endler's orchestration

Symph	Ms	Date	Fl	Ob	Bsn[a]	Hr1	Hr2	Cl1	Cl2	Tmp	Vl1	Vl2	Vla	Bs
c 1	1213/19	?									x	x	x	fig[b]
D 1	/25	?	x			x	x	x	x	x	x	x		fig
D 2	/8	?		x	x			x	xx[c]	x	x	x	x	x
D 3	/22	?	x*[d]					x	x		x	x	x	fig
D 4	/2	1/1/50	x			x	x	x	xx	x	x	x		x
D 5	/27	8/25/50		x	x	x					x	x	x	fig
D 6	/28	1/1/51	x	x		x	x	x	xx	x	x	x		x
D 7	/30	1/1/52	x			x	x	x	x	x	x	x	x	fig
D 8	/16	1/1/54	x			x	x	x	x	x	x	x		fig
D 9	/9	1/1/55	x			x	x	x	xx	x	x	x	x	x
D 10	/5	8/25/56	xx					x	x	x	x	x		fig
D 11	/11	4/16/57	x			x	x	x	x	x	x	x	x	fig
D 12	/24	8/25/57						x	x	x	x	x		x
D 13	/6	4/16/58						x	x	x	x	x	(x)[e]	fig
D 14	/1	8/25/58	x			x	x	x	x	x	x	x	x	fig
D 15	/23	1/1/59	x			x	x	x	xx	x	x	x	x	fig
D 16	/17	8/25/59	**			x	x	(x)	x)	x	x	x		fig
D 17	/29	1/1/60	x	x		xx	xx	x	xx	x	x	x	x	fig
D 18	/3, /26	8/25/60	x	x		x	x	x	x	x	x	x		x
D 19	/10	1/1/61	x			x	x	x	xx	x	x	x	x	x
d 1	/4	?									x	x	x	fig
Eb 1	/12	?		x				x	x	x	x	x		fig
Eb 2	/14	?		x				x	xx	x	x	x	x	fig
Eb 3	/18	?						x	x		x	x	x	fig
Eb 4	/20	1/1/57	xx**[f]	x				x	xx	x	x	x	x	fig
e 1	/7	?									x	x	x	fig
F 1	/15	4/16/48	xx			x	x	x	x	x	x	x	x	fig
F 2	/13	8/25/49		x	x	x	x	x		x	x	x		fig
G 1	/21	?	x			x	x				x	x	x	x

a. The bassoon was always present as part of the basso continuo group. It is mentioned explicitly here only when it has a designated solo in one of the inner movements.

b. "fig" indicates the presence of a figured bass. A simple x indicates no figures.

c. The presence of a third clarino part is indicated by xx under "Cl 2."

d. An asterisk is used to indicate a recorder ("flauto dolce").

e. Parentheses indicate a part named on the title page but not found in the extant material.

f. This symphony offers alternative parts for two transverse flutes or two recorders. They could not have been played simultaneously because the parts were written on two sides of one sheet of paper.

de [sic] Trompettes" are written in the parts (the tempo, *Allegro*, is at its usual place, above the first line of music). Also in the parts, the additional words "1. Posten" and "2. Posten" stand before the exposition, and "3. Posten" and "4. Posten" before the beginning of the development section. The same is true of the timpani part. This would seem to suggest first that there were at least eight trumpeters and two timpanists (using a minimum of four timpani), and secondly, that they were separated physically into two groups. Perhaps the trumpeters even marched in at their respective entries and paraded around the room (the movement is entitled *Marche* after all). Since there is no notated music for the trumpeters' and timpanists' *Marche*, they presumably played music of their own devising for this stunning entrance, something the Darmstadt trumpeters were trained to do, and even did at inappropriate times.[40] Table 4 offers a schematic rendering of this whole, six-movement symphony, demonstrating both the variety of soloistic groupings within this one work, as well as the variety of forms, meters, keys, and so on, that Endler mustered within one single work.

Endler's orchestration ranks among the most brilliant and original characteristics of his symphonies. It did, however, make up a potential problem for their dissemination at the time: the large number of instrumentalists required—especially of brass and, to a lesser extent wind instruments—and the high caliber of playing needed to master these parts, as well as the fact that the brass parts, and soloistic wind parts, were not *ad libitum*, made these pieces simply unplayable at most contemporary courts. To my knowledge there is only one surviving copy of an Endler symphony at another court, namely Symphony F 1, his earliest dated symphony (1748), which is housed now at Karlsruhe, in the Badische Landesbibliothek, under *Anonyma*. The Darmstadt princess Caroline Luise, who had been a pupil of Endler's, married the margrave of Baden-Durlach in 1751, three years after this symphony was performed at her father's court in Darmstadt, a fact that could explain its transmission to Baden.[41]

---

40. Noack, *Musikgeschichte Darmstadts*, 225, relates a story about *Hoftrompeter* Schneider, who tried to insist on having his own pieces played for a *Tafelmusik* in 1742, because with the planned pieces no special impression could be made. His were too difficult for the elder trumpeters, however.

41. Jan Lauts, *Karoline Luise: Ein Lebensbild aus der Zeit der Aufklärung* (Karlsruhe: C. F. Müller, 1980), 14; interestingly, this symphony features two F-clarinos in the highest register, suggesting that this uncommon usage of the instrument was perhaps somewhat more widely disseminated at the time than generally assumed now.

Table 4. Endler's Symphony D 11, overview

Movement Key Meter	Form	Orchestra	Special Feature
I. Marche de Trompettes—Allegro D-Major 2/4	Sonata	2 Cl; Timp; 2 Vl; Vla; Bc (fig)	Solo trumpets and timpani, apparently issuing from different parts of the room, at beginning and middle of the movement
II. Presto D-Major 2/4	Tri-ritornello	2 Cl, Timp, 2 Vl, Vla, Bc.	One episode features 2 trumpets with timpani bass, the other strings; harmonic expansion to include key of submediant.
III. Arioso G-Major 3/8	Binary, with internal repeats	Fl (or Vl), 2 Hr, 2 Vl, Vla, Bc.	Solo treble voice (marked "Flauto o Violino") accompanied by 2 Hr (piano throughout) and pizzicato strings.
IV. Vivace G-Major ₵	Binary, with internal repeats (gavotte-like in time signature and two quarter-note upbeats)	2 Hr, 2 Vl, Vla, Bc.	Full of little harmonic surprises, sudden unison minore gestures.
V. Minuet 1 & 2 D-Major 3/4	Large-scale ternary (minuet-trio-minuet) made up of small-scale, repeated binary forms	Minuet 1: 2 Tr, Timp, 2 Vl, Vla, Bc; Minuet 2 (=Trio): same instruments, but alternating and piano	Trio section alternates piano strings, solo trumpets (with pianissimo timpani bass) and tutti sections.
VI. Rigaudon 1 & 2 D-Major ₵	Large-scale ternary made up of small-scale, repeated binary forms	Rigaudon 1: 2 Tr, Timp, Str, Bc; Rigaudon 2: high strings only	Rigaudon 2: Vl 1 melody line accompanied by Vl 2 and Vla. No bass, no brass or winds.

Closing Remarks

The North German symphonic scene was dominated by the Italian three-movement model, but with contemporary commentators still cherishing fond memories of the old-fashioned overture-suite. As we have seen, some composers chose another model, most consistently Johann Samuel Endler in Darmstadt. Some commentators have contended that his suite-symphonies are generically merely overture-suites.[42] Were he and Graupner perhaps really selling their old-fashioned suites with a false, new-fangled title? Old wine in new skins?

I would argue that the Darmstadt composers, and to a certain extent the two Kassel *Kapellmeister*, were indeed creating something new and original through their interesting synthesis: Endler showed a full-blown sonata form already in the first movements of his earliest datable works, and not as the result of some kind of "evolution," branching out to experiment with other forms only later; both he and Graupner used sonata principles, often—in some inner movements—married to concerto ideas; Endler expanded some of his dance forms through the use of sonata practice or rondo form to make substantial, more complex movements which could hold their own against the long and lovely slow movements and the weighty first movements. At the same time, they still retained numerous standard dances and also character pieces in their older forms, something that pleased through the combination of the familiarity of their types with the surprising touches, especially in the realm of orchestral color, which these composers utilized so masterfully. Both wrote for winds and brass in a brilliant manner not to be found in contemporary Italianate symphonies.

That the question of the impact of these works on the development of symphonic music in Germany around the middle of the eighteenth-century is intimately linked to its dissemination is clear. What is not clear is what the actual source situation was at the time. When we surmise that the composers at the nearby court of Hessen-Kassel, with its verifiable contacts with the Hessen-Darmstadt musical establishment, could well have been influenced by

---

42. Ludwig Finscher, in his article "Symphonie" in MGG2, dismisses Endler's symphonies simply as "ausnahmslos französische Suiten" (without exception French suites). MGG2, Sachteil, vol. 9, col. 29. His section on the symphony in Darmstadt largely repeats the appraisal and errors of Friedrich Noack's 1954 entry in MGG1 on Endler (*Die Musik in Geschichte und Gegenwart*, ed. Friedrich Blume, vol. 3, Kassel and Basel, 1954, cols. 1342–1343) with some additional recognition of Peter Cahn's 1987 essay on Graupner.

Endler and Graupner—and that the suite-symphony type might have wandered thereafter from Kassel to Johan Helmich Roman in Sweden, who also composed suite-symphonies[43]—we are immediately frustrated by the loss of the music collections of both the Kassel landgrave, Chelleri's patron, and of his son Maximilian, Agrell's employer. (Dynastic connections existed both between the two Hessian courts and also between Hessen-Kassel and the Swedish royal court. Frequent travel between members of the princely families of Darmstadt and Kassel that included musicians in their entourages is assumed.)[44]

The use of *concertante* episodes throughout many of the movements is a signal characteristic of both composers' symphonies. In addition, their common use of multiple solo voices within the symphonic context reveals an early and original use of the synthesis of concerto and symphonic structure and texture that predates the Mannheim *symphonie concertante* by ten to twenty years. An inquiry about the potential influence of the Darmstadt composers' writing on the *symphonie concertante* in Mannheim is also frustrated by the loss of the contemporary Mannheim collection. Endler's composition student Christoph Schetky spent considerable time in Mannheim (overstaying his leave substantially), studying cello with Anton Fils, who had joined the Mannheim *Hofkapelle* in 1754.[45] Did he bring Darmstadt compositions with him? We cannot know.

Back to our original question about symphonic "evolution." Where do the suite-symphonies belong? Are they simply generic peculiarities? Are these questions even legitimate? Perhaps we have succumbed to the destructive idea of symphonic "progress" and "evolution," and their musicological equivalent, something we might call the "dissemination of the fittest." It is now time to finally give up our search both for a single line of development toward the Viennese triumvirate and for signs of historical "progress" toward some kind of symphonic goal. To recognize the amazing variety of symphonic activity in the mid-eighteenth-century and its usage of both the new styles and the familiar old friends is a gain for both our scholarship and our concert halls. And in terms of influence/

---

43. Sherrin, "Agrell," in *The Symphony*, Series C, Vol. 1, xx, writes that Roman became an active composer only after Agrell had left Sweden, and that Agrell sent copies of music to Roman in Sweden in 1742.

44. Ibid., xxiii.

45. Schetky's connection to Fils is documented in a notice in the *Allgemeine Musikalische Zeitung* of 16 October 1799, col. 35–36. See Biermann, *Endler*, 45–46 for the text.

modeling/appropriation and whatever else we might call it, we must recognize the inherent limits to what we can know given the complexity of dissemination, and the accidents of extancy.

Appendix: Endler's Symphony D 2, Fanfaron (iv)

The Suite-Symphony

47

The Suite-Symphony

The Suite-Symphony

51

"Ein Musikdirector hat an einem Instrumente Mangel":
Obbligato Organ in the Bach Cantatas

EVAN PHILIP CORTENS

J. S. Bach made much greater use of the organ as an obbligato instrument in his sacred cantatas than the vast majority of his contemporaries.[1] This observation in itself constitutes nothing new, but what has yet to be fully explored is the true nature of Bach's use of the instrument in this context.[2] Rarely does a part written for organ remain on that instrument; the reverse is also true, as parts often conceived for other instruments are later played by the organ. It is not enough to simply say that Bach accorded the instrument a special status; its role is more complex than this.

My thanks to David Yearsley—in whose Spring 2009 seminar on Bach's organ works this paper began—as well as to William Cowdery, Mathieu Langlois, Joshua Rifkin, and Andrew Shryock for their invaluable feedback on earlier drafts.

1. To my knowledge, neither Georg Philipp Telemann, cantor in Hamburg from 1721, nor Christoph Graupner, *Kapellmeister* in Darmstadt from 1709, wrote a sacred cantata movement with obbligato organ. However, Matthew Cron reports that Gottfried Heinrich Stölzel, Bach's contemporary at Gotha, wrote twenty-seven sacred cantata movements with obbligato organ ("The Obbligato Organ Cantatas of J. S. Bach in the Context of 18th-Century Practice" (PhD diss., Brandeis University, 2004), 809–815). Communication between Bach and Stölzel certainly took place, as evidenced by the former's inclusion of the latter's music in both the *Clavier-Büchlein* for Wilhelm Friedemann (BWV 929) and Anna Magdalena (BWV 508). Furthermore, Marc-Roderich Pfau found that Bach performed Stölzel's "Saitenspiel" cantata cycle in 1735–1736 (see "Ein unbekanntes Leipziger Kantatentextheft aus dem Jahr 1735—Neues zum Thema Bach und Stölzel," *Bach-Jahrbuch* 94 (2008): 99–122), and Peter Wollny showed that Bach based "Bekennen will ich seinen Namen" (BWV 200) on Stölzel's "Dein Kreuz" from his 1720 Gotha passion (see "'Bekennen will ich seinen Namen'—Authentizität, Bestimmung und Kontext der Arie BWV 200. Anmerkungen zu Johann Sebastian Bachs Rezeption von Werken Gottfried Heinrich Stölzels," *Bach-Jahrbuch* 94 (2008): 123–158). Finally, Andreas Glöckner, ("Ein weiterer Kantatenjahrgang Gottfried Heinrich Stölzels in Bachs Aufführungsrepertoire?" *Bach-Jahrbuch* 95 (2009): 95–116, goes further to show that Bach also performed cantatas from Stölzel's "Namenbuch" cycle in 1733, from Estomihi (15 Feb) to Trinity 4 (28 Jun). Cron's list of Stölzel movements reveals that none of them are to be found in these two cycles.

2. George B. Stauffer's recent article ("Bach's Cantata and Passion Movements with Obbligato Organ," in *Pro Organo Pleno: Essays in Honor of Ewald Kooiman*, ed. Hans Fidom, Jan Luth, and Christoph Wolff (Veenhuizen: Boeijenga, 2008), 19–41) makes a strong contribution to this literature, but space permits only short consideration of the issue of substitution (pp. 40–41).

Obbligato Organ in Bach Cantatas

Throughout his career, Bach composed twenty-six cantata movements making use of the organ in an obbligato capacity, shown in Tables 1 through 4.[3] What becomes immediately apparent is that sixteen (roughly two-thirds) of these movements were written in 1726, Bach's third year as cantor in Leipzig. (The remaining ten movements divide evenly before and after this year.) Why this sudden abundance of solo organ movements? Laurence Dreyfus suggests that they were "yet another in the myriad of experiments in Bach's cantata cycles,"[4] perhaps similar to Bach's extended use of chorale melodies a few years earlier. Yet this explanation does not fully satisfy. He goes on to imply another possibility, saying that "as a modest melodic voice that arbitrarily replaces a more usual obbligato instrument, the organ adds little to Bach's cantata orchestration. Certain movements even tend to highlight a sense of posing, as if the composer called on the organ as a temporary, auxiliary aid."[5] Gregory Butler has followed

Table 1. Transcriptions from instrumental works

BWV/Mvt	Occasion	First Perf. Date	Type	Model
146/1	Easter 3	12 May 1726?	Sinfonia	1052/1
146/2	Easter 3	12 May 1726?	(Chor)	1052/2
35/1	Trinity 12	8 Sep 1726	Concerto	1059/1
35/5	Trinity 12	8 Sep 1726	Sinfonia	1059/3
169/1	Trinity 18	20 Oct 1726	Sinfonia	1053/1
169/5	Trinity 18	20 Oct 1726	Aria (A)	1053/2
49/1	Trinity 20	3 Nov 1726	Sinfonia	1053/3
188/1	Trinity 21	17 Oct 1728	Sinfonia	1052/3
120a/4	Wedding	Apr–May 1729	Sinfonia	1006/1
29/1	Town Council	27 Aug 1731	Sinfonia	120a/4

---

3. Though twenty-seven movements are listed in these four tables, BWV 29/1 reworks the music of BWV 120a/4. Throughout this paper, I use a slash to separate the BWV number and the movement; thus, BWV 29/1 refers to the first movement of BWV 29.

4. Laurence Dreyfus, "The Metaphorical Soloist: Concerted Organ Parts in Bach's Cantatas," in *J. S. Bach as Organist: His Instruments, Music, and Performance Practices*, ed. George Stauffer and Ernest May (Bloomington: Indiana University Press, 1986), 173.

5. Ibid., 188.

Table 2. Originally for another instrument, later for organ

BWV/Mvt	Occasion	Date	Type	Original Instrument
172/5	Pentecost	20 May 1714	Aria (SA)	Violoncello
63/3	Christmas	25 Dec 1714–1715	Aria (SB)	Oboe d'amore
73/1	Epiphany 3	23 Jan 1724	(Chorale + Recit)	"Corno"
128/4	Ascension	10 May 1725	Aria (AT)	Oboe d'amore[6]
170/3	Trinity 6	28 Jul 1726	Aria (A) Trio son?	(Vn/Ob?)
170/5	Trinity 6	28 Jul 1726	Aria (A)	Oboe d'amore
35/4	Trinity 12	8 Sep 1726	Aria (A)	Violoncello (piccolo?)
27/3	Trinity 16	6 Oct 1726	Aria (A)	Cembalo

Table 3. Originally for organ, later for another instrument

BWV/Mvt	Occasion	Date	Type	Later Instrument
70/3	Trinity 26	21 Nov 1723	Aria (A)	Violoncello[7]
170/5	Trinity 6	28 Jul 1726	Aria (A)	Traverso[8]
47/2	Trinity 17	13 Oct 1726	Aria (S)	Violin[9]

---

6. Alfred Dürr (*Neue Bach Ausgabe* [hereafter *NBA*], I/12 Kritischer Bericht [hereafter KB], 188–189) concludes that the most likely explanation for the "Organo" inscription in the score (CH-Winterthur, facs. *NBA*, I/12, x) is that Bach originally intended the movement for this instrument, but ultimately had it copied for oboe; the *Bach Compendium* (1:311) and Dreyfus, "Metaphorical Soloist," 175, agree. However, Joshua Rifkin ("Some Questions of Performance in J. S. Bach's *Trauerode*," *Bach Studies* 2 (1995): 147, n. 108) determined that the inscription was actually in the hand of Wilhelm Friedemann, and dated from after 1750. Thus, this movement fits most appropriately in this table, but with the caveat that the later performance was not under Sebastian's direction.

7. Perhaps originally conceived for cello; see below.

8. Perhaps originally conceived for oboe d'amore; see below.

9. The obbligato part for this movement shows signs of having been entered first in *Chorton* and then corrected to *Kammerton*. See note 18. Perhaps it was originally conceived for violin, but Bach was forced to substitute at the last moment; only some years later was the original scoring restored.

Table 4. Written for, and only ever played on, the organ

BWV/Mvt	Occasion	Date	Type
71/2	Town Council	4 Feb 1708	Duet
35/2	Trinity 12	8 Sep 1726	Aria (A)
169/3	Trinity 18	20 Oct 1726	Aria (A)
49/2	Trinity 20	3 Nov 1726	Aria (B)
49/6	Trinity 20	3 Nov 1726	Aria (SB)
29/7	Town Council	27 Aug 1731	Arioso (A)

up on this issue, finding documentary evidence to show that at the times Bach relied especially heavily on the organ he was missing key personnel.[10]

Dreyfus, having said that the organ "adds little," then goes so far as to question the very appropriateness of its presence as melodic instrument. He quotes Johann Friedrich Reichardt (1752–1814), who says that the organ "is such a resourceful instrument . . . [that] one man can represent a complete and powerful orchestra."[11] It is interesting to note in this context that Bach does, at least once, work in this manner: organ *as* ersatz orchestra rather than organ *within* actual orchestra. All but one (BWV 646) of the "Schübler" Chorales, BWV 645–650, published in the later 1740s, are direct transcriptions for organ with two manuals and pedal of pre-existing cantata movements.[12] Here we see the organ playing "cantata music" in a manner we might think most appropriate for it: multiple manuals with obbligato pedal, registration indications, etc.[13]

---

10. Gregory Butler, "'Instrumente Mangel': The Cantata Movements with Obbligato Organ as a Reflection of Bach's Performing Forces," *Keyboard Perspectives* 3 (2010): 131–146.

11. Dreyfus, "Metaphorical Soloist," 172. Reichardt's quotation, from 1791, is given in full in Hans-Joachim Schulze, ed., *Dokumente zum Nachwirken Johann Sebastian Bachs, 1750–1800*, Bach-Dokumente 3 (Kassel: Bärenreiter, 1972), 508 (No. 961).

12. BWV 646 may well be a transcription of a cantata movement as well, in which case this cantata is lost. See *NBA* IV/1 KB, 156–159. Also, BWV 527/4 is a transcription of the sinfonia that begins the second half of BWV 76. Interestingly, this same trio sonata is also reworked in concerto form in a movement of BWV 1044.

13. See facsimile edition: Hans Schmidt-Mannheim, ed., *Sechs Choräle von verschiedener Art* (Innsbruck: Edition Helbling, 1985). By registration indications, I mean the indications of register (e.g., "2. Clav: 16 Fuß.") found at the beginning of the second and third chorales, and not of specific stops.

However, though the organ has the ability to substitute for the orchestra does not necessitate that it always do so. This same flexibility mentioned above by Reichardt allows Bach to use the organ either *as* the orchestra or *in* the orchestra, a capability perhaps possessed by no other instrument.[14]

The focus of this study then is to reconcile these two apparent opposites, namely the use of organ for its own sake and its use as "mere" substitute. I argue that it is the organ alone which is capable of bridging this gap. The four tables show the four different ways in which Bach uses the organ in his cantatas: as the solo instrument in a concerto transcription (Table 1); as a substitute for another instrument (Table 2); as initial instrument eventually replaced by another (Table 3); and finally for its own sake (Table 4). This last category is, perhaps surprisingly, the smallest. In this discussion, I shall dwell especially on the second and third categories—discussing BWV 170, 70, and 27—before concluding with an exploration of the organ's significance in Bach's cantatas and the impact this has on our notion of the work, the editorial process, and performance.

* * *

The clearest example of last-minute substitution is to be found in the solo alto cantata "Vergnügte Ruh, beliebte Seelenlust" (BWV 170), written for the sixth Sunday after Trinity and first performed on 28 July 1726. The compositional origins of the third movement, "Wie jammern mich doch die verkehrten Herzen," have been discussed at length by Gregory Butler.[15] He reaches the conclusion that the movement was transcribed from a trio-sonata-like piece, and that the organ alone plays what two separate instruments, possibly violin and oboe, once did.[16] In Bach's day, the organs at the two principal churches in

---

14. Save, perhaps, the harpsichord; one thinks immediately of the *Italian Concerto*, BWV 971, or the concerto transcriptions, BWV 972–987, in which the harpsichord represents the orchestra. This relationship certainly comes into play with BWV 27, discussed below.

15. Gregory Butler, "The Origins of J. S. Bach's 'Wie jammern mich doch die verkehrten Herzen,' BWV 170/3," in *Music and Its Questions: Essays in Honor of Peter Williams*, ed. Thomas Donahue (Richmond, VA: OHS Press, 2007), 227–236, and Butler, "Instrumente Mangel," 135–138.

16. To support this, he notes the generally clean appearance of the score (in contrast to the first and fifth movements), the one-stroke bar lines through all four staves, numerous transposition errors from *Kammerton* to *Chorton* in the organ parts, and the very layout of the score itself with the organ parts on top, rather than above the continuo. See Butler, "Origins," 227–229. The addition of a vocal part to a pre-existing texture is

Obbligato Organ in Bach Cantatas

Leipzig—the Thomaskirche and Nikolaikirche—sounded a whole-tone higher (*Chorton*) than the other orchestral instruments (*Kammerton*).[17] This meant that parts intended for performance on the organ were transposed down one whole-tone in order that they may be played together with the ensemble. In this movement, the organ part is entered into the score already transposed, and thus suitable for performance.[18]

The fifth-movement aria, "Mir ekelt mehr zu leben," stands in opposition to the third movement. The autograph score (Figure 1) is now clearly a composing one, and the obbligato line is the top line of the system—the standard location for a wind or string part, but certainly not a keyboard part.[19] The part is

---

not without precedent in Bach's works, and Butler mentions BWV 169/5 to this effect; I would add BWV 146/2. As to adding a fourth part to a trio, Forkel (perhaps on the basis of information from C. P. E. Bach) says that Bach "even went so far, as when he was in a cheerful humor and in the full consciousness of his powers, as to add extempore to three single parts a fourth part, and thus make a quartet of a trio." (Translation from Hans T. David and Arthur Mendel, eds., *The New Bach Reader: A Life of Johann Sebastian Bach in Letters and Documents*, rev. Christoph Wolff (New York: Norton, 1998), 435.)

17. See, for instance, Laurence Dreyfus, *Bach's Continuo Group: Players and Practices in His Vocal Works* (Cambridge: Harvard University Press, 1987), 7; Ulrich Prinz, *J. S. Bachs Instrumentarium* (Stuttgart: Internationale Bachakademie, 2005), 631. Throughout this paper, I will refer to the former situation (*Chorton*) as "transposed" and the latter (*Kammerton*) as "untransposed."

18. Butler, "Origins," 233, suggests that the score placement of the organ part indicates that perhaps Bach intended to retain the use of two melody instruments here. I find this argument less convincing, given their notation in *Chorton* throughout. It is perhaps conceivable that when Bach entered the clefs, he intended to maintain two separate melody instruments, but he must have abandoned this plan as soon as he began to write the part in its transposed version. Doubtless not more than a few minutes would have passed between one action and the other. Contrast this with BWV 47/2, in which Bach clearly began writing out the top staff transposed (in C minor), but changed his mind and corrected it to *Kammerton* (D minor). That the obbligato part was entered on the top staff suggests, perhaps, that Bach initially conceived this movement for an instrument other than organ, but was forced, perhaps for lack of time, to play it himself.

19. That this is a composing score is indicated by the bar lines, which are drawn in two separate strokes (cf. note 30), and the clear tendency toward Bach's composing script (*Gebrauchsschrift*), especially evident with the down-stemmed "black" notes, which are virtually all stemmed on the right. See Yoshitake Kobayashi, *NBA*, IX/2/2, 15–16. Robert Marshall, *The Compositional Process of J. S. Bach* (Princeton: Princeton University Press, 1972) of course discusses this issue throughout (especially in the first chapter), but does not provide as much detail as Kobayashi does, relying on the descriptions of Bach's handwriting in Georg von Dadelsen, "Beiträge zur Chronologie der Werke Johann Sebastian Bachs," *Tübinger Bach Studien* 4/5 (1958).

Figure 1. "Vergnügte Ruh, beliebte Seelenlust," BWV 170, original autograph score (*NBA* A), mvt. 5 (P 154)

[The figures used in this chapter are reproduced by kind permission of the Staatsbibliothek zu Berlin—Preußischer Kulturbesitz, Musikabteilung mit Mendelssohn Archiv.]

Obbligato Organ in Bach Cantatas

entered untransposed throughout (unlike the previous aria) and on stylistic and range criteria, seems to have been originally intended for oboe d'amore.[20] Then, after the movement was completely written out in score, Bach instead decided that the oboe d'amore would not play this part; it was never entered into any performance part.[21] Rather Bach wrote "Organo" above the top system and filled in a basic left-hand part in keyboard tablature (also in *Kammerton*).[22] This is perhaps one of the clearest instances of a last-minute substitution of the kind adumbrated earlier.[23]

---

20. The part descends as low as A3, the lowest pitch on the Baroque oboe d'amore. See *NBA*, I/17.2, vi; *NBA*, I/17.2 KB, 105 (Reinmar Emans). There is a part for this instrument in the original performing materials, but it merely doubles the violin part in this movement. Since this doubling is not indicated in the score, the most likely explanation for the existence of the part is a verbal direction by Bach to the copyist, Christian Gottlob Meißner.

21. Butler also reaches this conclusion, saying that Bach must have made the decision to use obbligato organ "fairly soon." See Butler, "Instrumente Mangel," 140.

22. This part consists mostly of a simple octave alternation, filling in the rests in the continuo line. It is thus entirely possible that the organist doubled the continuo line throughout, as the *NBA* proposes, although this would be rather difficult.

23. The performance materials for the obbligato movements in this cantata would seem to argue for this being an instance of so-called dual continuo, namely the participation of multiple keyboard instruments. The obbligato parts for movements three and five are not entered into a separate part for the original 1726 performance. There is however a transposed and figured continuo part extant, the eighth numbered part of *NBA* Source B (*NBA* B 8). (The first movement is in the hand of Anon. IIf, the remainder in the hand of a singular scribe. The figures are autograph. Anon. IIf seems to be found most commonly in sources from the mid-1720s, suggesting further that the part dates from that time.) Movement three in this part is marked "Aria senza Violon: tacet," so there exists the possibility that the organist playing from the continuo part then played movement three from the score. Butler does not exclude the possibility that the bassetto was doubled in the organ's pedal part, though both Dreyfus and Schering do. (Butler, "Origins," 234.) For the fifth movement, however, this could not have been the case. Either the continuo went unrealized, doubtful given that Bach figured the part himself and would have known by that time—if one is convinced by the previous discussion—that the obbligato part would be played by organ. One must then consider the possibility that there were two organs in the choir loft for this performance, and with it Arnold Schering's thesis concerning the Thomaskirche's so-called "Trauungspositiv." (See *NBA*, I/23 KB and Schering, *Johann Sebastian Bachs Leipziger Kirchenmusik* (Leipzig: Breitkopf & Härtel, 1936), chap. 17.) However, more recent research has shown Schering's supposition that the *Trauungspositiv* was tuned to *Kammerton* to be incorrect, it was in fact at *Chorton* pitch, and was not reconfigured as a *Kammerton* instrument until after Bach's death. (See Dreyfus, *Bach's Continuo Group*, 21–22; Wolfgang Sandberger, *Das Bach-Bild Philipp Spittas* (Stuttgart: F. Steiner, 1997), 131 n. 242.) The organist who played the obbligato part would then

This cantata was revived a final time around the years 1747–1748, and Bach himself prepared a traverso part containing only the obbligato line for the fifth movement, without "tacet" markings (Figure 2).[24] The obbligato line in this movement has come full circle: from wind instrument (oboe d'amore) to organ and back again.[25]

The first version of the cantata "Wachet! betet! betet! wachet! " (BWV 70a) was performed on 6 December 1716 for the second Sunday of Advent in Weimar. In 1723, Bach revived the cantata, but reworked it for the twenty-sixth and last Sunday after Trinity, 21 November (BWV 70).[26] BWV 70a, BWV 186a, and BWV 147a form a trio of similar works, composed for three successive Weimar Sundays in Advent, for which music was prohibited in Leipzig. All three were expanded, principally through the addition of recitatives, into two-part cantatas and reperformed on different liturgical occasions during Bach's first Leipzig year. Interestingly, all three have continuo arias of some kind: BWV 70a/2, 186a/2, and 147a/3.

---

likely have been Bach himself, given the messiness of the score as well as the necessity of sight-transposition for the fifth movement.

24. This part, though on the same paper as the others (Weiß No. 132), is datable on the basis of Bach's handwriting, which shows all the hallmarks of his so-called "Spätschrift." See Yoshitake Kobayashi, "Zur Chronologie der Spätwerke Johann Sebastian Bachs: Kompositions- und Aufführungstätigkeit von 1736 bis 1750," *Bach-Jahrbuch* 74 (1988): 56. At the same time, Bach also crossed out the first word of "Organo obligato" on the title page for the original parts (St 94), otherwise in Meißner's hand, and replaced it with "Flauto" (facs. *NBA*, I/17.2, ix). Again, on the basis of script, this adjustment must be roughly contemporaneous with the preparation of the new part. This change is rather strange, for there is no indication that the third movement obbligato line was moved to an instrument other than organ.

25. A performing edition of the traverso part alone is given in *NBA*, I/17.2, 89–90, comparable to what one sees in the *NBA* edition of BWV 63/3.

26. Though only two weeks earlier in the liturgical year, this represents a sizable theological shift. Rather than located at the beginning of the church year, celebrating the coming of Christ as savior, it has moved to the end of the liturgical year, the time at which eschatological imagery reaches its height in the Biblical readings: Christ is now figured as eternal judge at his second coming. No autograph score for this cantata is extant, though likely one would have been prepared for the Weimar version at least. The only extant materials for the first version are the principal copies of the two violin parts (*NBA* A 7 and 9) and the viola part (*NBA* A 11); these parts are on Weimar paper ("Gekrönter sächsischer Rautenkranz-Schild," Weiß No. 36). The new Leipzig parts were mostly prepared by Bach's principal copyist Johann Andreas Kuhnau (Hauptkopist A) in 1723 on Leipzig paper ("IMK in Schrifttafel/kleiner Halbmond," Weiß No. 97).

Obbligato Organ in Bach Cantatas

Figure 2. "Vergnügte Ruh, beliebte Seelenlust," BWV 170, Traverso (*NBA* B 2), mvt. 5 (St 94), scribe: J. S. Bach (Spätschrift)

The first aria from BWV 70 "Wenn kömmt der Tag" is scored for alto voice. As the Weimar materials for this aria no longer survive, we cannot know its original scoring. One might imagine that in 1716 there was no separate continuo line; in other words, the 1723 obbligato line *was* the 1716 continuo line. For this scenario, the comparison between BWV 208/13 (the "Hunting" cantata) and BWV 68/2 ("Also hat Gott die Welt geliebt") is instructive. The former, dating also from Weimar, was an aria for voice and continuo alone. When it was reconfigured for performance in Leipzig, now part of a sacred cantata, the original continuo line became an obbligato line in its own right, assigned to the violoncello piccolo. Bach then composed a new continuo line, derived musically from the now-obbligato part. The final version is shown in Example 1. Looking at BWV 70/3, we see a similar relationship between the two parts as has just been observed, shown in Example 2. The obbligato part, also in the bass register, is really a filled-out version of the continuo, or vice versa: the continuo is a pared-down version of the obbligato. However it would seem to be more likely,

Example 1. Obbligato violoncello piccolo and continuo from BWV 68/2, mm. 1–4

Example 2. Obbligato violoncello and continuo from BWV 70/3, mm. 1–4

given the source evidence—namely that the surviving Leipzig parts were copied from some now-lost *Vorlage*—that the 1723 configuration closely parallels the original.

The original instrumental designation, though, remains an open question.[27] The obbligato line seems clearly to have been composed with the cello in mind. Stylistically, it strongly recalls this instrument, in its extended use of arpeggiation for one thing; furthermore the part never descends below C2, the cello's lowest note. Nevertheless, the first extant part to contain the obbligato line dates from 1723 and is for organ (Figure 3). The likely situation is thus as follows: the aria was originally written for voice, obbligato violoncello, and continuo. In 1723, for the revised version, Bach transferred the obbligato line to the organ, perhaps because his new cellist found the part too difficult. The simpler continuo line in this performance would have been played then by the melody instruments in the continuo group, including cello and bassoon.

The cantata was revived again for performance on 18 November 1731, but this time with the obbligato part reconfigured.[28] J. S. Bach's second son, C. P. E. Bach, prepared a part for violoncello (Figure 4), containing only the obbligato line (perhaps copied from a now-lost Weimar *Vorlage*) for the third movement without any "tacet" markings. As with the new keyboard part for BWV 27/3, this suggests that either this movement was played alone, or played by an instrumentalist working from another part for the remaining movements. When viewed in concert with the new continuo part (Figure 5), which does contain all eleven movements, it becomes clear that the latter took place. This part thereby makes the previous figured continuo part obsolete.[29]

---

27. As it seems that the oboe at least and possibly the trumpet as well were later additions to the Leipzig version (see Joshua Rifkin, "Zur Bearbeitungsgeschichte der Kantate 'Wachet! betet! betet! wachet!' (BWV 70)," *Bach-Jahrbuch* 85 (1999): 127–132), it is entirely possible that other instrumentation changes were made, including reassignment of the obbligato part.

28. Trinity 26 occurred a total of eleven times during Bach's tenure, however 1731 is the only year for which this paper (Weiß No. 122, "MA auf Stegen, mittelgroße Form") was used and the copyists J. L. Krebs and C. P. E. Bach overlap. See *NBA,* IX/3, 118–121, 126–128 and *NBA,* IX/1/1, 95–99.

29. According to the critical report, the first movement of A 16 (the new continuo part) may well have been copied from A 15 (the 1723 continuo part), but the remaining movements show transposition errors and thus appear to have been copied from one of the untransposed parts (A 13 or 14). (See *NBA,* I/27 KB, 109–110.) This certainly is very

The sources thus ultimately suggest a situation very similar to that seen in BWV 170/5. This movement was conceived originally for violoncello obbligato with simple continuo and performed as such in 1716. For the 1723 performance, Bach moved the obbligato line to the organ, the most expedient choice to fill in for a less-qualified (or ill?) cellist. In 1731, some fifteen years after the first performance, the original scoring was ultimately restored. This thus complicates the scenario first proposed in Table 3: while it is true to say that the first verifiable performance was on the organ, it was likely not the first ever performance.

One final example may be drawn from the cantata "Wer weiß, wie nahe mir mein Ende" (BWV 27), first performed on 6 October 1726 for the sixteenth Sunday after Trinity. Its third movement, "Willkommen will ich sagen" was originally conceived as an aria for alto voice, with harpsichord and oboe da caccia obbligato. Bach began the piece as such, going so far as to enter the first sixteen and one-half measures of the da caccia part, before changing his mind (see Figure 6). The score for this movement, of the composing variety, was initially laid out on five staves: oboe da caccia (alto clef), alto voice (alto clef), violone (bass clef), harpsichord right hand (treble clef) and harpsichord left hand (bass clef).[30] Likely Bach composed several measures of the oboe part (perhaps even all sixteen and one-half?),[31] before returning to enter the bass line

---

strange, as the only musical change in A 16 is the movement three change to continuo from obbligato. Why not simply copy all the movements, except that one, from A 15? Regarding whether the movement was performed alone or not, *NBA*, I/27 KB, 112, posits this source situation as a possible step in a larger plan by Bach that was to remain unrealized.

30. The bar lines are clearly entered first in the top staff, the oboe da caccia line, in a slow, heavy stroke. They are then finished in a separate quicker, thinner stroke through all five staves. This feature is characteristic of Bach's composing scores. On the second system (lines 14–17), Bach even misses the separate completing stroke. The critical report (*NBA*, I/23 KB, 98, ed. Helmuth Osthoff and Rufus Hallmark) states that when the movement continues on four staves it is because the vocal part has been omitted, possible in an instrumental ritornello. This would argue that Bach laid out the staves with the toccata-like figuration in mind. However, it is equally likely that he laid out the remaining two systems with the final version of the harpsichord part in mind, and the staves are thus oboe, voice, harpsichord, bass. It is worth noting that this is how the staves are laid out in the final version, on fol. 4v.

31. The pace of composition must have been frenzied, for Bach was in such a hurry to finish his musical idea that he completed the ritornello melody in tablature at the bottom of the page.

Figure 3. "Wachet! betet!," BWV 70, Continuo (NBA A 15), mvts. 1 (end), 2, and 3 (start) (St 95). Scribe: Anon. Ic

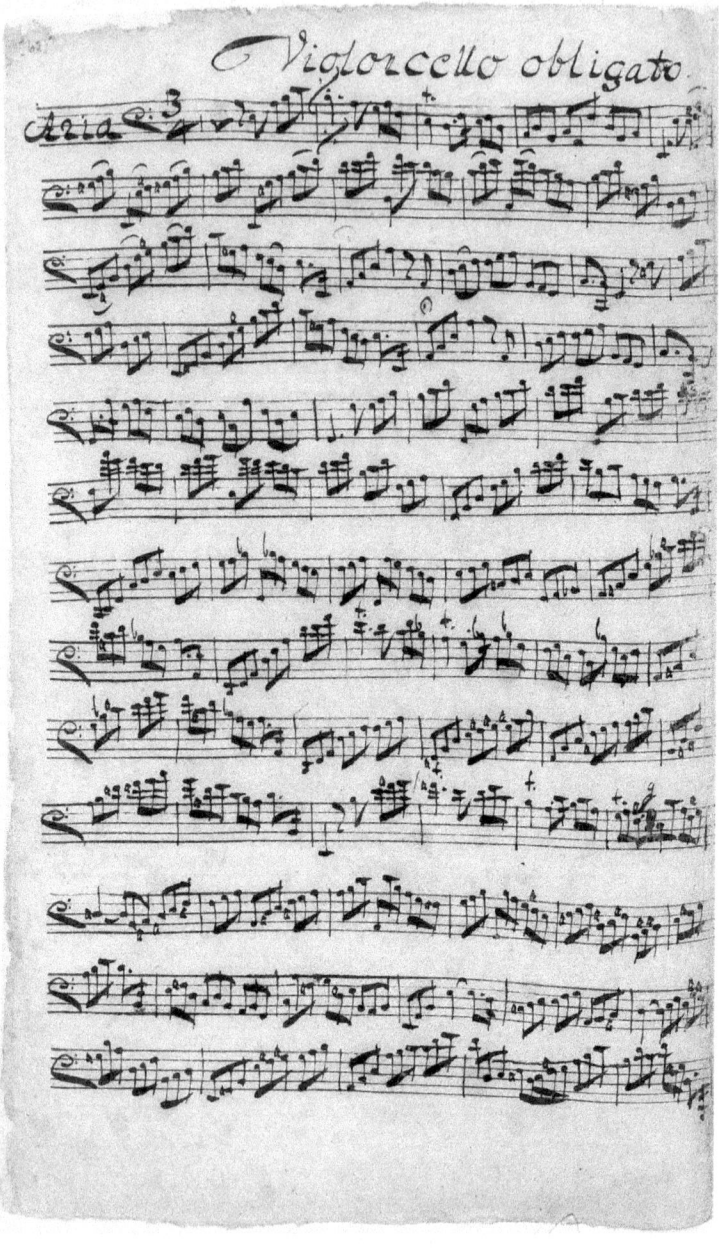

Figure 4. "Wachet! betet!," BWV 70,
Violoncello obligato (NBA A 12), mvt. 3 (St 95). Scribe: C. P. E. Bach

Obbligato Organ in Bach Cantatas

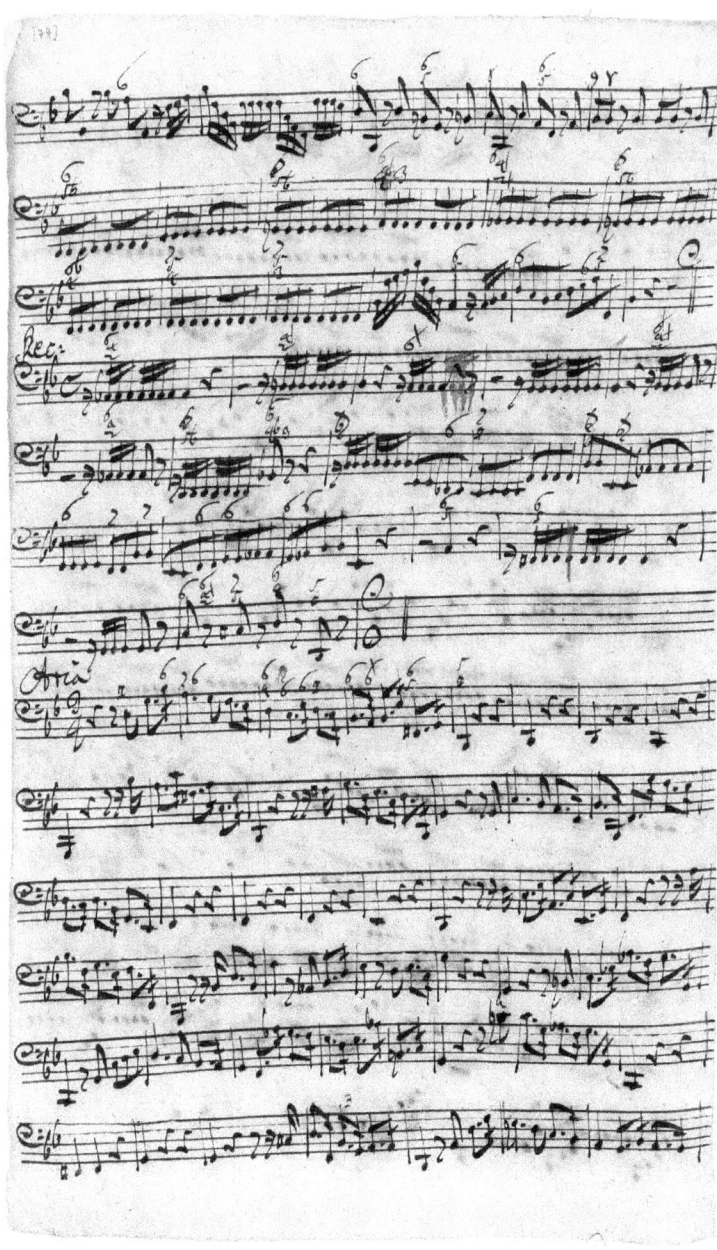

Figure 5. "Wachet! betet!," BWV 70, Continuo (NBA A 16), mvts. 1 (end), 2, and 3 (start) (St 95). Scribe: J. L. Krebs.

Figure 6. "Wer weiß, wie nahe mir mein Ende!," BWV 27, original autograph score (NBA A), mvts. 2, 3 (draft) (P 164)

Obbligato Organ in Bach Cantatas

and obbligato harpsichord part. The original conception of the latter was for it to consist of toccata-like figuration, using both the keyboardist's hands, thus precluding doubling of the continuo in the left hand. Bach wrote out one and one-half measures in this manner before crossing it out. He then reconceived of the obbligato keyboard part as suitable for a single hand and entered it instead on the second line, intended originally for the alto soloist, without correcting the clef; he entered four full measures in this manner.[32] At this point, for an unknown reason, Bach crossed the entire draft out and began anew on the verso side of the same page.[33]

The composer retained the oboe da caccia part at the top of the score; the first measure is even identical, and the remainder bears a strong resemblance to the draft (see Figure 7). The other obbligato part—entered now on the third line of the system, directly above the continuo line—has a much different character: gone is the two-handed toccata figuration to be replaced by a line on one staff, vaguely suggestive of violinistic string crossing.[34] Again, this line is reminiscent of the (second) draft of the harpsichord line on the recto side. Though Bach does not specify the instrument for which this part was intended, it must surely be a keyboard, or else he would have entered it above the vocal part, as with any other obbligato part. In the absence of any new designation contradicting the harpsichord indication on the previous page, one must assume the instrument has not changed.

The untransposed keyboard part containing the obbligato line for this movement, *NBA* B 15, has proven difficult to date, using as it does different paper and a different scribe than the other fourteen parts (St 105). In the first

---

32. The valid harpsichord part in this draft is stylistically appropriate for the violin, perhaps suggesting that Bach was working from a model originally for this instrument. He intended to give the harpsichord a more idiomatic part, but ran out of time and reverted to the original form. That being said, this score is clearly a composing one. Thus the considerations were perhaps internal: Bach conceived the movement for harpsichord, considered moving it to violin, but ultimately stuck with his original plan.

33. This sketch is transcribed both in the critical report (*NBA*, I/23 KB, 97–98, ed. Helmuth Osthoff and Rufus Hallmark) and, in much greater detail, in Marshall, *Compositional Process*, vol. 2, number 18. As discussed above in note 31, that the oboe part forms the basis of the complete ritornello is clear in these transcriptions. The sketch concludes with a cadential figure in the oboe line, ending with a quarter note on scale degree 3.

34. Cf. note 32.

Figure 7. "Wer weiß, wie nahe mir mein Ende!," BWV 27, original autograph score (NBA A), mvt. 3 (start) (P 164)

edition of his chronology, Alfred Dürr dated it to "1735–1750 (1737?)," principally on the basis of its watermark;[35] the "1737 (?)" was repeated by Dreyfus.[36] For the revised version of his chronology, the specific year is gone; Dürr keeps only the fifteen-year range, again with the watermark as evidence.[37] In the intervening years, however, the scribe for the part has been identified as Christian Gottlob Meißner, and his dates of activity as Bach's copyist firmly established as 1723–1729.[38] This, as Hans-Joachim Schulze points out, makes the dating of this part to 1737 untenable.[39] Furthermore, the vast majority of his activity as a copyist took place in the four-year period from 1723 to 1726.[40] The performance of BWV 27 in this latter year strongly suggests that the part was in fact prepared for the first performance, and not a second one some eleven (or even a few) years later. The confounding factor is the watermark, Weiß No. 74. It occurs only two other times in Bach's music, in BWV 29 and 102, and the score for the former bears an incredibly rare autograph date "Beÿ der Rahts-Wahl [sic] 1731."[41] However, I think it far more likely that Meißner prepared the obbligato keyboard part in 1726—making this the first use of Weiß No. 74—than that he copied it out five years later, after his service to Bach had essentially ended. Indeed the first performance of BWV 102 also took place in this year, some six weeks earlier. It thus makes more sense to adjust our dating of this watermark earlier than to attempt to explain the presence of a copyist long after his principal years of service to Bach were over. The part lacks "tacet" markings for the other movements, suggesting either that this movement was performed alone, or more likely, that this part was used in combination with another continuo part.

---

35. Alfred Dürr, "Zur Chronologie der Leipziger Vokalwerke J. S. Bachs," *Bach-Jahrbuch* 44 (1957): 156.

36. Dreyfus, "Metaphorical Soloist," 175.

37. Alfred Dürr, *Zur Chronologie der Leipziger Vokalwerke J. S. Bachs* (Kassel: Bärenreiter, 1976), 118, 156.

38. *NBA*, IX/3, 38. Meißner (b. 1707) was a student at the Thomasschule during this time. In 1729, he moved to the University of Leipzig and continued to serve as a copyist at the Neukirche. In 1731, he left Leipzig entirely to become cantor in his hometown of Geithain, where he remained until his death in 1760.

39. Hans-Joachim Schulze, *Studien zur Bach-Überlieferung im 18. Jahrhundert* (Leipzig: Edition Peters, 1984), 105.

40. Ibid., 51.

41. "For the town-council election [i.e., 27 Aug], 1731." See *NBA*, I/32.2 KB, 15.

Given that the part was untransposed, it would have been suitable for performance on the harpsichord.[42]

The curious tale of this keyboard part resumes some fifteen years later, around 1741. The heading on the part, "organo obbligato," was originally thought contemporaneous with the music.[43] The *NBA* editors, however, speculated that it may have been a later addition,[44] and Hans-Joachim Schulze confirmed this, assigning it to Dürr's Anonymous Vm.[45] Thus, when first prepared by Meißner, the part bore no instrumental designation, and as stated above, in the absence of conflicting evidence an untransposed keyboard part was surely performed on the harpsichord. Our understanding of this later scribe increased significantly when Peter Wollny realized that he was the same individual as Dürr's Hauptschreiber I, and identified him by name as Georg Heinrich Noah (1716–1762).[46] While a mere inscription on a part otherwise clearly intended for harpsichord might not be enough to convince us that it was performed on organ, perhaps a broader view of this copyist will help. As shown in Table 5, the first four tasks Noah performed for Bach all relate to organ parts. Though by no means airtight, given that Noah was writing out full organ parts for other cantatas at this same time, it is certainly conceivable that the part in question was repurposed for that instrument as well. Wollny suggests that Noah, being too old for matriculation at the Thomasschule, may well have been a private student of Bach, and likely a keyboardist himself.[47] While it is perhaps tempting to imagine that Noah performed the obbligato for this movement in 1741–1742, given the difficulty of sight-transposing this part to the required D-flat major,

---

42. The likely candidate is *NBA* B 14, the only other figured continuo part extant. However, this part is transposed and thus suitable for realization on organ. Perhaps for this second performance, the continuo player sat at the organ throughout, but for the third movement moved to the harpsichord and played the obbligato part. In this scenario, the continuo would not have been realized chordally.

43. The first published edition of this cantata, Wilhelm Rust, ed., *Bach Gesellschaft Ausgabe*, vol. 5.1 (Leipzig: Breitkopf and Härtel, 1855) assigns the obbligato part unproblematically to the organ. There are a number of reasons for this, not least a confusion of scribal hands (both in the part and on the title wrapper) and an (ahistorical) anxiety about the use of harpsichord in sacred works.

44. *NBA,* I/23 KB, 106.

45. Schulze, *Bach-Überlieferung*, 105.

46. Peter Wollny, "Tennstädt, Leipzig, Naumburg, Halle—Neuerkenntnisse zur Bach-Überlieferung in Mitteldeutschland," *Bach-Jahrbuch* 88 (2002): 29–33.

47. Ibid., 32.

Obbligato Organ in Bach Cantatas

it is perhaps more likely that, if the part was performed on organ at all, it was played by Bach himself.[48]

Table 5. Earliest copyist activity of G. H. Noah

Occasion	Date?[49]	BWV	Activity
Trinity 16	17 Sep 1741	27	"Organo obligato" heading (St 105, NBA B 15)
Christmas 3	27 Dec 1741	64	Organo part (St 87, NBA A 14)
Trinity 4	17 Jul 1742	177	Added mvts 2–5 to organo (St Thom, NBA B 13)
Trinity 15	2 Sep 1742	100	Organo part (St 97, NBA B 28)

* * *

In light of these findings, which show a diversity of motivations for the introduction of the organ into Bach's cantatas, what can be said more generally about his use of the instrument or his attitude towards its role in concerted music? In his *Anleitung zu der musikalischen Gelahrtheit* published in 1758, Jakob Adlung says the following:

> When sometimes it happens that a traverso part[50] is played either in the left or in the right hand [of the organ], then either the composer has wished to do it intentionally or the music director has been short an instrument (ein Musikdirector hat an einem Instrumente Mangel) and transcribes this melody into the continuo [part].[51]

---

48. Though well outside the scope of this paper, it is interesting to note that in a part prepared in the later eighteenth or early nineteenth century, the oboe da caccia line from the third movement is assigned to the viola. That this part was a later addition was not noticed by the first round of library cataloging, hence it is numbered "13," in sequence with the other parts from Bach's lifetime. It is designated Source B' in *NBA*, I/23 KB, 107.

49. With the exception of course of BWV 27, all the parts in this table are on Weiß Nos. 65 or 68. Wollny ("Neuerkenntnisse," 31) suggests that these two watermarks are actually the same. This is sufficient to locate the parts around 1741–1742. I have assigned these, speculatively, on the basis of the liturgical function of the cantata in question. I have placed BWV 27 first, given that, as Wollny says, it makes sense to think of a copyist beginning first with a smaller role before proceeding to a larger one. That being said, source evidence does not rule out a date of 9 Sep 1742.

50. Adlung may also be referring to a traverso organ stop here, given that this quotation occurs in the context of a discussion of registration. This reading does not alter the meaning of the passage however.

51. "Hierbei wird bisweilen eine Traverse zu spielen vorgelegt, entweder in der linken, oder in der rechten Hand; entweder hat der Setzer es mit Vorsatz also beliebt, oder ein Musikdirector hat an einem Instrumente Mangel, und schreibt solche Melodie in

Adlung's choice of language is interesting. *Instrumente Mangel* can simply mean a missing instrument; however *Mangel* may also mean a deficiency or fault, an imperfection.[52] Perhaps then this gives us an insight into the role of the organ in Bach's cantatas: it does not merely fill in for an absent instrument, but in doing so restores the perfection of the composition. Mattheson's "vollkommene Kapellmeister," the perfect *Kapellmeister*, can do all things, but need not do them all at once.[53] For Bach, the organ serves almost as an extension of himself, filling in where necessary. As an instrument then, the organ is not so much perfect ('vollkommen') itself, but rather it is perfecting ('vervollkommnen'): when faced with a deficiency ('Mangel'), the organ alone can reconstitute the perfect whole.

In this context, it has become almost obligatory to quote the description J. M. Gessner, rector of the Thomasschule (1730–1734), gives of Bach's cantata performances:

> If you could seem him . . . watching over everything and bringing back to the rhythm and the beat, out of thirty or even forty musicians [symphoniaci], the one with a nod, another by tapping with his foot, the third with a warning finger, giving the right note to one from the top of his voice, to another from the bottom, and to a third from the middle of it—all alone, in the midst of the greatest din made by all the participants, and, although he is executing the most difficult parts himself [cum difficillimis omnium partibus fungatur], noticing at once whenever and wherever a mistake occurs . . .[54]

---

den Continuo." Jakob Adlung, *Anleitung zu der musikalischen Gelahrtheit* (Erfurt, 1758), 488–489. My thanks to Gregory Butler for bringing this passage to my attention; the translation here is from Butler, "Instrumente Mangel," 131.

52. The 68-volume *Zedler-Lexikon*, published in Leipzig 1732–1754, implicitly endorses this interpretation, listing "unmangelhafft" as a synonym for "vollkommen, vollkömmlich, völlig and vollständig." (vol. 50, col. 485.)

53. Johann Mattheson, *Der vollkommene Capellmeister* (Hamburg, 1739); rev. and trans. Ernest Charles Harriss as *Johann Mattheson's Der vollkommene Capellmeister: A Revised Translation with Critical Commentary* (Ann Arbor: UMI Research Press, 1981).

54. Werner Neumann and Hans-Joachim Schulze, eds., *Fremdschriftliche und gedruckte Dokumente zur Lebensgeschichte Johann Sebastian Bachs, 1685–1750: Kritische Gesamtausgabe*, Bach Dokumente 2 (Kassel: Bärenreiter, 1969), 335–336 (No. 435); translated in *The New Bach Reader*, 328–329. It should be noted that Philipp Spitta (*Johann Sebastian Bach* (Leipzig: Breitkopf und Härtel, 1880), 2:90), with his background in classical philology, translates "cum difficillimis omnium partibus fungatur" as "obgleich er von allen die schwierigste Aufgabe hat" ("although he has the most difficult

Obbligato Organ in Bach Cantatas

We can certainly imagine Bach at the head of the ensemble, executing an obbligato line from a hastily-prepared score, transposing at sight, while still having the wherewithal to direct the instrumentalists and singers.

The realization that the organ may serve as perfectly valid substitute has, I believe, a wide-ranging impact, not only on the ontological status of the musical work,[55] but for the editorial process and, especially, for performance. First, there is no *Urtext*, no 'primal version,' of this music—or at least no one *Urtext*. Bach is not revising his works with an eye toward some imagined artistic ideal, as the Gustav Mahler we see through the eyes of Natalie Bauer-Lechner does.[56] Rather, each version is the equal of every other; the "Fassung letzter Hand" holds no sway here.[57] Take as an example BWV 170/5, discussed above: though the obbligato line was initially conceived for oboe d'amore, it was first performed on organ, and then some years later, given on traverso. In some sense, the artistically ideal version is the first, for oboe—but this was never heard. Is the true version then the one for organ, since it was the first to be performed? Or the version for traverso, for the opposite reason? Surely it would be pure folly to arbitrate this hypothetical dispute. Though the findings in this paper have called into question the initial constitution of Table 3, showing that even these three movements seem to have been conceived initially for another instrument, this does not invalidate the organ version.

I would not, however, go as far as some and declare Bach's music to be entirely abstract—simply the interplay of pure tones—and thus declare instrumental timbre insignificant. If this were the case, why would Bach ever bother to designate an instrument at all? Again, rather than argue against the importance of timbre, our realization speaks in support of the organ's versatility. In fact, Adlung

---

task of all"). This suggests a reading wherein Bach is not performing, but only conducting. See Rifkin, "Trauerode," 147, n. 104.

55. For the seminal study of this phenomenon, see Lydia Goehr, *The Imaginary Museum of Musical Works: An Essay in the Philosophy of Music* (Oxford: Oxford University Press, 1990).

56. Natalie Bauer-Lechner, *Erinnerungen an Gustav Mahler* (Leipzig: E. P. Tal, 1923), trans. Dika Newlin as *Recollections of Gustav Mahler* (Cambridge: Cambridge University Press, 1980).

57. Gregory Butler, in his "J. S. Bach's Kanonische Veränderungen über 'Vom Himmel hoch' (BWV 769): Ein Schlußstrich unter die Debatte um die Frage der 'Fassung letzter Hand,'" *Bach-Jahrbuch 86* (2000): 9–34, makes this same argument with respect Bach's Canonic Variations on "Vom Himmel hoch," BWV 769.

continues on after the quote above to exhort the organist to use the stops which will most accurately recall the replaced instrument.[58] While Adlung's statements cannot be taken as unproblematically representative of Bach's beliefs, that a contemporary source would make the point so strongly would seem to argue against the aforementioned position.

For scholars however, the revision distinction need not be a sharp one. The issue of scoring is not unlike the well-known A♯/A♮ debate in Beethoven's "Hammerklavier" sonata, op. 106, wherein the former note is found in Beethoven's two sketches, the latter in the first edition, and no autograph survives.[59] The performer, of course, must play one note or the other, while in a critical score, footnotes and appendices ameliorate the difficulty of choosing a preferred version. The *Neue Bach Ausgabe*, in its edition of the Christmas cantata "Christen ätzet diesen Tag" (BWV 63) for instance,[60] prints the score of the third movement with the obbligato line given to the oboe.[61] A footnote over the instrumental designation directs the reader to an appendix containing the organ part alone on a grand staff, in a manner suitable for performance.[62] While this still privileges one reading (the oboe version) over another by including it in full score with the other movements, it is an improvement over what is found in many of the other cantatas: a notation buried deep in the critical report.

This is exactly the case with BWV 70/3, the movement discussed earlier. In the *Neue Bach Ausgabe*, the score includes only the cello version; the presence of the organ is relegated to a note in the critical report. This is certainly why every readily available recording uses cello. Even Ton Koopman, who is himself

---

58. "Hierbei richtet man sich so viel möglich nach solcher Stimme, welche man vorstellen soll." Adlung, *Anleitung*, 489.

59. The passage in question is in the retransition of the first movement, mm. 224–226. See James Grier, *The Critical Editing of Music: History, Method and Practice* (Cambridge: Cambridge University Press, 1996), 1–2 and n. 1.

60. *NBA*, I/2 (Alfred Dürr, 1957).

61. I should note that this example is by no means the only instance of this sort of thing in the *NBA*. Another instance where the instrument heading is used to direct the reader to a later version is BWV 170/5, where the flute version is included as an appendix. See note 25.

62. The instrument heading itself reads as follows: "Oboe I Solo | (spätere Fassung: | Organo obligato)," and the footnote is: "Die Organo-obligato-Stimme ist auf Seite 61 mitgeteilt."

an organist, has not recorded the obbligato organ version.[63] As I have stated, I believe both versions to be equally valid interpretations of the piece. The approach that should be taken here is the same as was taken with BWV 63: the organ part should be included in the main score and the violoncello should be provided either as an *ossia* or, better, as an appendix, with appropriate footnotes.

While in live performance one particular version must be chosen, many listeners will have their first, and sometimes only, experience with this music through boxed complete cycles. The earliest such cycles, for instance those by Nikolaus Harnoncourt, Gustav Leonhardt, and Helmuth Rilling, record each movement once, but more recent cycles, especially those by Ton Koopman and Masaaki Suzuki, often include a few additional, appendix tracks at the end of a given disk. In fact, Koopman records two versions of both BWV 47/2 and 63/3: in the case of the former, the obbligato organ version is the principal track and the violin version the appendix; for the latter, the oboe version is the principal and the organ given in appendix.[64] It is surely no coincidence that both movements have alternates given in the *Neue Bach Ausgabe*, whereas BWV 70/3 does not.

Even in a brief survey, both the facility and variety Bach found in the organ is readily apparent. It plays a role in everything from full-scale sinfonia settings with brass and wind instruments (e.g., BWV 29/1) to the most intimate chamber textures (e.g., BWV 170/3). As described by Adlung, Bach seems to have conceived obbligato parts with the organ originally in mind (e.g., BWV 71/2, 29/7) as well as used it when he found himself short a qualified soloist (e.g., BWV 170/5, 47/2). We have also seen that Bach's constant modification of instrumental forces problematizes the preparation of a critical edition, and precludes any possibility of an *Urtext*. "Indeed," as Dreyfus says, "the ideal of a fixed text to which all philology aspires cannot help but misrepresent Bach's constantly shifting working conditions."[65] It is my hope then that we can come to an understanding of these movements which does not privilege one version over another.

---

63. *J. S. Bach Cantatas*, vol. 9, dir. Ton Koopman, Challenge Records 72209.

64. *J. S. Bach Cantatas*, vol. 18, dir. Ton Koopman, Challenge Records 72218; *J. S. Bach Cantatas*, vol. 3, dir. Ton Koopman, Challenge Records 72203.

65. Dreyfus, *Bach's Continuo Group*, 4.

A Tale of Two Brothers: Friedemann and Emanuel Bach

DAVID SCHULENBERG

In the 1941 German film *Friedemann Bach*, Gustaf Gründgens played the title character as a proto-Romantic misunderstood genius. In one memorable scene, the elector of Saxony (also king of Poland) applauds Friedemann's performance while rebuking him for being a rebel. Although the scene is completely imaginary—it was Johann Sebastian Bach, not his oldest son Wilhelm Friedemann, who was to have competed with the French harpsichordist Louis Marchand at Dresden[1]—the music that Friedemann plays in the scene is really his, comprising portions of his two fantasias in D minor (F. 18 and 19) and the one in A minor (F. 23).[2] We never see his hands at the keyboard, but he is seated before a large audience at an instrument that looks like the so-called white harpsichord by Michael Mietke now at Charlottenburg Palace in Berlin.[3]

Although Friedemann Bach indeed held his first professional position from 1733 to 1746 in Dresden, as organist at the Sophienkirche, it is unlikely that the elector of Saxony ever berated him for being a rebel. Surely it would be anachronistic to suppose that the Romantic (or perhaps post-Romantic) view of art and rebellion as kindred forms of self-expression would have occurred either to that ruler or to one of Sebastian Bach's sons. And certainly the instruments on which Friedemann Bach played sounded very different from the jangling early twentieth-century harpsichord that we hear on the soundtrack. Yet in one respect the scene comes surprisingly close to what one might have heard in Friedemann's real-life performances. For Friedemann's performance of an appar-

---

1. The story of Sebastian's aborted contest with Marchand was first related in 1739 by Johann Abraham Birnbaum, whose account is translated in Hans T. David and Arthur Mendel, eds., *The New Bach Reader: A Life of Johann Sebastian Bach in Letters and Documents*, rev. Christoph Wolff (New York: Norton, 1998), 79–80 (item no. 67).

2. Friedemann's works will be cited by the numbers assigned to them in the thematic catalog published as an unpaginated supplement to Martin Falck, *Wilhelm Friedemann Bach: Sein Leben und seine Werke* (Leipzig: C. F. Kahnt Nachfolger, 1913).

3. On the Mietke instrument—whose maker remained unidentified in 1941 but which was presumably being kept at Schloss Charlottenburg—see Edward L. Kottick and George Lucktenberg, *Early Keyboard Instruments in European Museums* (Bloomington: Indiana University Press, 1997), 69–70. Although its decoration and stand were clearly modeled on those of the Mietke harpsichord, the instrument seen in the film is a prop, probably without a keyboard, as the latter is never shown in the film.

ently improvised medley of excerpts from favorite pieces may well correspond to the type of recital that he played later in life at Berlin and elsewhere.[4]

This Nazi-era film was hardly the first fictional treatment of the oldest son of J. S. Bach. Two operas and a best-selling novel preceded it, reflecting popular fascination in a figure often said to have been the most brilliant of the Bach sons.[5] Yet barely a hundred of his works are known. He never held a major position, ending his career unemployed and, supposedly, a drunk selling off his father's manuscripts as his own.[6] Carl Philipp Emanuel Bach, four years younger, held prestigious positions at the royal Prussian court (1740 or 1741 to 1767) and as cantor at Hamburg (1768–1788). From Emanuel there survive roughly a thousand works, not to mention his famous *Versuch über die wahre Art das Clavier zu spielen*.[7] It would be natural to see Friedemann's music as representing

---

4. See, for example, the account of two 1774 Berlin performances in *Bach-Dokumente III: Dokumente zum Nachwirken Johann Sebastian Bachs*, ed. Hans-Joachim Schulze (Kassel: Bärenreiter, 1972), 264 (item no. 786). In the film we hear the eight opening measures of F. 18, followed by mm. 11–20 of F. 19 and most of the closing *Prestissimo* of F. 23 (skipping mm. 52–66). Only a few notes at the transitions between these passages are altered, much as in Friedemann's two large fantasias in C minor (F. 15 and 16), which themselves incorporate portions of other works. For further discussion of these and other works mentioned here, see David Schulenberg, *The Music of Wilhelm Friedemann Bach* (Rochester: University of Rochester Press, 2010).

5. The 1941 film is based loosely on Albert Emil Brachvogel's popular novel *Friedemann Bach: Ein Roman*, 3 vols. (Berlin: Janke, 1858, revised edition in his *Ausgewählte Werke*, 1, Berlin: Janke, 1872); more than a century later the book appeared in an abbreviated English translation by Emanuel W. Hammer as *Albert Emil Brachvogel's Friedemann Bach* (New York: Pageant Press, 1959). Brachvogel's novel directly or indirectly inspired the obscure 1901 opera *Friedman* [sic] *Bach* by Luigi Gustavo Fazio as well as Paul Graener's better-known *Friedemann Bach* (libretto by Rudolph Lothar, Berlin: Bote und Bock, 1931). Even Dominique de Rivaz's 2003 film *Mein Name ist Bach*, although primarily about Sebastian Bach, contains ahistorical matter traceable to Brachvogel's novel.

6. Falck, *Wilhelm Friedemann Bach*, 53–55, expresses skepticism about the report of Friedemann's drinking in Johann Friedrich Reichardt's *Musikalischer Almanach* (Berlin: Unger, 1796), 61, and argues that claims for Friedemann's poor stewardship of his father's manuscripts are overstated. Nevertheless, the altered attribution of BWV 596 (Sebastian's organ arrangement of Vivaldi's concerto op. 3, no. 11) is visible in the autograph, Staatsbibliothek zu Berlin (henceforth SBB), Mus. ms. Bach P 330.

7. 2 vols. (Berlin, 1753–1762); new edition by Tobias Plebuch, *Carl Philipp Emanuel Bach: The Complete Works*, vols. 7/1–3 (Los Altos, CA: Packard Humanities Institute, 2011); English translation by William J. Mitchell as *Essay on the True Manner of Playing Keyboard Instruments* (New York: Norton, 1949).

the same so-called *empfindsamer* style as Emanuel's. Yet despite obvious parallels, their work, like their careers, shows striking differences, raising the question of how both could have emerged from the same household, after receiving presumably similar training.

Wilhelm Friedemann Bach was born at Weimar in 1710; Carl Philipp Emanuel followed in 1714. Early in 1720, the nine-year-old Friedemann received from his father the famous Little Keyboard Book;[8] probably when he was fifteen, he was sent to study violin with Johann Gottlieb Graun, brother of the opera composer Carl Heinrich Graun and a significant composer in his own right.[9] Sebastian helped Friedemann gain his first position in 1733, as organist at the Sophienkirche in Dresden.[10] There he composed keyboard pieces, concertos, and probably other instrumental works. In 1746 he moved to Halle, where he served as director of church music, composing perhaps several dozen church cantatas.

By then Emanuel had gained a far more illustrious position as chamber musician to King Frederick II "the Great" of Prussia. During thirty years in Berlin, Emanuel produced numerous keyboard sonatas and concertos, of which a significant fraction was published. Meanwhile, in 1764, Friedemann quit his church job and seems to have wandered in search of a position. He was not alone in doing so; Georg (Jiří Antonín) Benda would likewise leave an apparently stable but provincial position at the court of Gotha in 1778, traveling to Hamburg and Vienna.[11] Friedemann eventually came to Berlin, but only after

---

8. *Clavierbüchlein vor Wilhelm Friedemann Bach*, now in the Yale University Library (without shelf mark).

9. The exact dates of Friedemann's study have not been ascertained (see Falck, 21). Friedemann acknowledged Graun as his teacher in a letter of 1749, edited in Carl Hermann Bitter, *Carl Philipp Emanuel und Wilhelm Friedemann Bach und deren Brüder*, 2 vols. (Berlin: Wilhelm Müller, 1868; facsimile in one volume, Leipzig: Zentralantiquariat der Deutschen Demokratischen Republik, 1973), 370.

10. Friedemann's letter of application, including the signature, is in his father's hand (text in Falck, 12–13), and it is sometimes supposed that Friedemann played the praeludium in G, BWV 541, as part of his audition; see the article on Friedemann Bach by Peter Wollny in *Grove Music Online* (the electronic version of *The New Grove Dictionary of Music and Musicians*, 2nd ed., London: Macmillan, 2001, at oxfordmusiconline.com, accessed 6 January 2012).

11. According to the *Grove Music Online* article by John D. Drake et al. (accessed 6 January 2012).

Emanuel had departed for Hamburg. For the rest of his life, Friedemann presumably eked out a living through the sale of his compositions and as a private teacher, although he reportedly claimed that he did not give instruction.[12]

That report is odd, for we know of many distinguished pupils, including the composer Friedrich Wilhelm Rust and the theorist Johann Samuel Petri at Halle, and the *salonnière* Sara Levy at Berlin. Zelter, although not acknowledging Friedemann as a teacher, wrote about him to Goethe in a way that suggests he was a generous mentor to younger musicians.[13] Yet it was Emanuel who wrote the famous treatise on performance, as well as large numbers of pedagogic pieces. Although he had few known pupils, Emanuel seems to have been expected to train or at least coach other court musicians.[14] This could explain why he owned the king's copy of an aria from the opera *Cleofide* by Johann Adolf Hasse; Emanuel might have used this manuscript to coach one of the court castratos in

---

12. Falck, 51. On possible concert trips by Friedemann during the 1760s, see Peter Wollny, "'... welche dem größten Concerte gleichen': The Polonaises of Wilhelm Friedemann Bach," in *The Keyboard in Baroque Europe*, ed. Christopher Hogwood (Cambridge: Cambridge University Press, 2003), 169–183. The claim that Friedemann did not teach during his Berlin years is based on an addendum (Beylage) attached to Zelter's letter to Goethe dated 6 April 1829. The document is absent from most editions of the Zelter-Goethe correspondence and I have found it only in *Briefwechsel zwischen Goethe und Zelter in den Jahren 1796 bis 1832*, ed. Friedrich Wilhelm Riemer, vol. 5 (Berlin: Duncker und Humblot, 1834), 209–10. Peter Wollny, "Anmerkungen zur Bach-Pflege im Umfeld Sara Levys," in *"Zu groß, zu unerreichbar": Bach-Rezeption im Zeitalter Mendelssohns und Schumanns*, ed. Anselm Hartinger et al. (Wiesbaden: Breitkopf und Härtel, 2007), 39–49 (cited: 42), mentions a "statement of Kirnberger's, according to which W. F. Bach categorically refused to give keyboard instruction during his Berlin period," but the source for this is not further identified.

13. Letter of 6 April 1829 in Max Hecker, *Briefwechsel zwischen Goethe und Zelter* (Frankfurt: Insel, 1987) 3:163 (no. 665); page 203 (no. 648) in the edition by Riemer cited in the previous note.

14. On his training of the Berlin court harpist Franz Brennessell, see Christoph Henzel, "Neues zum Hofcembalisten Carl Philipp Emanuel Bach," *Bach-Jahrbuch* 85 (1999): 176–177. Emanuel furnished a model, if not actually providing lessons, for his younger fellow court keyboardist Carl Fasch; see Karl Friedrich Zelter, *Karl Friedrich Christian Fasch* (Berlin: Unger, 1801), 14–16. He also taught F. W. Rust, previously Friedemann's pupil, and the teenaged duke of Württemberg, dedicatee of the six keyboard sonatas W. 49, during the latter's extended visit to Berlin in the 1740s—doubtless with royal approval, although Württemberg nevertheless turned against Prussia during the Seven Years' War.

the approved manner of improvising embellishments and cadenzas, which the king himself added to the manuscript.[15]

The king's embellishments recall the heavy reliance on ornament and variation in Emanuel's own music, which thus reflects musical preferences in the circle of the Prussian court. A number of his early works, including several flute sonatas, contain variations, raising the possibility of royal influence.[16] Friedemann, on the other hand, rarely wrote elaborately embellished melodic lines into his music, avoiding variation as both a musical form (as in a theme with variations) and as a compositional technique. But although Friedemann thus disregarded a virtuoso device particularly associated at the time with operatic performance, in other respects his music shows greater theatricality and more outright virtuosity than that of Emanuel. It was Friedemann, too, who is thought to have been present in 1731 at the premiere performance in Dresden of Hasse's opera *Cleofide*.

Neither Friedemann nor Emanuel wrote any operas. Both, however, were composing keyboard concertos by the late 1730s, and those of Friedemann are particularly theatrical. For instance, one work, composed at Dresden, incorporates echoes of the aria "Son qual misera columba" from *Cleofide* (Example 1a). The A section of the aria, originally sung by Hasse's wife Faustina Bordoni, is a stunning display of vocal virtuosity. The B section concludes dramatically with a chromatic passage that leads to a cadenza. The first movement of Friedemann's

---

15. SBB, Mus. ms. autograph Friedrich II; facsimile edited by Wolfgang Goldhan as *Friedrich II.: Auszierung zur Arie "Digli ch'io son fedele" aus der Oper Cleofide von Johann Adolf Hasse* (Wiesbaden: Breitkopf und Härtel, 1991). Emanuel himself added the information beneath the title that the embellishments were for the castrato Porporino (Antonio Uberti).

16. See the flute sonatas W. 123, 124, 126, and 128, as well as the oboe sonata W. 135 and the keyboard variations W. 118/7 on a theme from Locatelli's flute sonata op. 2, no. 10. Berlin sources provide numerous examples of written-out embellishment, including those in chapter 13 of Johann Joachim Quantz, *Versuch einer Anweisung die Flöte traversiere zu spielen* (Berlin: Johann Friedrich Voss, 1752, translated by Edward R. Reilly as *On Playing the Flute*, 2nd ed. (New York: Schirmer Books, 1985) and in Emanuel's own so-called *Reprisen-Sonaten* (*Sechs Sonaten mit veränderten Reprisen*, W. 50), published at Berlin in 1760 with a dedication to the king's sister Anna Amalie. On King Frederick's possible patronage of Emanuel, once considered unlikely, see Mary Oleskiewicz, "Like Father, Like Son? Emanuel Bach and the Writing of Biography," in *Music and Its Questions: Essays in Honor of Peter Williams*, ed. Thomas Donahue (Richmond, VA: Organ Historical Society Press, 2007), 253–279.

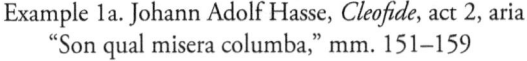

Example 1a. Johann Adolf Hasse, *Cleofide*, act 2, aria "Son qual misera columba," mm. 151–159

D-major concerto F. 41, although not literally in da capo form, contains an analogous passage that employs comparable harmonic progressions and syntax (Example 1b).[17] Elsewhere in the work, hand-crossings and related techniques involve the player in a sort of choreography whose impact is as much visual as musical. Sebastian and Emanuel used such tricks rarely, and almost never in their concertos. Yet these virtuoso devices are almost as common in Friedemann's keyboard music as in the sonatas of Domenico Scarlatti. Example 2 shows passagework involving the rapid alternation of the hands (indicated by the alterna-

---

17. Friedemann's work is dated by the handwriting and paper of the autograph score of the first movement (SBB, Mus. ms. Bach P 329), as established by Falck, 101; see also the modern edition by Peter Wollny (Stuttgart: Carus, 2000). A cadenza, indicated by a fermata in Example 1b, can also be assumed in Example 1a on the basis of the 6/4-chord and adagio marking in the penultimate measure.

Example 1b. Wilhelm Friedemann Bach, Concerto in D, F. 41, mvt. 1, mm. 90–98

tion between upward and downward note stems) from another of Friedemann's Dresden concertos.

Example 2. W. F. Bach, Concerto in A minor, F. 45, mvt. 3, mm. 205–209 (strings omitted)

This is one of the passages incorporated into the Dresden scene from the 1941 film, a happy choice presumably attributable to Mark Lothar, who is credited with the score.[18] Emanuel Bach would later describe hand-crossing as "a type of natural magic" that had been popular in his youth.[19] Emanuel evidently had little use for this technique, which is almost unknown in his work except in his early Menuet W. 111 and in the opening movement of the sixth "Probestück" sonata (W. 63/6, published in conjunction with his *Versuch*). Perhaps he failed to recognize that Friedemann's use of virtuoso devices was more than mere showmanship; like Domenico Scarlatti, or Sebastian in his inventions and the Goldberg Variations, Friedemann uses hand-crossing and other types of ostentatious passagework to compose out harmonic progressions through rigorous if often counter-intuitive motivic work.

This contrast between the two brothers extends to their vocal works. The sacred music of both includes the types of coloratura typical of the *galant* style. But Friedemann's vocal music is more demanding, as in Example 3, from his first

---

18. A prolific composer for film and opera, Lothar worked alongside Gründgens at the Preussische Staatstheater through most of the Nazi period. Presumably he found the fantasias in the editions by Hugo Riemann and Carl Banck cited by Falck (85–86). That the survival of one of these works (F. 19) was due to Friedemann's Jewish pupil Sara Levy, who had owned the only manuscript copy known at the time (SBB, Mus. ms. Bach P 702), of course goes unremarked in the film. Also Jewish was Rudolf Lothar (librettist of Graener's opera *Friedemann Bach*), born Rudolf Lothar Spitzer and unrelated to the composer Mark Lothar (also a pseudonym, born Lothar Hundertmark).

19. *Versuch über die wahre Art das Clavier zu spielen*, part 1, chap. 1, para. 97. By "natural magic" (natürliche Hexerey) Emanuel may have referred to the types of popular scientific and mathematical entertainments described in such works as Johann Conrad Gütle, *Versuche, Unterhaltungen und Belustigungen aus der natürlichen Magie* (Leipzig and Jena, 1791).

Example 3. W. F. Bach, *Wer mich liebet*, F. 72, mvt. 4, "Süße, Liebe, hohes Gut," mm. 92–109

Halle cantata.[20] In this aria he also gave himself a florid part for obbligato organ, almost overshadowing the bass voice, who must execute elaborate passagework, such as occurs here on the word *Glut* (cinders or embers). Through such writing, Friedemann demonstrated that he could bring the style of *opera seria* to his new church position. But he also showed that he could participate as an equal partner with the singer, as he had imitated Dresden singers in his concertos. Nothing

---

20. The example is transcribed from the sole source, the autograph SBB, Mus. ms. Bach P 322.

Friedemann and Emanuel Bach

of the sort occurs in Emanuel's vocal works, which seem not to incorporate any obbligato keyboard parts.

The Friedemann Bach of stage and screen is a revolutionary artist who cares only for the integrity of his art. Although anachronistic, there may be some truth to this image. Certainly Friedemann was less willing than Emanuel to make concessions to public taste. Emanuel's works of the 1740s are full of striking ideas, as in the slashing gestures of the opening ritornello in the D-minor concerto W. 23 of 1748 (Example 4). By the 1750s and 1760s, however, Emanuel's music was growing more suave, less challenging, as is evident above all in the little teaching pieces that he began to compose and publish in large numbers after his father's death in 1750.

Example 4. Carl Philipp Emanuel Bach, Concerto in D minor, W. 23, mvt. 1, mm. 1–10

This, like the other differences between the two brothers mentioned up to this point, is chiefly one of general musical character. Others reflect fundamental distinctions in how the two conceived musical structure. Example 5 is taken from a concerto in G minor that has only recently been recognized as a work of Friedemann Bach.[21] Its third movement opens somewhat like the D-minor

---

21. The sole source, SBB, Mus. ms. Bach St 174, gives the attribution only on a wrapper, and Falck considered the work doubtful (unsicher), but see the discussion in Schulenberg, *The Music of Wilhelm Friedemann Bach*, 190–196. Peter Wollny kindly informs the author that the work will appear under his editorship in a volume of *Wilhelm Friedemann Bach: Gesamtausgabe / Collected Works* (Stuttgart: Carus, 2009–).

Example 5. W. F. Bach, Concerto in G minor, mvt. 3, mm. 1–6

concerto; in both works, the melody, although irregular and punctuated by leaps and rests, is supported by a simple bass line that initially descends by step.[22] Emanuel's bass, however, descends through the equivalent of a full octave, beginning on d, before the interruption on a remarkable chromatic appoggiatura in m. 9. The G-minor concerto, on the other hand, strikes an augmented sixth already in m. 3 and then repeats it, as the bass becomes stuck on the half step e♭–d. The insistent repetition of a striking harmonic idea, often over a tortuously chromatic or enharmonic bass, is a common feature in Friedemann's music; Example 6 shows further examples from his keyboard works. In each case the rhetorical emphasis on a repeated harmonic gesture, sometimes very early in a composition, can be understood as something that is vividly theatrical in a way that Emanuel's music rarely is.

The descending bass of the ritornello theme in W. 23 is one of many scalar bass lines underlying not only themes but sometimes extensive passages in the body of Emanuel's works.[23] Such basses are rare with Friedemann. Emanuel spelled out his understanding of musical structure in the famous concluding chapter of his *Versuch*.[24] Figure 1 shows two pages from that chapter, which presents a series of scalar bass lines with figures meant to serve as the basis for im-

---

22. The melodic resemblance was noted by Peter Wollny, "Studies in the Music of Wilhelm Friedemann Bach: Sources and Style" (PhD diss., Harvard University, 1993), 60–62, who tentatively assigned the concerto to Friedemann's brother-in-law Johann Friedrich Altnickol in the work-lists for Friedemann Bach in *Die Musik in Geschichte und Gegenwart*, 2nd ed. (Kassel: Bärenreiter, 1994–2007) and *Grove Music Online* (accessed 6 January 2012).

23. For further examples, see David Schulenberg, *The Instrumental Music of Carl Philipp Emanuel Bach* (Ann Arbor, MI: UMI Research Press, 1984), 34ff.

24. Part 2, chap. 41.

Example 6. W. F. Bach, (a) Polonaise in C minor, F. 12/2, mm. 5–8;
(b) Fantasia in D minor, F. 19, mm. 17–21;
(c) Sonata in G, F. 7, mvt. 2, mm. 17–24

provisation. At the end of the chapter, Emanuel demonstrates how a complete composition, a free fantasia, could emerge through the elaboration of a figured bass line, given as an example; the fantasia itself (W. 117/14) was published on a supplementary engraved sheet. Friedemann left nothing like this; his most ambitious fantasias tend rather to comprise fragments that are either drawn from previously composed pieces or sound as if they could have been, as in the examples incorporated into the film soundtrack.[25]

As Heinrich Schenker recognized, Emanuel's doctrine of invention through variation could apply to any tonal composition.[26] Variation technique

---

25. Of Friedemann's ten surviving fantasias, six are of this type: F. 15 (in c), 16 (in c), 19 (in d), 20 (in e), 21 (in e), and 23 (in a).

26. See Heinrich Schenker, "Die Kunst der Improvisation," in his *Das Meisterwerk in der Musik* (Munich: Drei Masken, 1925–1930), 1, 12; here he equates composition with the "art of diminution," that is, the composing out of a harmonic progression such as is represented by the figured bass line that underlies Emanuel's fantasia, or by Schenker's own analytical sketches.

328   Ein und vierzigstes Capitel.

spielen bedienen können, ist diese: daß man die auf- und abstei
gende Tonleiter der Tonart, woraus gespielet werden soll, mit
allerhand Bezifferungen (a), und einigen eingeschalteten halben
Tönen (b), in, und ausser der Ordnung (c) mit einer gewissen
Vorsicht, zum Grunde leget, und die dabey vorkommenden Auf=
gaben gebrochen, oder ausgehalten in einem beliebigen Tempo
vorträget.   Die Orgelpuncte über der Prime sind bequem, die
erwählte Tonart bey dem Anfange und Ende festzusetzen (d). Vor
dem Schlusse können auch sehr wohl Orgelpuncte über der Do=
minante angebracht werden (e):

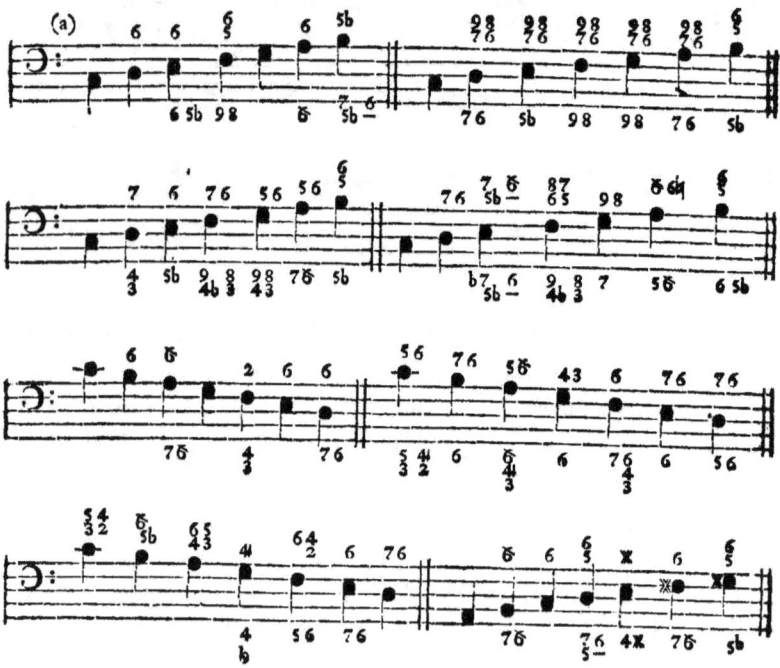

Figure 1. C. P. E. Bach, *Versuch über die wahre Art das Clavier zu spielen*,
vol. 2 (Berlin, 1762), pp. 328–329

Friedemann and Emanuel Bach

Figure 1 continued

in this sense was fundamental for Emanuel not only in the initial composition but in the revision of many works. He frequently returned to earlier compositions, embellishing and otherwise varying them, even writing two three-movement keyboard sonatas that are measure-for-measure variations of an earlier one.[27] Even where variation technique as such is absent, his melodic material is often conceived as a variation on a template, as in the ritornello theme of his D-minor concerto; that theme might have been conceived as a realization of one of the scalar bass lines shown in the *Versuch*.[28]

So important is this way of conceiving musical invention in Emanuel's music that it would be natural to suppose that Sebastian taught it.[29] Yet Friedemann's music shows little evidence of such thinking, and he left but a single substantial example of variation form. Emanuel evidently viewed themes and melodies as single-line variations on paradigmatic voice-leading progressions. Friedemann, on the other hand, seems to have conceived of thematic material as comprising motives within a polyphonic texture. The music of both is contrapuntal in the sense that there is always a strong, independent bass line. But Friedemann's basses are more likely than Emanuel's to incorporate imitations of the upper part, and his inner voices are more independent as well. In orchestral works, Emanuel usually writes in just three parts, with the two violins frequently in unison; in this he followed Hasse, the Grauns, and other older contemporaries. Friedemann usually writes for orchestral strings in four real parts, and these tend to involve frequent imitations of recurring motives.

All these features are evident in the opening ritornello of the one movement that Friedemann completed of his keyboard concerto in E-flat, F. 42 (Example 7a). Similar writing occurs in the work's solo episodes, where the strings continue to receive little imitative entries (Example 7b). Solo passages in concertos by Emanuel and other contemporaries tend to be simpler in texture,

---

27. W. 65/35 and 36, both "varying" the sonata in C W. 51/1; the latter is described as "nachhero 2 mal durchaus verändert" (afterwards twice varied throughout) in the posthumously published catalog of Emanuel's estate, the *Verzeichniß des musikalischen Nachlasses des verstorbenen Capellmeisters Carl Philipp Emanuel Bach* (Hamburg: Schniebes, 1790), 16 (item no. 119). For an online synoptic score presenting all three versions simultaneously, see http://faculty.wagner.edu/david-schulenberg/c-p-e-bach-pages/.

28. Compare the third and fourth bass lines in Figure 1.

29. This was the underlying assumption in the present author's "Composition and Improvisation in the School of J. S. Bach," in *Bach Perspectives* 1 (Lincoln: University of Nebraska Press, 1995), 1–42.

Friedemann and Emanuel Bach

Example 7a. W. F. Bach, Concerto in E-flat, F. 42,
mvt. 1, mm. 1–19 (letters indicate recurring motives)

the accompaniment of solo passagework typically limited to sustained chords. This is another reason for assigning the G-minor concerto to Friedemann, for it too contains many polyphonic passages, as in Example 8.

In short, Friedemann's conception of the musical surface is more genuinely contrapuntal and more profoundly motivic than that of Emanuel, who could vary the melodic surface of an entire sonata—including its motivic content—without altering its form. This distinction on the surface of the music re-

Example 7b. W. F. Bach, Concerto in E-flat, F. 42, mvt. 1, mm. 134–140
(letters indicate the same recurring motives as in Example 7a)

flects one at the formal level. Both composers employ the same basic varieties of sonata form, ritornello form, and da capo form in their sonatas, concertos, and arias. Yet the movements of Emanuel's sonatas and concertos are more likely to follow the routine designs also used by their contemporaries. Such movements comprise three main sections, with a clearly articulated return—a restatement of the opening passage in the tonic—that marks the beginning of the final section or recapitulation.[30]

---

30. In this early version of sonata form, the first main section is not always clearly divided into distinct thematic groups or key areas, and the middle section is not usually so distinct in style or modulatory content to warrant being called a development; see Schulenberg, *The Instrumental Music of Carl Philipp Emanuel Bach*, 28.

Example 8. W. F. Bach, Concerto in G minor, mvt. 1, mm. 109–116

Friedemann employed this type of form less consistently than his younger brothers. In the opening movement of his relatively early keyboard sonata F. 1, he may even have eliminated a sharp break between what would later be called the end of the development and the beginning of the recapitulation. The two upper staves of Example 9 show an early version in which the middle section ("development") ends in m. 56, where a fermata calls for a cadenza.[31] The return, which follows after a pause, is of precisely the same type, inspired by the da capo aria, as in Example 1b. At some point Friedemann revised the present movement, as shown on the lower staves of Example 9. But rather than embellishing the upper line, as Emanuel might have done, Friedemann eliminated the cadenza, and while shortening the movement he also gave it a more fluid, less starkly articulated form.

---

31. The written-out cadenza shown in Example 9 is present only in one source, SBB, Mus. ms. Bach P 368.

Example 9. W. F. Bach, Sonata in C, F. 1, mvt. 1:
(a) early version, F. 1B, mm. 45–59;
(b) late version, F. 1A, mm. 44–52

Emanuel meanwhile seems to have been tending in the opposite direction, writing sonata and concerto movements that distinctly articulate the beginning of the recapitulation, marking it as the crux of the entire form, as in Classical works from the later eighteenth century. In concertos, this is accomplished by having the tutti re-enter at that point with a substantial portion of the opening ritornello, as in the first movement of W. 23 (Example 10, m. 253). The three main solo sections of such a movement, indicated in bold type in Table 1, correspond with those of a sonata-allegro form. The return, marked in the table by an asterisk, is preceded by a relatively short solo episode, which serves as the retransition.

In Friedemann's F-major concerto F. 44, on the other hand, the final solo episode, corresponding to the recapitulation, is significantly shorter than the first (Table 2). In the last movement, the tutti enter for a single measure (m. 166) to announce the beginning of the recapitulation. The first movement appears to contain something similar, but the return is displaced to the middle of the measure, where it is part of a series of imitative exchanges between strings and keyboard that have already modulated back to the tonic F major (Example 11). Thus the tutti entrance in the second half of m. 110 sounds merely like the continuation of the ongoing development of the opening theme. In some sonata movements by Friedemann the final section consists almost entirely of the restatement of the opening section—the first part repeated verbatim, the second transposed downward by a fifth. Friedemann avoided such a design in his concertos, however, preferring continued development over recapitulation.[32]

Nevertheless, at the conclusion of nearly every concerto movement, Friedemann repeats the entire ritornello. Emanuel does so only in early works; his mature concerto movements usually end with abbreviated ritornellos, the real recapitulation having already been completed by this point. In this respect, as in his freer treatment of the final solo section, Friedemann's concerto movements represent a somewhat earlier conception of concerto form, in which the main solo episodes correspond less precisely with the three sections of a sonata

---

32. To be sure, even in Classical works the modern expression recapitulation can obscure the considerable amount of development that may occur in the third section of a sonata form; on this point, see, e.g., Charles Rosen, *Sonata Forms*, rev. ed. (New York: Norton, 1988), 289–293, on what he terms the "secondary development" within the recapitulation section.

Example 10. C. P. E. Bach, Concerto in D minor, W. 23, mvt. 1, mm. 243–262

design. To put it more positively, his design for a concerto movement remains relatively fluid, and this, incidentally, is another reason to accept Friedemann as composer of the G-minor concerto, which follows the same formal principles as his more assuredly attributed works.

Table 1. C. P. E. Bach: Concerto in D minor, W. 23, first movement

section:	R	**S**	r	**S**	r	s	r*	**S**	r
key:	d	d	d-->	g	g-->	a	a-->	**d**	d
measure:	1	**44**	98	**126**	202	221	253	**262**	313

R = full statement of ritornello   r = partial statement of ritornello
S = one of the three principal solo episodes
   (corresponding to the sections of a sonata form)
s = additional solo episode   *passage functioning as retransition

Table 2. W. F. Bach: Concerto in F, F. 44, first and third movements

section:	R	**S**	r	**S**	r	s	r*	**S**	R
key:	F	F	F-->	C	C-->	d-->	F	F	F
measure:	1	**23**	45	**53**	73	83	110b	**112**	125

section:	R	**S**	r	**S**	4	s	r*	**S**	R
key:	D	F	F-->	C	C-->	d-->	F	F	F
measure:	1	**25**	65	**78**	116	127	166	**167**	194

R = full statement of ritornello   r = partial statement of ritornello
S = one of the three principal solo episodes
   (corresponding to the sections of a sonata form)
s = additional solo episode   *passage functioning as retransition

How many of these differences between the two composers point to distinctions in training? Sebastian was never routine as a composer, and the diversity of style in the music of his sons and pupils suggests that he likewise never fell into a routine as a teacher. His early biographer Forkel reported that Friedemann and Emanuel had consciously invented their own styles, since they could not imitate their father's.[33] Two such brothers must also have avoided deliberately imitating one another, although a number of close thematic parallels can be found.[34]

---

33. Johann Nicolaus Forkel, *Ueber Johann Sebastian Bachs Leben, Kunst und Kunstwerke* (Leipzig: Hoffmeister und Kühnel, 1802), 79; English translation probably by Augustus Frederic Christopher Kollman in *The New Bach Reader*, 458.

34. For examples of thematic parallels, see Schulenberg, *The Music of Wilhelm Friedemann Bach*, Examples 2.14 and 4.52, respectively, illustrating Friedemann's keyboard sonata in E-flat, F. 5, mvt. 3, and the corresponding movement of Emanuel's sonata in the same key, W. 65/7; and the opening ritornellos of Friedemann's Concerto in

Example 11. W. F. Bach, Concerto in F, F. 44, mvt. 1,
(a) mm. 1–2, (b) mm. 106–111

The theorist Friedrich Wilhelm Marpurg claimed to have discussed "certain matters concerning fugue" with Sebastian.[35] But only for Friedemann do

---

F, F. 44, mvt. 3, and the corresponding movement of Emanuel's Concerto in G, W. 4. This is not to mention the puzzle of the two alternating minuets W. 116/7, published as Emanuel's in *Musikalisches Vielerley* (Hamburg, 1770), which he edited; these are embellished versions of the minuets in Friedemann's keyboard sonatas F. 6A (mvt. 2a) and F. 1A (mvt. 2b), respectively, which recur as the pair of minuets that conclude Friedemann's Sinfonia in F, F. 67.

35. "als ich bey meinem Aufenthalte in Leipzig mich über gewisse Materien, welche die Fuge betrafen, mit ihm besprach"; Friedrich Wilhelm Marpurg, *Kritische Briefe über*

we have documentation for any comparable activity, in the form of several pages of studies in invertible counterpoint and the like, written jointly with his father.[36] Emanuel, by contrast, told Forkel that his father avoided the "dry species" of counterpoint.[37] Marpurg also reported that Friedemann had written a treatise on the "harmonic triad";[38] nothing survives of it, but the report suggests that Friedemann, like Marpurg, was an adherent to Rameau's harmonic theories. Emanuel, on the other hand, stated famously that neither he nor his father held to Rameau's theory of harmony.[39]

But Emanuel could not have known everything his father taught, and he might have had his own reasons for spinning posthumous views of Sebastian. In 1775, when Emanuel wrote several now-famous letters to Forkel, he must have known that Friedemann had visited Forkel two years earlier.[40] Friedemann had now moved to Berlin, where he was evidently causing trouble for Emanuel's

---

die Tonkunst, vol. 1 (Berlin, 1760), p. 266, letter no. 34 (9 February 1760) to Johann Mattheson; partial translation in *The New Bach Reader*, 363 (item no. 357a).

36. For an initial account of these collaborative exercises or sketches, see Peter Wollny, "Eine Quellenfund in Kiew: Unbekannte Kontrapunktstudien von Johann Sebastian Bach und Wilhelm Friedemann Bach," in *Bach in Leipzig—Bach und Leipzig: Konferenzbericht Leipzig 2000*, ed. Ulrich Leisinger (Hildesheim: Olms, 2002), 275–287. Further discussion in Schulenberg, *The Music of Wilhelm Friedemann Bach*, chap. 2.

37. Letter to Forkel of 13 January 1775, translated in *The New Bach Reader*, 289 (item no. 803). "Dry" in this context evidently meant "strict" and was not necessarily a pejorative term; compare, for example, the quotation from Friedrich Nicolai's *Anekdoten von König Friedrich II von Preussen* (Berlin and Stettin, 1792), 253–254, concerning the king's early taste for contrapuntal music, in Mary Oleskiewicz, "The Trio in Bach's Musical Offering: A Salute to Frederick's Tastes and Quantz's Flutes?," in *Bach Perspectives 4, The Music of J. S. Bach: Analysis and Interpretation*, ed. David Schulenberg (Lincoln: University of Nebraska Press, 1999), 84. But Marpurg, in the letter cited in note 35, has Sebastian equating "dry" (trocken) with "wooden" (hölzern) and "pedantic" (pedantisch).

38. *Abhandlung vom Harmonischen Dreyklang*; mentioned in *Kritische Briefe über die Tonkunst*, vol. 1, p. 241, letter no. 31 (19 January 1760) to Friedemann.

39. According to Johann Philipp Kirnberger, who quotes Emanuel's statement that his and his father's principles are "anti-Ramellian" ("Daß meine und meines seligen Vaters Grundsätze antirameauisch sind, können sie laut sagen."), *Die Kunst des reinen Satzes in der Musik* (Berlin, 1771–1779), 2:188.

40. The visit was recorded by Forkel's pupil Friedrich Conrad Griepenkerl in the preface to the latter's edition of Friedemann's polonaises F. 12; see *Zwölf Polonoisen für das Pianoforte von Wilhelm Friedemann Bach. Mit einer Beschreibung und Bezeichnung des wahren Vortrags wie derselbe von Friede[man]n Bach auf Forkel und von Forkel auf seine Schüler übertragen worden* (Leipzig: C. F. Peters, 1819).

friend Kirnberger.[41] In writing to Forkel, Emanuel might have been trying to set the record straight, as he understood it. The letters in which he did so have been taken as solid evidence for Sebastian's teaching.[42] But Emanuel's actual music, and Friedemann's, may provide more reliable, if less unequivocal, documentation for musical instruction and practice in the school of J. S. Bach.

---

41. Apparently Friedemann sought to have Princess Anna Amalie appoint him as her librarian or composition teacher in Kirnberger's place; see Falck, 52–53.

42. For instance, substantial extracts from three of them appear in *The New Bach Reader*, 395–400 (items nos. 393–395). The present more skeptical perspective on them has been influenced by Peter Williams's critical rereading of Sebastian's obituary—which was written in part by Emanuel Bach—in *The Life of Bach* (Cambridge: Cambridge University Press, 2004), passim.

Haydn's "Irregularities": Ambiguous Openings in the
B-minor String Quartets, op. 33/1 and op. 64/2

MATHIEU LANGLOIS

Musicologists have long associated Joseph Haydn's works—particularly his sonata-form movements—with formal irregularity, whether for their persistent defiance of our "normative" formal paradigms, or their penchant for devices of surprise.[1] In fact, "irregularities" is precisely the word Charles Rosen uses in his discussion of the famous op. 33/1 in B minor, whereby he allies Haydn with his older contemporary C. P. E. Bach under the banner of "eccentricity" in an informal fraternity of composers who occasionally liked to begin a piece in the "wrong key"—a device, he says, "deliberately outrageous to the eighteenth-century ear."[2]

The substantial critical literature on the D-major / B-minor twist in the opening measures of op. 33/1 (see Example 1) testifies to the fascination provoked by a work that subverts the listener's expectations no sooner than they are established—what is commonly referred to as an "ambiguous opening."[3] This

---

I am grateful to Evan Cortens, Ellen Lockhart, Annette Richards, and James Webster who read, and generously offered commentary on, earlier drafts of this paper.

1. For example, James Hepokoski and Warren Darcy, in their monumental *Elements of Sonata Theory*, figure this tendency for formal irregularity as evidence of Haydn's "pervasive originality of content and design." There is, however, clearly an element of difficulty in having to address the sheer variety of "deformations" of normative sonata procedures they find "rampant" in Haydn's works. James Hepokoski and Warren Darcy, *Elements of Sonata Theory: Norms, Types, and Deformations in the Late-Eighteenth-Century Sonata* (Oxford: Oxford University Press, 2006), 11 and 413.

2. Charles Rosen, *The Classical Style: Haydn, Mozart, Beethoven* (New York: Norton, 1972), 112. In mentioning these two composers, Rosen follows Tovey, who in turn follows a host of eighteenth-century commentators who drew comparisons between the works of Haydn and C. P. E. Bach. Tovey, however, was perhaps the first to assert that Haydn "got" the ambiguous opening device of op. 33/1 from C. P. E. Bach. See Donald Francis Tovey, *Essays and Lectures on Music* (London: Oxford University Press, 1949), 49. Rosen disputes Tovey's assertion, but mentions C. P. E. Bach's Sonata V in F Major (Wq 55/5), from the *Sechs Clavier-Sonaten für Kenner und Liebhaber, Erste Sammlung* of 1779, as an example comparable to op. 33/1. He is quick, however, to debunk any overt imitation on Haydn's part, and asserts that in Haydn's hands the false opening was a device "capable of greater elaboration." See Rosen, *The Classical Style*, 114.

3. A representative sampling of this scholarship, beyond Tovey and Rosen, would also include Markus Bandur, "Plot und Rekurs: 'eine gantz neue besondere Art'? Analytische

Example 1. Haydn, String Quartet in B Minor, Op. 33/1i, mm. 1–13[4]

Überlegungen zum Kopfsatz von Joseph Haydns Streichquartett op. 33, Nr. 1 (Hoboken III:37)," in *Haydns Streichquartette: Eine moderne Gattung*, ed. Heinz-Klaus Metzger and Rainer Riehn (Munich: Boorberg, 2002), 62–84; Floyd Grave and Margaret Grave, *The String Quartets of Joseph Haydn* (Oxford: Oxford University Press, 2006), 212; James Webster, *Haydn's "Farewell" Symphony and the Idea of Classical Style: Through-Composition and Cyclic Integration in His Instrumental Music* (Cambridge: Cambridge University Press, 1991), 127–130; and Gretchen A. Wheelock, *Haydn's Ingenious Jesting with Art: Contexts of Musical Wit and Humor* (New York: Schirmer, 1992), 103–106.

4. By kind permission of G. Henle Verlag, all musical examples in this paper unless otherwise indicated are drawn from the volumes of *Joseph Haydn Werke* edited by Georg Feder (Munich: G. Henle Verlag, 1963–1978), XII/2 *(Streichquartette "Opus 9" und "Opus 17")*, XII/3 *(Streichquartette "Opus 20" und "Opus 33")*, and XII/5 *(Streichquartette "Opus 64" und "Opus 71/74")*.

phrase is usually employed as a kind of convenient umbrella term, but is, at least from an analytical perspective, lacking in specificity. My aim here is twofold: first, to parse the notion of the ambiguous opening from an aesthetic standpoint, since the term itself encompasses a number of different effects; and second, to interrogate the notion that such devices demand and achieve a kind of resolution across a movement. I focus here on harmonic ambiguity and not metrical (though an exploration of the latter would certainly be possible), and do not aim to be comprehensive. My discussion revolves around the most frequently cited ambiguous openings in this oeuvre: the first movements of op. 33/1 (1781) and the lesser-known, but oft-cited op. 64/2, also in B minor (1791). Although these two quartets are frequently grouped together in the critical literature, they differ fundamentally from one another: Haydn treats the ambiguous opening of the latter in a way that challenges any expectations based on his other quartets regarding the long-term consequences of such a device within a movement.

James Webster, in his discussion of Haydn's quartet op. 33/3, distinguishes between tonal ambiguity and tonal instability[5]—the former suggesting a musical passage (however fleeting) in which insufficient harmonic information is supplied to definitively establish the key area, leaving the door open to multiple tonal interpretations; the latter implying a somewhat more clearly defined tonal area that is nevertheless vulnerable to disintegration and harmonic digression. I would add, furthermore, that in dealing with ambiguous openings it is useful to distinguish between compositional gambits that are tonally uncertain and those which are deceptive or misleading. The difference is essentially a function of a given musical passage's harmonic potential and the degree to which it is realized before being subverted: what is termed "ambiguous" typically engenders a sense of listener disorientation because of its multiplicity of potential interpretations, while that which is "deceptive" requires just enough of those potentialities to be realized for the listener to decide upon the apparent tonal context, before full elucidation of the harmonic orientation forces a change in his or her thinking on the matter.

Kofi Agawu defines ambiguity as a musical circumstance that gives rise to more than one potential meaning, with the caveat that "a musical situation is ambiguous if and only if its two (or more) meanings are comparably or equally

---

5. Webster, *Haydn's "Farewell" Symphony*, 131.

plausible, leaving the listener undecided about their future significance."[6] Within a select temporal span, this is well-aligned with the distinction I have proposed above. However, Agawu aims to take his definition of ambiguity much further: he seeks an ambiguity that is genuinely undecidable, a musical event that "remains ambiguous *after* a reflective analytical exercise" (emphasis original).[7] In fact, Agawu argues against the existence of genuine musical ambiguity, at least as it might occur within the context of the analysis of a musical work, concluding that "while ambiguity may exist as an abstract phenomenon, it does not exist in concrete musical situations," for "theory-based analysis necessarily includes a mechanism for resolving ambiguities at all levels of structure."[8] The "I do not know" kind of ambiguity—that is, the uncertainty the listener might experience in trying to determine the harmonic context of a given sonority within a select period of time—is relegated within Agawu's discussion to the "weak kind."[9] My purpose here is not to dispute Agawu's conclusions; it is, rather, to valorize the experiential element he marginalizes, for the "I do not know" kind of ambiguity is of critical importance to the listener. Furthermore, the skillful manipulation of such ambiguous events in time has the potential to form the defining feature of a composer's relationship with his or her audience. Within the confines of this paper then, I treat ambiguity not as an ideal theoretical concept (whose concrete existence may or may not be provable in analysis), but as a facet of perception which might plausibly be fostered by compositional strategies. Put simply, then, the ambiguity I discuss here resides in the gap between our expectations and the progress of the musical events themselves in time, a progression on which we as listeners and performers must formulate an interpretation.

Doris Silbert's 1950 article, "Ambiguity in the String Quartets of Haydn," recognizes the significance of these events in Haydn's compositions, in effect employing the word "ambiguous" to discuss musical events of all kinds that subvert the listener's expectations or introduce a "counter tension" against the "main

---

6. Kofi Agawu, "Ambiguity in Tonal Music: A Preliminary Study," in *Theory, Analysis and Meaning in Music*, ed. Anthony Pople (Cambridge: Cambridge University Press, 1994), 89.

7. Ibid., 90 and 93.

8. Ibid., 107. These form points Nos. 3 and 1 respectively of Agawu's four concluding propositions concerning musical ambiguity.

9. Ibid., 93.

Haydn's "Irregularities"

direction of movement" of the work.[10] It is common today, as it was apparently in his own time, to interpret these subversions as evidence of a kind of humor, wit, or irony.[11] As is widely recognized, one of the contemporary perceptions of Haydn was as a composer of characteristically "humorous" music.[12] We might posit, thus, that the openings of op. 33/1 and op. 33/3 had some bearing on Johann Friedrich Reichardt's review of the opus (1783), in which he asserts that these works are full of "the most original humor [Laune], the most lively, most agreeable wit"[13] (or, for that matter, on Carl Friedrich Cramer's review from the same year, in which he praises the quartets in much the same terms).[14] That such wit might connote not only special ingenuity, but also the potential for sleight of hand, is reflected in sources such as William Jackson's 1798 article "On Wit," in which he asserts that "wit . . . is the dextrous performance of a leger-

---

10. Doris Silbert, "Ambiguity in the String Quartets of Haydn," *Musical Quarterly* 36, no. 4 (1950): 564. Some of the "counter tensions" Silbert discusses include enharmonic shifts, delays or arrests of rhythmic motion, false reprises, changes in phrase length, and the "tonal ambiguities" of the openings of op. 33/1 and op. 64/2.

11. Silbert's discussion is a case in point here: she views these events as "jokes" intended for both listeners and the performers of the quartets. Ibid., 565.

12. It should be noted that the notion of "humor" in this context derives originally from theories of temperament having to do with the fluids of the body, and in the eighteenth century was not necessarily thought of as amusing or funny in the modern sense (though these meaning came increasingly to be aligned with one another later in the century). For the most thorough discussion of these distinctions, see Wheelock, *Haydn's Ingenious Jesting*.

13. "Diese beiden Werke sind voll der originälsten Laune, des lebhaftesten angenehmsten Witzes." Johann Friedrich Reichardt, *Musikalisches Kunstmagazin* 1 (Berlin, 1782; facsimile reprint, Hildesheim: Olms, 1970), 205. This review is also cited in Wheelock, *Haydn's Ingenious Jesting*, 49, and Steven E. Paul makes much the same observation in "Comedy, Wit, and Humor in Haydn's Instrumental Music," in *Haydn Studies: Proceedings of the International Haydn Conference, Washington, D.C., 1975*, ed. Jens Peter Larsen, Howard Serwer, and James Webster (New York: Norton, 1981), 450.

14. "Diese Werke werden gepriesen, und könnens auch nicht genug, in Absicht der allerorginellsten Laune, und des lebhaftesten angenehmsten Witzes, der darinnen herrscht." (These works have been praised and cannot be praised enough, in view of the most ingenious humor and the most lively, most agreeable wit that prevails in them.) Carl F. Cramer, *Magazin der Musik* 1 (Hamburg, 1783): 259–260. This too is cited and translated in Wheelock, *Haydn's Ingenious Jesting*, 114. As one might expect, Wheelock notes that the similarity between the two reviews suggests Cramer may have borrowed directly from Reichardt's assessment of op. 33.

demain trick, by which one idea is *presented* and another *substituted*" (emphasis original).[15] This provides an apt lens through which to view, for instance, the tonal shift the listener perceives in the opening of op. 33/1. And if, like Mark Evan Bonds, we accept musical irony as being produced through the violation of generic convention such that the audience is reminded of the underlying artifice of the work, Haydn's ambiguous openings may be seen as a means of "call[ing] attention to [the music's] own structural rhetoric."[16] Indeed, "irony" is precisely the term James Webster invokes in his own extended analysis of the first movement of op. 33/1.[17]

Musical ambiguity and subversions are thus significant in that they create several, sometimes contradictory effects depending on the angle from which one views them: they may insert a sense of authorial voice into a piece while simultaneously implying a self-conscious distance between composer and product, or serve to draw the listener into the music's roller-coaster progress while paradoxically reinforcing the fact that one may never entirely trust its trajectory. Nevertheless, we need to recognize a deeper level of significance to these devices, for ultimately surprise has limited currency. Is a device still ambiguous if left unaltered on repeated hearings? If it was amusing the first time, does it remain funny, or does its novel effect become tiresome and finally expire in the diluting process of repetition?

In the case of the ambiguous openings in Haydn's sonata-form quartet movements, the listener recognizes that the surprise event will recur on the repeat, and attention necessarily turns to the handling of the device and its implications within the larger musical context. If, on subsequent hearings, the effect of a musical jest is different, then, as Doris Silbert has argued, it is plausible that one might derive most pleasure from these "delusive moments" if already

---

15. William Jackson, "On Wit," in *The Four Ages, Together with Essays on various Subjects* (London, 1798), 122; facsimile available at *Eighteenth Century Collections Online*, http://www.galenet.galegroup.com (accessed 2 May 2009). Gretchen Wheelock emphasizes the fact that wit commonly connoted ingenuity, incongruity, and sudden amazement. She states, "the delights of surprise, of the unexpected and the novel, are commonly noted in eighteenth-century discussions of wit, though not always with complete assurance of benign intent." Wheelock, *Haydn's Ingenious Jesting*, 21.

16. Mark Evan Bonds, "Haydn, Laurence Sterne, and the Origins of Musical Irony," *Journal of the American Musicological Society* 44 (1991): 70.

17. Webster, *Haydn's "Farewell" Symphony*, 130.

Haydn's "Irregularities"

familiar with them.[18] They are thus turned on their heads: what began as a subversion of listener expectations becomes successful precisely when it begins to fulfill expectations.

But if its effects may vary after the initial statement, we have a potential shift in the value of the ambiguous device. The rationale behind this phenomenon can perhaps be best explained by being brought into alignment with eighteenth-century theories of contrast and variety. Scheibe's description of the chamber symphony in his *Critischer Musikus* (1745), while too early to be directly applicable to formal considerations in Haydn's sonata-form movements, is useful nevertheless in establishing a concern for the balancing of unity and variety in a way that is intimately linked to the effect of surprise. According to him, the composer must

> integrate the main theme with even the most foreign ideas in a most proper manner. Accordingly, the composer must surprise the rather unsuspecting listeners with quite unexpected events. But before they can make any judgment as to what has happened, everything must suddenly once again become linked and united with the main theme.[19]

A harmonically ambiguous opening of the first theme accords strikingly well with these compositional values, for it contains the latent possibility to form the basis of subsequent "unexpected events" while nonetheless never being entirely

---

18. Silbert, "Ambiguity in the String Quartets," 568–569. Both Wheelock and Edward T. Cone have also addressed the notion that the effect of a jest may vary upon repetition. See Wheelock, *Haydn's Ingenious Jesting*, 15; and Edward T. Cone, *Musical Form and Performance* (New York: Norton, 1968), 54–55.

19. The full quotation reads, "Es gehöret aber eine große Uebung, eine tiefe Einsicht in die Melodie, und keine gemeine Geschicktlichkeit darzu, alles wohl und natürlich mit einander zu verbinden, und auch die fremdesten Gedanken und Einfälle auf das ordentlichste wieder mit der Haupterfindung zu vergleichen. (But much experience, a deep insight into melody, and no ordinary skill is required in order to bind everything together skillfully and naturally, and in order to integrate the main theme with even the most foreign ideas in a most proper manner.) So müssen dahero ganz unerwartete Einfälle die Zuhörer gleichsam unvermuthet überraschen. Bevor sie aber darüber ihre Beurtheilung anstellen können, muss so fort alles wieder mit der Haupterfindung vereinbaret und verknüpfet werden." Johann Adolf Scheibe, *Critischer Musikus*, 2nd ed. (Leipzig: Breitkopf, 1745; facsimile reprint, Hildesheim: Olms, 1970), 624. I use here the translation given by Bellamy Hosler in *Changing Aesthetic Views of Instrumental Music in 18th-Century Germany* (Ann Arbor: UMI Research Press, 1981), 59–60.

divorced from the original thematic idea. In possessing the built-in potential to be simultaneously familiar and foreign, Haydn's ambiguous devices neatly accomplish Scheibe's task of effecting unforeseen turns while "uniting" everything with the "main theme" before the listener even fully comprehends it.

Such concerns are echoed by Sulzer in the *Allgemeine Theorie der schönen Künste* (1771–1774), for the article on "Mannichfaltigkeit" (variety) emphasizes the importance of unity and connectedness. Sulzer states:

> Variety must appear as the constantly varied effects of a single cause, or as the different forces that act upon a single object, or things of the same kind that are distinguished by their individual shadings. The closer things cohere in their variety, the more delicate will be the enjoyment they provide.[20]

Variety and unity must therefore co-exist in a tenuous balance, lest a superabundance of disparate ideas result in incomprehensibility. Sulzer asserts that it is the composer's task to "present the main idea in a variety of forms by changing its accompanying harmonies, developing it, and altering it through the addition of subordinate but still coherent ideas."[21] Again, the ambiguous opening, with its many possibilities for reworking over the course of a movement, is striking in its ability to meet these criteria.

---

20. "Das Mannichfaltige muß als die immer abgeänderte Würkung einer einzigen Ursache, oder als verschiedene Kräfte, die auf einen einzigen Gegenstand würken, oder als Dinge von einer Art, deren jedes durch seine besondere Schattirung ausgezeichnet ist, erscheinen. Je genauer die Dinge bey ihrer Mannichfaltigkeit zusammenhangen, je feiner ist das Vergnügen, das sie verursachet." Johann Georg Sulzer, "Mannichfaltigkeit," in *Allgemeine Theorie der schönen Künste* (1771–1774), 3:361–362; trans. in *Aesthetics and the Art of Musical Composition in the German Enlightenment*, ed. Nancy Kovaleff Baker and Thomas Christensen (Cambridge: Cambridge University Press, 1995), 47.

21. The full quotation reads, "Nur der Tonsetzer, der das zu seiner Kunst nötige Genie hat, weiß den Hauptgedanken in mannichfaltiger Gestalt, durch abgeänderte Harmonien unterstützt, vorzutragen, und ihn durch mehrere ihm untergeordnete, aber genau damit zusammenhangende Gedanken so zu verändern, daß das Gehör vom Anfang bis zum Ende beständig gereizt wird." (Only the composer possessing the necessary genius for his art knows how to present the main idea in a variety of forms. . .) Sulzer, "Mannichfaltigkeit," 362; translated in Baker and Christensen, *Aesthetics and the Art of Musical Composition*, 48.

Haydn's "Irregularities"

The special value of an ambiguous opening lies in its capacity to create diversity from a single event with significant economy of compositional means. In fact, three of the four quartets with ambiguous openings cited by Webster (op.17/4; op. 33/1; and op. 33/3)[22] involve the opening device in some significant fashion in the introduction of the second group,[23] as well as at many subsequent formal junctures.[24] The most striking (and famous) instance occurs in op. 33/1, where the second group is able to appear as the untransposed main theme specifically because of the tonal ambiguity at the beginning (see Example 2).

Example 2. Haydn, String Quartet in B Minor, Op. 33/1i, mm. 17–20

Ambiguous devices in Haydn's quartets, through their repetition and reinterpretation, thus often become formal instigators capable of effecting dramatic shifts of direction elsewhere in the movement.

Perhaps one of the most tempting interpretations of these events is to see resolution as a necessary outcome of the proposition offered by an ambiguous opening—the gesture a deceptively simple problem calling for a solution over the course of the following musical form. Arnold Schoenberg, in his essay entitled "New Music, Outmoded Music, Style and Idea," suggests that the fundamental purpose of any composition—the "idea"—lies in the restoration

---

22. Webster, *Haydn's "Farewell" Symphony*, 127 and 130.

23. Regarding terminology, I use "first group" and "second group" to refer to the sections of the exposition in a sonata form in the tonic and dominant respectively (i.e., what are often misleadingly referred to as the "first theme/subject" and the "second theme/subject"). Both the first and second groups may then contain several different ideas (i.e., thematic material which may vary in its prominence relative to any other ideas within a group).

24. The ambiguous opening may thus at times function comparably to main theme transposition at the beginning of the second group.

of balance to a state of unrest produced by the addition of tones to the "beginning tone" (or initial state of affairs).[25] While reading an entire movement as the act of finding resolution to an initial destabilization certainly seems a fitting model for harmonically ambiguous openings, we need to exercise caution in the manner in which we assert that such events find resolution over the course of an entire movement. Although a tonal resolution in the "home" key by the end of a movement is a fair generic expectation in this repertoire, asserting that the opening device in-and-of-itself is somehow reconciled is a less simple matter.

Op. 33/1 serves here as a useful example. Rosen, using the unfortunately unreliable Eulenburg scores, sees the first movement of this quartet as an extended attempt to resolve what appears to him a "'false' tonal opening"[26]—certainly a credible interpretation given that the Eulenburg score supplies double-stops (F-sharp and A-natural) in the violin II part in m. 1, thus creating a full D major triad not present in the original sources (see the comparison of the Eulenburg and JHW editions supplied in Examples 3a and 3b).[27] In his view, resolution to the large-scale dissonance this false opening creates is furnished by the use of the device in establishing the secondary key area for the second group, its expansion in the development section, and the fact that "the recapitulation—except for two measures at the beginning—insists dramatically on the tonic."[28] However, reiteration of the thematic material involved, especially within a development section, speaks to a preoccupation with the device, and does not provide a resolution in itself.[29] And the two measures to which he refers in the recapitulation

---

25. Arnold Schoenberg, "New Music, Outmoded Music, Style and Idea," in *Style and Idea* (London: Faber & Faber, 1975), 123. This passage of *Style and Idea* is also cited in Webster's discussion of "progressive form," in *Haydn's "Farewell" Symphony*, 124.

26. Rosen, *The Classical Style*, 120.

27. The modern *Joseph Haydn Werke* edition makes clear that Haydn supplied only a harmonizing F-sharp in the violin II part, thus, leaving open the possibility for the work to be in either B minor or D major until the introduction of the A-sharp in m. 3 (although the key is not fully confirmed until the cadence in mm. 10–11). Georg Feder and Sonja Gerlach point out that these alterations seem to have been first introduced in the edition of op. 33 edited by J. J. Hummel. See Georg Feder and Sonja Gerlach, "Vorwort," in *Joseph Haydn Werke*, XII/3: *Streichquartette "Opus 20" und "Opus 33"* (Munich: G. Henle Verlag, 1974), IX. See also Bandur, "Plot und Rekurs," 70–71.

28. Rosen, *The Classical Style*, 120.

29. Rosen's wording here is not entirely clear to me; it is also possible that he is referring to the "expanding" of not just the opening gesture, but the secondary key area within the development. If the latter is the case, there is indeed a section of the development which operates in B minor; however, the thematic material of the opening gesture

Example 3a. Haydn, String Quartet in B Minor, Op. 33/1i, mm. 1–2
(Eulenberg edition)

Example 3b. Haydn, String Quartet in B Minor, Op. 33/1i, mm. 1–2
(*Joseph Haydn Werke* edition)

(mm. 59–60) contain another reworking of the ambiguous device, this time harmonized with a tonally unstable augmented triad (see Example 4).[30] Although it is apparent here that the key is B minor,[31] one cannot call this a resolution of the tonal issues within the actual musical event; it is, rather, a perpetuation of them. Moreover, the first group in the recapitulation (mm. 59–71), much as it did until m. 11 of the exposition, actually prolongs the dominant and lacks any bass tonic (see Examples 1 and 4).[32]

---

is stated only once in the tonic in this B-minor section and is juxtaposed with several statements in other keys and at other pitch levels in the development.

30. This too would not have been apparent to Rosen, for the Eulenburg score does not preserve the augmented triad, substituting instead an A-natural in the violin II part.

31. This is made clear by the Ger6–V progression in m. 58.

32. Webster suggests precisely this in his analysis. See Webster, *Haydn's "Farewell" Symphony*, 130.

Example 4. Haydn, String Quartet in B Minor, Op. 33/1i, mm. 59–73

Webster's view is that Idea 2 (thematic material first introduced in m. 11) functions to concretely establish B minor within the expositional first group, and is subsequently reinterpreted as the beginning of the second group in the recapitulation (m. 72 of Example 4).[33] This theory does directly address the tonal instability of the beginning. Nonetheless, it is not the ambiguity within the original event that is resolved in the recapitulation, but the larger-scale formal dissonance it creates. If, during the course of the movement, the ambiguous event as a *discrete* entity does find tonal resolution to the D-major / B-minor dichotomy it contains, I would offer that it is actually in the *expositional* 2Gr, where the theme is harmonized unambiguously in the relative major (refer to Example 2). The treatment of these events across a movement thus does not necessarily take on the characteristics of a strictly teleological narrative. Moreover, while tonal resolution may be theoretically possible for deceptive or misleading musical openings (by which I mean to suggest that the specific, internal harmonic tension of the event may come to be resolved in a later statement), resolution of a truly "ambiguous opening" in the broader sense, if possible at all, can really only take the form of an exploration of its harmonic potentialities over the course of the movement. This is a useful way of viewing, for example, op. 33/3 in C major and op. 17/4 in C minor, in which each recurrence of the ambiguous device offers alternate potential harmonizations and marks many of the subsequent formal junctures.

Op. 33/3 opens with a dyad, lacking one crucial member of a full triad (see Example 5).[34] Unlike the first measures of 33/1, however, the opening dyad of 33/3 contains the root of the chord, although technically it would be possible to hear the movement in A minor until the entry of the note G in m. 2 realizes one of the potential harmonizations of the open interval. While the opening of 33/3 does not offer a suggestive treatment of the sonority only to be subverted later (as in 33/1 or 64/2, which I would term genuinely misleading), each introduction of this thematic material allows for variation that, while simultaneously recalling the opening, presents the opportunity for subverting the listener's expectation. In effect, the eighth-note motive from m. 1 becomes the harbinger of each new area of exploration, altered in ways which undermine tonal stability at nearly every appearance. Not only does it introduce the expositional second group at m. 27 (without a root) and the development (with an unstable dimin-

---

33. Ibid.
34. For the sake of simplicity during the analysis, I hereafter refer to the first movements of the quartets under discussion as 33/1, 33/3, 64/2, and 17/4 (i.e., without "op.").

Example 5. Haydn, String Quartet in C Major, Op. 33/3i, mm. 1–6

Example 6. Haydn, String Quartet in C Major, Op. 33/3i, mm. 107–113

Haydn's "Irregularities"

ished harmony reinterpreted in the following measure as a dominant-seventh in third inversion), its entry at the recapitulation in m. 108 retains the key of E minor two measures longer than expected before modulating back to the home key C major (see Example 6).

The potential for dislocation of thematic and harmonic return based on such an ambiguous opening is also made apparent in 17/4 in C minor (see Example 7). Here the opening event again becomes a defining element at later formal junctures within the movement. The first two notes in m. 1 of the violin I part (an ascending E-flat and G) might suggest the possibility of continuing on

Example 7. Haydn, String Quartet in C Minor, Op. 17/4i, mm. 1–11

117

in triadic fashion to a B-flat (if we as listeners assume the first note to be the tonic); however, the note C is sounded in both the first violin and the cello on the downbeat of the following measure. Although no deception occurs here, in that the first measure lacks enough clues to concretize the impression that we are operating in E-flat major, the length of the half-notes in the first measure (which Steve Larson calls a "lengthened anacrusis"[35]) heightens anticipation through temporal play. This phrase is followed immediately in mm. 9–10 with a repetition of the opening melodic gesture which does indeed proceed to the B-flat (though we do not land on an E-flat-major sonority in m. 10). Subsequent permutations of the opening gesture see it recur as the harmonic accompaniment of the second group (m. 20), and as the marker for the beginning of the development (m. 54). But at the recapitulation, the potential of the gesture to suggest E-flat major to the listener is employed so as to bring us back into the "correct" key later than expected, in effect realizing the alternate potential of the opening gesture (see Example 8). The return of thematic correspondence with the expo-

Example 8. Haydn, String Quartet in C Minor, Op. 17/4i, mm. 86–95

---

35. Steve E. Larson, "Recapitulation Recomposition in the Sonata-Form Movements of Haydn's String Quartets: Style Change and Compositional Technique," *Music Analysis* 22 (2003): 152–153.

sitional first group begins in m. 87 (since m. 87 represents a direct transposition of m. 3 into the relative major), but it is not until m. 93 that we arrive firmly in C minor (at which point the opening melody is again recalled). Haydn thus exploits the implications of the opening device such that the listener is forced to question whether mm. 86–91 represent a "false" recapitulation, or the gesturally and thematically "real" recapitulation in the incorrect key.[36]

But if any quartet unseats assumptions about compositional treatment of the ambiguous opening, it is Haydn's later string quartet in B minor, op. 64/2 (1791). This quartet has been somewhat overshadowed in the literature by its predecessor, 33/1, yet the two are frequently cited in the same breath. Beginning at least with Tovey, musicologists have reiterated the fact that the two quartets share some common features, including a correspondence of keys between their respective opuses (C major, G major, D major, B minor, B-flat major, and E-flat major), and most importantly, an opening that plays with the ambiguity between D major and B minor.[37] Tovey calls this a "great work, unduly neglected,"[38] and Hans Keller perceives it as an outdoing of its B minor predecessor, saying that it betrays evidence of Haydn's "maturest adventurousness."[39] Despite the movement's frequent mention, however, the long-term consequences of the opening of 64/2 seem not to have received detailed attention with respect to the quartet's better-known counterpart, 33/1.[40]

---

36. These layers of ambiguity are pointed out by Larson, who, in a tongue-in-cheek downward semantic spiral, posits that we could be dealing with a "false false recapitulation," or a "false 'false false' recap," or perhaps even a "doubly disguised 'false double recap.'" Larson, "Recapitulation Recomposition," 155.

37. Markus Bandur (who calls it "perhaps ironical self-quotation"), "Plot und Rekurs," 73; Floyd and Margaret Grave, *The String Quartets*, 266; Paul Griffiths, *The String Quartet: A History* (London: Thames & Hudson, 1983), 64; Hans Keller, *The Great Haydn Quartets: Their Interpretation* (London: J. M. Dent & Sons, Ltd., 1986), 151; Rosen, *The Classical Style*, 140; Silbert, "Ambiguity in the String Quartets," 568–569; Tovey, *Essays and Lectures*, 62; and Webster, *Haydn's "Farewell" Symphony*, 127.

38. Tovey, *Essays and Lectures*, 62.

39. Keller, *The Great Haydn Quartets*, 151. Keller does note that its beginning is "differently conceived and constructed" than its predecessor.

40. To my knowledge, the only published analysis of the exposition and recapitulation of 64/2i is that of William E. Caplin in *Classical Form: A Theory of Formal Functions for the Instrumental Music of Haydn, Mozart, and Beethoven* (Oxford: Oxford University Press, 1998), 114, 116, and 175–177. Caplin's primary interests in this quartet movement have to do with the beginning of the "subordinate theme" in the exposition and the complex recomposition of its recapitulation.

Not only is the opening event of 64/2 constructed and handled differently from 33/1 on the local level, the movement as a whole takes on an entirely different cast. The opening two-measure violin solo implies D major, not only because it is the first and longest note the listener hears, but also because of the repetition of the C-sharp lower neighbor and emphasis on what we perceive as the third scale-degree, F-sharp (see Example 9). However, the crucial A-natural/A-sharp ambivalence that pervades 33/1 (see the striking introduction of this dissonance

Example 9. Haydn, String Quartet in B Minor, Op. 64/2i, mm. 1–40

Haydn's "Irregularities"

Example 9 continued

in m. 3 of Example 1) is not prolonged in 64/2; it is put to rest from the moment the other voices enter in m. 2, the sudden harmonic twist emphasized by *forte* dynamic indications. Moreover, the first group (mm. 1–8) consists of a period whose consequent phrase reiterates the material from the first four measures unambiguously in B minor. Thus, although the two quartet movements share an ambiguity between the same key areas and a common emphasis on deceptive harmonic motion within the first group (see mm. 3 and 7 of 64/2, and mm. 4 and 8 of 33/1), they differ in that B minor is established unequivocally before the sounding of the first perfect authentic cadence in 64/2 (elided at m. 9). And where the opening thematic material recurs at the recapitulation, the addition of a new three-note pick-up including the leading-tone A-sharp (m. 67), as well as a synthesis of the opening two phrases (since mm. 68–69 correspond to mm. 5–6; and mm. 70–71 to mm. 3–4), cause the listener to hear the melody this time as distinctly in B minor (refer to Example 10).

Because the tonal issue is put to rest earlier than in 33/1, the exposition of 64/2 is able to dispense with the first group in a mere eight measures, and includes a transition section beginning at m. 9 (a section entirely absent in 33/1).[41] It thereby attains the mediant key (m. 13) without the dramatic juxtaposition between minor tonic and relative major heard at mm. 17–18 in 33/1 (refer to Example 2). Moreover, 64/2 differs from all other examples I have mentioned in that the expositional second group neither represents main theme transposition nor utilizes the opening thematic material as a kind of formal marker.

Strikingly, the exposition of 64/2 is filled with a variety of other events which might be construed as disorienting and ambiguous (though in entirely different respects), and which have no specific relation to the opening gesture. I refer here namely to the beginning of the second group (m. 15, labeled Idea 2 in Example 9), which is harmonically consequent to the previous phrase, consists of a long chromatic descent and sequence (mm. 17–19), and has an aesthetic effect of continuing melodic instability.[42] (Although this placement of the second group is normative in that the transition is placed at the only available half cadence in m. 15, its rhetorical undermining in this fashion might nevertheless tempt a listener to hear mm. 15–20 as still part of the transition and the material beginning at m. 20 as the second group. There is here, in other words, a non-coincidence of structural/tonal and aesthetic disposition.) More striking still is the amorphous expansion section (mm. 26–31, labeled Idea 4) which

---

41. In 64/2, the transition begins with a transposition of Idea 1 onto B as home pitch, presented in unison (with the cello at the octave), thus articulating in effect a kind of vehement response to the tonal questions posed by mm. 1–2. Despite this tonal affirmation, the event paradoxically precipitates a destabilization, becoming the formal marker from which the transition spins off.

42. Caplin, whose terminology differs from that which I employ in this essay, terms this the beginning of the "subordinate theme," and notes that it is "especially difficult to determine because little in the way of any rhythmic, textural, or dynamic change helps articulate the boundary between the transition and the subordinate theme." Caplin, *Classical Form*, 114 and 116.

Example 10. Haydn, String Quartet in B Minor, Op. 64/2i, mm. 66–108

Haydn's "Irregularities"

Example 10 continued

SECM in Brooklyn 2010

Example 10 continued

upends closure of the second group (see Example 9). Here we see the temporary evacuation of both goal-oriented harmonic progression and melodic coherence, the latter reduced to disjunct leaps presented in unison and at the octave. The second group is thus book-ended in the exposition by unstable passages which problematize its formal boundaries from the listener's perspective. In fact, compositional preoccupation with these events later supersedes concern for the opening gesture. Unlike the examples above, the opening ambiguity itself is not the primary fodder for Haydn's compositional process; rather, it represents a foreshadowing of the large-scale interplay to come between stable and unstable events. The opening of 64/2 acts thus a self-conscious calling-of-attention to the type of processes the movement will explore, which in-and-of itself is subverted, for contrary perhaps to the expectations of a listener familiar with 33/1, the deceptive opening is ultimately surpassed in import.

As mentioned above, Webster posits a reinterpretation of formal divisions in 33/1 such that Idea 2, originally part of the first group in the exposition, becomes the beginning of the second group in the recapitulation.[43] Haydn's re-composition of the recapitulation of 64/2, however, is much more radical than in 33/1 (see Example 10). Measures 68–79 of the recapitulation of 64/2 represent in essence a contraction, or a shifting forward in formal function, of the most significant expositional themes.[44] Measures 68–71 combine what was formerly eight measures of first-group material (Idea 1) into the four-bar antecedent of a period; however, the consequent phrase is now devoted to former transition material (mm. 72–73) and second-group material (mm. 74–76), culminating in a perfect authentic cadence in m. 77. I thus read the recapitulatory first group as extending to the perfect authentic cadence in m. 77, the transition as consisting of what was formerly second-group material and extending to the caesura in m. 83 (which has no clear counterpart in the exposition), and the recapitulatory second group as commencing in the latter part of m. 83.

Haydn thus adumbrates the principal ideas of the expositional first group, transition, and second group in the scant fifteen bars between mm. 68–83, which now constitute the recapitulatory first group and transition. The recapitulatory second group is then entirely devoted to further exploration of the most transitory, digressive, and unstable events of the exposition. After heightening suspense by reiterating the medial caesura in mm. 85–86, the second group

---

43. Webster, *Haydn's "Farewell" Symphony*, 130.
44. Caplin also recognizes how substantially recomposed the recapitulation of 64/2i is, stating that, "from the point of view of motivic ordering and specific formal design, Haydn creates a recapitulation that has little relation to the exposition." He demonstrates, however, that the recapitulation does contain moments of closure which allow it to "retain the overall shape of a standard recapitulation but distribute the material of the exposition in an entirely different way." The formal demarcations he indicates are largely in agreement with those I outline above (albeit, using different nomenclature), although his rationale for the distribution of thematic material in the recapitulation differs somewhat from my own. See Caplin, *Classical Form*, 175–176.

presents the material of the original transition and the unstable Idea 2 in reverse order, fused with an echo of Idea 4 in m. 97 (see Example 10).

I have argued against necessarily construing ambiguous devices as demanding and achieving resolution in-and-of themselves (although the large-scale tonal dissonances they propose do need to be resolved); however, one encounters in mm. 97–102 a rare case in which we can say an ambiguous event really does find resolution. What was in the exposition a nearly directionless melodic and harmonic interruption of the second group (Idea 4) has undergone substantial change over the course of the movement. In the development, the presentation of this thematic material (mm. 52–59) recalls that of the exposition with a distinct difference (see Example 11): after only two measures of unisons (mm. 53–54) melodic correspondence with Idea 4 is restricted to the first violin, now harmonized by the other voices such that the music modulates towards B minor on the downbeat of m. 59 and then just as quickly veers off again. The appearance of Idea 4 in the recapitulation, however, is fully reinvigorated with a functional harmonic progression (refer to Example 10). Over the course of

Example 11. Haydn, String Quartet in B Minor, Op. 64/2i, mm. 51–59

Haydn's "Irregularities"

its three statements (exposition: mm. 26–31; development: mm. 52–59; and recapitulation: mm. 97–102), the passage achieves gradual reintegration with the surrounding harmonic context. In its final statement its melodic leaps are wider, but are constrained to one voice, and are clearly re-purposed so as to act as a concerto-like rhetorical heightening of tension, culminating in the structural cadence of m. 102 and the introduction of the closing group (labeled Idea 5).[45]

Not only does 64/2 thus derail any rigid theorizing about the nature of a compositional process based upon an ambiguous opening, it turns the conventions of other examples on their heads. It is to some extent an undoing of 33/1, since the opening ambiguity plays a less significant role than its counterpart in terms of introducing new formal sections and in establishing a problematized, large-scale tonal duality. This, however, should not mean that we see the opening gesture of 64/2 as simply an isolated and discarded idea, little more than a momentary diversion for the listener.

What 64/2 demonstrates is that an ambiguous opening can acquire meaning not just through its immediate surprising effect, nor its relation to an abstract formal model, but also through a discursive and fluid relationship with other handlings of the same trope. In this case, if the ambiguous opening gains meaning, it is precisely through its defiance of the expected preoccupation with the device. In a sense, 64/2 is the exception that proves the rule: it is the very fact that ambiguous openings are so often devices of more than humor or irony alone which makes the gesture's failure here to produce the expected fecundity of melodic, harmonic, and formal invention such an effective calling-of-attention to the rhetoric of the work. A listener steeped in Haydn's quartets, who might reasonably perceive this as a chronological continuation of the discourse of 33/1, encounters here a kind of self-conscious, double layering of subversion. The ambiguous opening, in its many potential guises, thus furnishes the composer with opportunities for clever play on multiple levels.

To describe the ambiguous opening gesture as "eccentric" or "irregular" effectively calls attention to its unique nature amongst eighteenth-century compositions, but we should guard against the potential for such terms to suggest that

---

45. The rhyme of this cadence with m. 32, and the stability of the subsequent, transposed (but otherwise unchanged) closing group, play a crucial anchoring function for the listener after the thorough recomposition of the recapitulatory second group. It is worth noting, moreover, that we encounter the same stability of closing group in opus 33/1.

these gestures may be perceived as mere oddities. While the immediate, jarring effect of an ambiguous opening might indeed seem to contribute to the perception of Haydn as a formally "aberrant" composer, closer investigation reveals the extensive calculation and potential layering of meanings underpinning the gesture's use. Moreover, the remarkable variety of treatments of the ambiguous opening Haydn explores in just the few quartets described above demonstrates the irreducibility of these openings to straightforward narratives of resolution. By virtue of their capacity to provide focal points of invention and listener engagement, it is precisely in these events that the artfulness of the composer's strategies is revealed.

Issues of Authenticity and Chronology in the Sacred Music of Leopold Hofmann

ALLAN BADLEY

Around 650 manuscript copies of sacred works with attributions to the eighteenth-century Viennese composer Leopold Hofmann have survived into the present day.[1] Few of these copies are in score and none, bar a brief *Alleluja* setting, is indisputably in the composer's hand. Most of Hofmann's sacred works are preserved in manuscript parts of varying degrees of reliability and, all too often, of uncertain provenance. Few of these parts offer much help in the matter of establishing the works' authenticity let alone reliable composition dates. Some, indeed, complicate matters further by introducing major textual variants that appear to be authorial in origin with the attendant problem of determining the primacy of the versions. These variants are not always apparent from entries in contemporary thematic catalogs or more recent bibliographical sources. How then does one combine this frequently unhelpful bibliographical evidence with the slender biographical information we possess to construct a tolerably accurate account of the career of such an important figure in eighteenth-century Viennese music?

As the title of this study suggests, authenticity and chronology are highly problematic issues in Hofmann research. The 650-odd extant manuscript copies represent something in the order of 185 works about most of which little or nothing is known. Among the immediate problems facing the scholar working on this repertory is the difficulty in distinguishing between authentic works, works of questionable authorship, and spurious works. There are also numerous challenges in evaluating multiple versions, musical variants, and *contrafacta*. Related to all of these issues is the overarching question of how we might begin to create a chronological framework for Hofmann's extensive output. There are no simple solutions to any of these problems but it is possible to make some sense out of the confusing jumble of extant sources through reconstructing Hofmann's working repertory at the two churches with which he was associated longest: St. Peter's (1764–1793) and St. Stephen's Cathedral (1772–1793). This

---

1. All information concerning sources and the numbering system employed throughout this paper are derived from the writer's draft thematic catalog of Hofmann's complete works.

reconstruction does not provide all the answers but it does allow us to separate works that were performed at—and possibly composed for—these institutions from those that may have been written for other purposes.

Leopold Hofmann was a church musician by profession and wrote sacred music throughout his career. In his 1774 application for the post of *Hofkapellmeister*, Hofmann wrote that he had composed church music from his earliest years and that his works had been received with approbation in all the great churches in Vienna.[2] This was no exaggeration. Hofmann joined the chapel of the Empress Dowager Elizabeth Christine as a chorister in 1745 and around the same time began studying keyboard playing and composition with the chapel's organist, Georg Christoph Wagenseil. After the dissolution of the chapel in 1750, he continued his studies with Wagenseil, who seems to have thought a good deal of his young pupil. Wagenseil certainly helped further Hofmann's career in Vienna through his connections with the Imperial Court[3] and he may also have arranged for Venier to publish six of Hofmann's symphonies in Paris in 1760.[4] The earliest known work by Hofmann is a short *Alleluja*

---

2. "[Ich habe] von meiner Jugend an mich zu der Kirchenmusik, und Composition, vorzüglich verwendet, und durch mehrer Jahre in den ansehnlichsten hiesigen Gottes Häussern die Proben meiner Fähigkeit mit jedesmahligen Beyfalle abgeleget habe." (From my youth I have applied myself especially to church music and composition, and over many years and in the most important Houses of God, the proofs of my capability have met each time with approval.) Translation by the author. Vienna, Haus-, Hof- und Staatsarchiv: Obersthofmeisteramtsakt Nr.10 ex 1774.

3. "Da sich bald sein grosser Hang zur Tonsetzkunst entwickelte, liess ihn sein Vater von dem berühmten Hofcompositor und Hofklaviermeister Wagenseil in Klavier und der Composition unterrichten. Er machte auch hierin so grosse Vorschritte, daß ihn sein Lehrer dem Hofe als Klaviermeister vorschlug, in welcher Eigenschaft er die Erzherzoginnen Elisabeth, Amalie, Josephe und Theresie, die Tochter Kaiser Josephs II, der unseren Hofmann selbst für sie wählte, unterrichtete. Auch componierte er schon damals zu gänzlichen Zufriedenheit seines nicht leicht zu befriedigenden Lehrers." (As an aptitude for composition quickly grew in him, his father sent him to the famous court composer and keyboard master Wagenseil for lessons in composition and keyboard playing. He made such progress here as well that his teacher recommended him to the court as keyboard master, in which capacity he taught the archduchesses Elisabeth, Amalie, Josephe, and Theresie, the daughter of Emperor Joseph II, who had personally chosen our Hofmann for them. Already at that time he was also composing to the complete satisfaction of his not-easy-to-please teacher.) See Johann Georg Meusel, *Neue Miscellaneen artistischen Inhalts für Künstler und Kunstliebhaber* (Leipzig, 1799), 46.

4. Cari Johansson, *French Music Publishers' Catalogues of the Second Half of the Eighteenth Century* 1 (Stockholm: Swedish Academy of Music, 1955), facs. 118, col. 2.

setting scored for four-part choir with an accompaniment of two violins, basso, and organ that is preserved in autograph in the archive of the Gesellschaft der Musikfreunde in Vienna.[5] Written on a single leaf of fourteen-stave hand-ruled paper, the work may represent a student exercise. The rather informal style of the signature—"*Da Leop. H: D: S: M: 1756*"—suggests that the work was not written with wider circulation in mind. It is a simple yet effective setting that reveals a number of stylistic fingerprints encountered frequently in the composer's later works. Two years later, when the twenty-year-old Hofmann married, he gave his occupation as *musicus* (probably a violinist) at St. Michael's. One of the witnesses at the wedding was Johann Nepomuk Boog, *regens chori* at St. Peter's. Whether we can infer from this that Hofmann also played in the orchestra at St. Peter's is uncertain but it does suggest that the two men knew each other well and that Hofmann's appointment as Boog's successor in 1764 may have been made on the recommendation of the older composer.

It is impossible to determine how much sacred music Hofmann had composed by this time. Only a handful of works can be dated up to and including 1764 but these surely represent only a fraction of his output from these early years.[6] Copies of two of these works are preserved in the music archive at St. Michael's.[7] Unfortunately, neither can be dated with confidence and, as both works achieved wide circulation during the eighteenth century, it is possible that the copies were acquired after Hofmann's professional association with the church ended.

Little is known about the early years of Hofmann's professional life beyond his connection with St. Michael's. As the salary of a rank and file violinist in mid-eighteenth-century Vienna was modest, he may have held multiple positions in churches around the city or, perhaps, in one or more of the many private musical establishments maintained by wealthy members of the nobility. One of these churches was the Obere Jesuitenkirche (Kirche am Hof) where, according to Abbé Stadler, Hofmann was organist around the years 1762–1763.[8]

---

5. A Wgm A460: *Alleluja Da Leop. H: D:S:M: 1756*.
6. In addition to the *Alleluja* (see above) only five works can be confidently dated before 1764: Masses **C10** (A H 456, 1760), **C14** (A GÖ, 1760), **C6** (A GÖ, 1762), **C10a** (A GÖ, 1764), and **F1a** (A Wn S.m. 22269).
7. Masses **C6** (A W Mich 22) and **C10** (A W Mich 19).
8. "Während meiner Studien in Wien wurde ich mit den berühmtesten Musikern und Komponisten bekannt, als mit Reuter, Bonno, Vanhall, Haydn, Hofmann, Ziegler,

Interestingly, one of the early masses (**C10** and its variant **C10a**) includes an elaborate organ solo in the *Benedictus* that Hofmann may have played. The wide range of genres that he cultivated during the early 1760s suggests that his professional life was hectic and his duties varied. Although this pattern continued in his later career, there is no doubt that his appointment as *regens chori* at St. Peter's caused Hofmann to concentrate his energies on the composition of church music and that this inevitably precipitated a decline in his output of instrumental works, particularly symphonies.

Hofmann's appointment as *Kapellmeister* at St. Stephen's may represent the pinnacle of his professional career but in many respects his early years at St. Peter's are the most important of his career. During the period 1764–1772 he composed the bulk of his works in all genres, consolidated his international reputation as a composer, secured a lucrative appointment as *Hofklaviermeister* (in 1769) and, three years later, arguably the most sought-after musical post in Vienna, at St. Stephen's. Hofmann's significance and the respect in which he was held during these years is evident both from the tone and the specificity of the references in the well-known article "Von dem wienerischen Geschmack in der Musik," which was published in the *Wiener Diarium* in 1766.[9]

Gassmann, Mittelmayr Domorganist lud mich öfter ein, die Orgel in der Domkirche zu spielen, wie auch Hofmann bey den oberen Jesuiten." (During my studies in Vienna I became acquainted with the most famous musicians and composers, such as Reuter, Bonno, Vanhall, Haydn, Hofmann, Ziegler, Gassmann, and Mittelmayr, the cathedral organist, often invited me to play on the organ at the cathedral as did Hofmann at the upper Jesuit church.) From Anton Stadler, *Entwurf meiner Biographie* (ca. 1815). See Gerhard Croll, "Eine zweite, fast vergessene Selbstbiographie von Abbé Stadler," *Mozart Jahrbuch* (1964), 176.

9. "**Herr Leopold Hoffmann**, his path soars ever upwards. The **serious** with the **pleasant**, **melody** with **correctness**, characterize his pieces above all others. He is the only one to approach the church style of **Hrn von Reuttern**. His Masses are full of majestic and grand thoughts, which elevate and inflame the praise of God and the prayer in the temple. His **musical Oratorio**, which was performed last year by the Carmelites in the Leopoldstadt and was composed in honour of Saint Johann Nepomuk, shows us a genius who was born for lyrical poetry. Who does not feel everything that one can feel about a bloodthirsty tyrant, when the horrid words of the Hoffmann movement sound: 'ut irrita consilia in vanum abeant &c'? The menacing pride which lurks in these words flashes from every note, every bar awakes terror in the breast, as the listener hears of the innocent's death. But serious though this style is, as pleasant and attractive is he in his symphonies, concertos, quartets and trios; one may say that **Hoffmann**, after **Stamitz**, is the only one to give the transverse flute the proper lightness and melody." Translated by H. C. Robbins Landon in *Haydn: Chronicle and Works*, vol. 2, *Haydn at Eszterháza 1766–1790* (London: Thames & Hudson, 1978), 129.

The Sacred Music of Leopold Hofmann

The St. Peter's music archive has formed part of the Music Collection of the Austrian National Library for many years. It is the richest church music archive in Vienna after the *Hofkapelle* and is, without question, the most important source for Hofmann's sacred works. When Carl Rouland was appointed *Kapellmeister* in 1897 he found the archive in a very disorganized state. By his own account, "only the repertory pieces lay to hand; all the remaining music, smothered in finger-thick dust, lay about in a disorganized manner in great higgledy-piggledy piles."[10]

Rouland reorganized the music, made new scores of some of the more interesting items for use in modern performances and, most importantly, he published in 1908 a catalog of the entire music archive including a list of instruments owned by the church. Only one Hofmann work listed in Rouland's catalog, the motet *Gaude coelum et mirare*, has been lost or misplaced since 1908; and of even greater significance is the fact that the works listed in this catalog match in number and genre those listed in a catalog of the collection prepared in 1824 by the *Dechant und Pfarrer* Joseph Sauermann and *Kirchenprobst* Ignaz Anton Figl (see Figures 1 and 2).[11] Thus, the current collection of works, cataloged under the rubric Fond 24 St Peter Wien, probably comes close to representing Hofmann's working repertory during his tenure as *regens chori*. Some works have undoubtedly been lost, including Hofmann's only known setting of the *Stabat mater* of which only the wrapper survives.[12]

---

10. "Als ich im Jahre 1897 dasselbe übernahm, befand es sich einem sehr vernachläßigten, chaosartigen Zustande. Nur die Repertoir-Stücke lagen zu Hand, alle übrigen Musikalien befanden sich, von fingerdickem Staub bedeckt, in großen Stößen kunterbunt durcheinander." See Carl Rouland, *Katalog des Musik Archives der St. Peterskirche in Wien, zusammengestellt von Carl Rouland, Kapellmeister* (Vienna: Kommissions-Verlag von Anton Böhm & Sohn, 1908), Vorwort.

11. A Wn Inv 1 Peterskirche 1a. The *Inventarium* divides the music into two broad categories: usable and unusable. If Hofmann's works provide a reliable basis upon which to consider these two categories, it is clear that the prime factors in categorizing works as unusable were genre and style. Unusable works are typically smaller compositions like offertories with their overreliance on the da capo aria form; mass settings, for the most part, were still considered usable.

12. See A Wn St Peter C1. The wrapper, which reads "#/Stabat Mater / à / 4 Voci Soprano Conc^{to} / 2 Violini Rip^{ni} / 2 Trombini / con / Organo Conc$_{to}$ / Del Sigl Leopoldo de Hoffmann / M:D:C: di Sancto Steffano / ad chorum Sancti Petri / Partes 18," has been turned inside out and reused for twelve short settings of the *Ave Maria*. These are cataloged as anonymous works but they are without question by Leopold Hofmann. His designation as *Kapellmeister* at St. Stephen's indicates that the wrapper was written after 1772.

Fond 24 St Peter Wien includes fifty-three works by Hofmann: fourteen masses, one Requiem, seven litanies, twenty-three motets, three offertories, one Te Deum, and several miscellaneous works. As a group, these works represent under a third of the extant sacred works attributed to the composer. The St. Peter's copies are the closest we come to a corpus of authentic performing material for Hofmann's sacred music, yet they offer at best mixed evidence in relation to internal chronology. One of the most puzzling aspects of these copies is that not a single manuscript part or wrapper identifies Hofmann as either *regens chori* or *Maestro di Capella* at St. Peter's whereas ten attribute the works to "Signore Leopoldo de Hoffmann, Maestro di Capella di Santo Steffano." The unusual form of the composer's name and the uniformity of the handwriting indicate that these wrappers were likely produced by the same copyist. The reference to Hofmann's position at St. Stephen's establishes a convenient *terminus ante quem* of April 1772, the month he succeeded Georg Reutter the Younger as *Kapellmeister* at St. Stephen's. Performances are recorded on a number of the St. Peter's wrappers but none of these predates 1772. Purely on the basis of the physical evidence, there is nothing to suggest that any of Hofmann's works were performed at St. Peter's in the 1760s or indeed that he was connected professionally with the church. Such evidence—or the lack of it—highlights the pitfalls of restricting oneself to a literal interpretation of the bibliographic record, however well intentioned the motivation for doing so.

One interesting aspect of the performance data is the revelation that many of these performances took place outside St. Peter's. The most common venue is St. Stephen's, all of the performances of record taking place there within the first year or two of Hofmann's appointment as *Kapellmeister*. Performances at other churches are also noted although it is unclear whether Hofmann himself directed these or whether the annotations on the wrappers merely record the loan of the parts to the churches concerned. Hofmann's use of music from St. Peter's for services at the cathedral suggests that in the early years of his tenure, there cannot have been a great deal of his music, if any, in the archive. He doubtless set about rectifying this as quickly as possibly, building up a library of his own works that he supplemented from time to time with the use of borrowed material. The combined resources of the two collections provided him with the bulk of his working repertory for the remaining twenty years of his life.

Unlike the St. Peter's archive that survives intact, the music archive at St. Stephen's was largely destroyed in May 1945 when the cathedral burned for

The Sacred Music of Leopold Hofmann

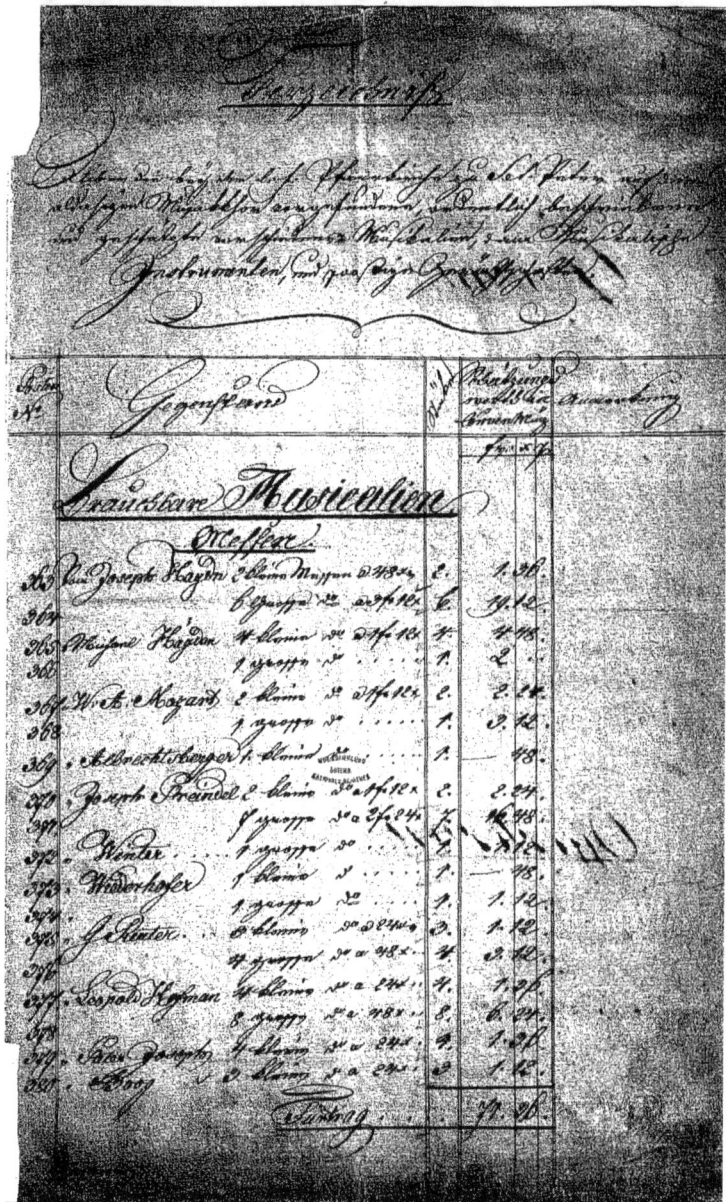

Figure 1. *Verzeichniß* (1824). A Wn INV. I. Peterskirche/a.
Twelve of Hofmann's sixteen mass settings in this collection were still considered usable in the 1820s.

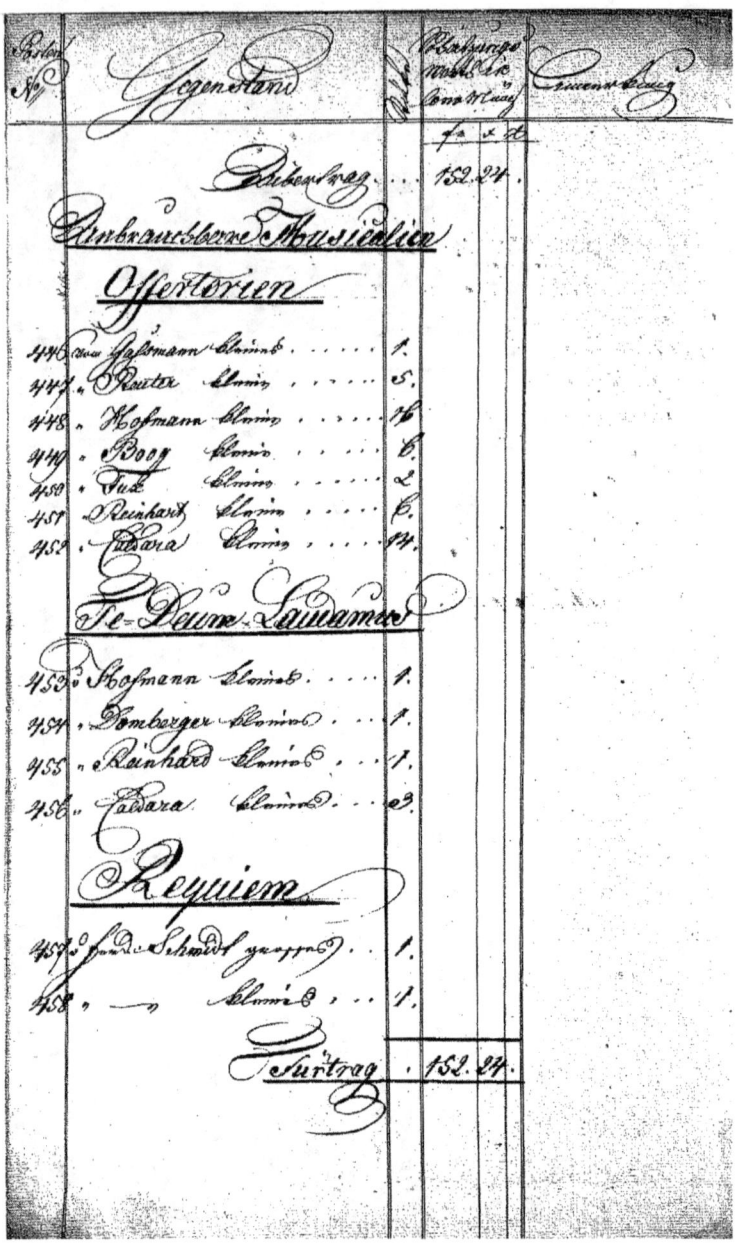

Figure 2. *Verzeichniß* (1824). A Wn INV. I. Peterskirche/a. Smaller works, such as offertories, fell into disuse far more readily than masses.

The Sacred Music of Leopold Hofmann

several days after being hit by Russian artillery fire. Although most of the works were destroyed—and among them, all of those attributed to Hofmann—we are in the fortunate position of being able to identify them with a strong degree of certainty.

Our knowledge of the cathedral's holdings of Hofmann's music comes from three sources, the most widely known of which is the list of works Robert Eitner includes under the entry for the composer in his *Quellenlexikon*.[13] Eitner's list makes it possible to identify works with distinctive or unique texts, such as motets and offertories, but not generally those with liturgical texts like masses and litanies. Whether Eitner actually saw these works or simply included information about them from a Viennese correspondent is uncertain. What is clear, however, is that the works included in the *Quellenlexikon* correspond exactly with those found in two nineteenth-century catalogs of the cathedral music archive. The first of these is a non-thematic catalog drawn up in December 1824 that includes, in addition to a list of all the music and instruments belonging to the cathedral, an inventory of the furniture in the *Kapellhaus*.[14] The works listed under the rubric "Domkapellmeister—Hofmann" are given in Table 1.

A second thematic catalog, copied in 1837 by the contrabassist Joseph Perschl from a version prepared ten years earlier by the then *Domkapellmeister* Johann Baptist Gänsbacher,[15] enables us to complete the identification of the works and make a comparison between this collection and the archive at St. Peter's. A number of points stand out.

Firstly, a significant number of works duplicate those found in the St. Peter's archive. These presumably represent compositions that Hofmann performed regularly and felt were essential to have in both locations even though the St. Peter's material was freely available and lay in close proximity to the cathedral.

---

13. Robert Eitner, *Biographisch-bibliographische Quellenlexikon der Musiker* (Leipzig: Breitkopf und Härtel, 1906).

14. Vienna, Domarchiv: "Inventorium / Uiber die der Domkirche St. Stephan angehörigen Instrumente, Musikalien, und Mobilien in dem Kapellhause, welche von denen am Ende Unterschriebenen am 6ten December 1824 vorgefunden, und der Ordnung nach beschrieben worden sind."

15. Vienna, Domarchiv: "Catalog / sämtlicher Musicalien, welche der Kapellmeister / der Dom=Kirche St Stephan / in Verwahrung hat. / verfasset / vom / Joan: Bapt. Gaensbacher. / Dom=Kapellmeister / in den Jahren 1827 u: 1828 / abcopirt vom Jos: Persechl. Contrabassist / in der Dom: Kapelle 1837."

Table 1. Hofmann works listed in the *Inventorium* of 1824

Domkapellmeister: Hofmann

13 Solemn Masses	7	4	1		
	C	D	Eb		
1 Missa brevis	Bb				
14 Graduals and Offertories	5	2	4	1	2
	C	D	Eb	F	c
1 Veni Sancte	C				
2 Te Deum laudamus	2 C				
1 Salve Regina	C				
1 Solemn Litany	C				
1 4-part Panga Lingua	C				
1 Vidi Aquam	C				
1 Sequence	C				
1 4-part Antiphon - Miserere	a				
1 Requiem	C minor Kyrie – Dies Irae				
2 Motets	C	d			
2 Motets	2 Eb				
1 Exaudi Domini	F				
1 4-part Confitebor de Angelus	d				

Secondly, eight of the St. Peter's copies show evidence of having been used for services at St. Stephen's in 1772 and 1773.[16] As four of these works are listed in the St. Stephen's catalogs[17] it is probably safe to infer that the cathedral copies were acquired *after* 1773. The other works may not have been borrowed again

---

16. A Wn F24 St Peter F20: Motet/Offertory **D4** *Huc adeste* ['1773/ 2 May S: St: chor']; A Wn F24 St Peter F33: Motet/Offertory **Bb7** *In tuo nomine* ['14 decemb. 1773 S: St:']; A Wn F24 St Peter F37: Motet/Offertory **c2** *O Sancte Michaël* ['1773/ 25 Aug S: St: chor; 26 Nov S: St:; 6 Decemb.; 25 Aug: S: St: chor / 1774 / 3 April S. St: hora 9']; A Wn F24 St Peter F34: Motet/Offertory **F1** *Omnia sunt plena insidiis* ['1772/ 16 Nov S: St:; 1773/ 6 Juny S: St: chor']; A Wn F24 St Peter F15: Motet/Offertory **C5** *Quid hostem times* (I) ['[1772] 2 Decemb. S: St: hora 11']; A Wn F24 St Peter A146: Mass **C2a** *Sanc. Barbarae* ['1772/ 15 Nov S: St: hora 9 Kyrie/glor:']; A Wn F24 St Peter A150: Mass **Eb2** *Omnium Sanctorum* ['1773/ 8 April S: St: … 31 Oct. S: St:']; A Wn F24 St Peter A147: Mass **F1** *Sta Catharinae* ['1772/ 28 Nov S: St:'].
17. Motet/Offertory **Bb7**; Motet/Offertory **c2**; Motet/Offertory **C5**; Mass **Eb2**.

The Sacred Music of Leopold Hofmann

but it is also possible that the lack of performance data post 1773 simply signifies that the practice of recording performances on wrappers was abandoned. Given the close links between the two musical establishments, it seems reasonable to suppose that Hofmann also borrowed music from the St. Stephen's archive from time to time for performances at St. Peter's; the destruction of the cathedral archive makes verification of this impossible.

Thirdly, and perhaps most importantly, the question arises as to whether the works listed in the St. Stephen's catalogs that are *not* found in the St. Peter's archive were composed later in his career or, at the very least, not prior to his appointment as *Kapellmeister* in 1772. The evidence for this is tenuous at best but it remains a possibility, if only because so few of Hofmann's works in the St. Peter's archive can be confidently dated after 1772. Only two works, the motets **C4** and **Bb7**, have wrappers that describe Hofmann as *Kapellmeister* at St. Stephen's;[18] these copies, for obvious reasons, are unlikely to have been acquired before April 1772. Unfortunately, (motet) **C4** is not among the works listed in the St. Stephen's catalogs. If we accept that the unduplicated works in the cathedral archive were composed later, then we need to consider whether they were written in the first instance for the cathedral or merely acquired at a later date for use there. The evidence will be considered later in this study.

Finally, the positive identification of the works in the St. Stephen's catalog allows us to consider the relationship between the music archives there and at St. Peter's. Hofmann's was the guiding hand in building up both collections of his music and it is clear that he intended the two to be complementary; in other words, that he considered the two collections in effect to comprise a single large depository of his sacred music. This is evident both from the distribution and the types of works found in each collection. St. Peter's, for example, has nearly double the number of motets, offertories, and graduals (the designations are frequently interchanged in Hofmann sacred music sources); it has four *sinfonie pastorali* to none in the St. Stephen's archive; it also has seven litany settings to St.

---

18. A Wn F24 St Peter F109: [Motet/Offertory **C4**] "Gradual o [Offertorium] / Chorus /a / 4 Voci / 2 Violini / 2 Tromboni / 2 Clarini / Tympani / e / Organo / St: Peter / Parti 21 / Del Sigl Leopoldo de Hoffmann / M:D:C^{la} di Santo Steffano"; A Wn F24 St Peter F 33: [Motet/Offertory **Bb7**] "# / No. / Mottetto / de Beata Maria Virgine / et de / omni Tempore / a / 4 Voci / Soprano in conc^{to} / 2 Violini, 2 Tromboni Rip^{ni} / con / Organo, Violone, e Violoncello / Ad Chorum Sti Petri 20 Part / Del Sigre Leopoldo Hoffmann / M:D:C: di St° Steffano".

141

Stephen's one duplicate copy. St. Stephen's, on the other hand, has ten antiphons to St. Peter's five (to which can also be added five duplicates). The most important category, masses, is evenly divided between the two with fourteen works in each archive, six of which are duplicated. What is surely of great significance, however, is the fact that the St. Stephen's catalogs list eight masses that are not part of the St. Peter's collection. Two of these are otherwise unknown and may represent works that were composed specifically for the cathedral. The six works that are preserved in other sources warrant further discussion (see Table 2).

Table 2. St. Stephen's non-duplicated masses (excludes two lost masses)

Mass	Dedication	Other Sources	Comments
C1	Sti Ignatii	A WMich 27	
		A Wn HK 470 "No.7"	Earliest perf. date Nov. 1792
		D HR III 4 ½ 2 151	ca. 1780
C3		A Wgm Q598	incomplete
		A WMi A 68	Earliest perf. date 1796
C8	Sti Vincenti	A Gd	
		A Wa 494 "No.47"	Early 19th-century copy
		A WMich 25 "Sti Vincentii"	
		A Wn S.m.513 "No.20"	
D5	Sti Peregrini	A HE II e	
		A Wn S.m.22264	
		A WPi 84	ca. 1780?
		A WSk	
		H PH Mus.sacr. Ant. H10	
Bb2	Sta Anna	A H 455/2	
Bb4	Stae Theclae	A LA M33	
		A WIL 484	Copy Festl 1860

The first thing that strikes one about this list is that none of the copies—with the possible exception of Lambach M33—can be dated confidently to earlier than around 1780 and two of these (or possibly three) were made after Hofmann's death. Only one of the works (**C8**) has a dedication that is found in another source although a number of Hofmann's other masses listed in the St.

Stephen's catalog have dedications identical to those found in copies elsewhere.[19] None of the "unduplicated" works was widely disseminated in Hofmann's lifetime; neither, with the exception of the copies alluded to above, were the copies made after his death. Those that do survive, however, are found for the most part in locations that are important sources for Hofmann's sacred music. In several instances—St. Michael's, the *Hofkapelle,* and St. Augustine's—we know that Hofmann had personal associations with the institutions concerned; this may also be true for the Piaristen and the Schottenkirche since Hofmann was such a prominent figure in Viennese church music, but here the evidence is considerably weaker. It is unsurprising that some of these works should have found their way into monastic collections, but their absence from Göttweig, Melk, Seitenstetten, and Herzogenburg, to name four very important Austrian monasteries with substantial collections of Hofmann's church music, is interesting to say the least. It is also noteworthy that none of these works is preserved in a Czech or Slovakian source.

While there is a strong degree of parity between the mass holdings in the two archives the same cannot be said for another important category of works—that designated variously motet, offertory, or gradual: St. Peter's, with twenty-five, has nearly twice the number of works in this category than are listed in the St. Stephen's catalogs. Nonetheless, St. Stephen's owned copies of five works that at no point appear to have been owned by St. Peter's. One of these, the gradual *Matrem Dei honorate,* is otherwise unknown. The remaining four works tell a rather different story to that of the St. Stephen's masses (Table 3): with the exception of (motet) **A2** (*Te summa bonitas*), which is preserved in only one other source, the remaining works were disseminated relatively widely.

These teasing scraps frankly do not add up to a great deal. But, when considered alongside other factors such as general distribution patterns for Hofmann's music, a picture emerges that appears to be consistent with what we know about the composer's professional circumstances. Although it is hardly a reliable indicator, Hofmann's earlier works tend to survive in much higher numbers than his later works. This is true not only of his sacred music but also of his instrumental works. The relative paucity of sources for some of the masses in the St. Stephen's catalog argues for a relatively late composition date whereas

---

19. Mass **C2** *Sancta Barbarae*; Mass **D8** *Sti Aloysii*; Mass **Eb2** *Omnium Sanctorum.*

Table 3. Unduplicated motets in the St. Stephen's catalogs

'Motet'	Other Sources	Title/Function/Comments
D2	A Ed B 84	De Beata
	A MT	
	A Wa 498A Mi 502	
	A Wn S.m. 2728	De Venerabili clientes
	CZ Pnm XLVI C 178	
	CZ Pnm XLVI C 179	
	CZ Pnm XLIX E 32	
	CZ Psj 318; 319	
	HR Vu 69	
	SK BRnm Mus.VII 86	
	SK BRnm Mus.X 127	
D5	A KN 985/5	
	A M II 75	"Pastorella"
	A Wsj 316	
	A Wsjm G 139	
	A Wk 476	Ms. ca. 1810
	A WMich 345	De Nativitate Domini
	A Wn S.m.00692	
	A WPi 307	Chorus pastoralis
	A Wsfl 315	Pastorale
	CZ NYd	
	D PO Hofmann 37	
Eb1	A Ed B83	De Tempore
	AGÖ 1777	lost
	A KN 985/4	
	A SL	4 copies
	A St Lambrecht	2 copies
	A TU207	De Tempore
	A Wk XI 473	De Tempore
	A Mich 176	
	A Mi 508	
	A Wn F.5 Mödling 935	
	A Wn S.m.22166	De Tempore
	H P H 134	
A2	A Wn HK482	Copy post 1778?

the motets have distribution patterns similar to those found in works Hofmann composed in the 1760s and early 1770s.

The ninety-nine manuscript copies of Hofmann's sacred works that comprise this single musical resource represent eighty-two individual works or slightly less than half of the extant works of this type that are attributed to our com-

The Sacred Music of Leopold Hofmann

poser. This total certainly includes a number of works that Hofmann composed prior to his appointment as *regens chori* at St. Peter's,[20] but there must also be a large number of works that were written later and it is these works that urgently need to be authenticated and, if possible, dated. Distinguishing between the two groups is problematic enough and it is even more difficult to determine when and for whom the works may have been composed. The scant documentary record helps only in that we know that Hofmann devoted a great deal of energy to his freelance activities—enough certainly to get him into serious trouble with his employers at the cathedral[21]—and that, according to his widow Maria Anna Hofmann, "he received many flattering letters from foreign cities and commissions for his works."[22]

An obvious difficulty that arises from the use of the term "city" is its precise definition. Does "city" imply a major metropolitan center like Prague or even a significant one like Passau, or is it used more loosely to include important monastic centers such as Melk, Göttweig or Seitensetten? Copies of Hofmann's sacred works are found in many locations in Central Europe and there is evidence from the wrappers that works were borrowed and lent by churches and monastic foundations on a quite regular basis.[23] The sources from which these

---

20. See note 6.
21. Our principal knowledge of Hofmann's activities as *Domkapellmeister* is found in a report compiled in 1784 by one Andreas Furthmoser, *Kirchenmeister* at St. Stephen's. Furthmoser was a member of a commission set up to examine the classification of church music personnel at the cathedral following the introduction of new regulations governing church music promulgated by Joseph II in the previous year. The commission was soundly abused by Hofmann who later received a written censure condemning his disrespectful and unseemly behavior and warning him of the unpleasant consequences should a repetition occur. Furthmoser's hostile report accuses him of arrogance, gross professional negligence, and avarice. Among the more damning broadsides are the accusations that Hofmann only worked sixty hours a year in his official position and that in twelve years of service to date (that is, 1772–1784) he had composed only one piece of music for the cathedral. At the heart of Furthmoser's damaging rant is the extent of Hofmann's professional activities at other churches, even more so than the fact that he is rarely seen in church on Sundays or feast days and spends all summer at his house in Döbling virtually leaving the singers to direct themselves. See Vienna, Stadtarchiv, Rathaus: "Hauptregistratur" Facs. 19 Nr.38/784.
22. "Aus verschiedenen fremden Städten wurden ihm schmeichelhafte Briefe zugesant, und Bestellungen auf seinen Arbeiten gemacht." Maria Anna Hofmann, quoted in Meusel, *Neue Miscellaneen*, 47.
23. For example, A WMi 508: "Mottetto ex Eb / a 4 Voci in pienno / 2 Violinis / 2 Trombonis / Organo con Violone / Del Sigl Leopoldo de Hoffmann. Pro choro

copies were made are unknown and likely to remain that way unless sensational new information is uncovered. Nonetheless, it is possible that some of the more important collections of Hofmann's sacred music include works that were acquired directly from the composer or his agent and that some of them may have been commissioned. The evidence as always is frustratingly incomplete, but certain patterns do emerge from the current distribution of manuscripts as is evident from a study of the masses that are neither part of the St. Peter's archive nor listed in the cathedral catalogs. The majority of these works fall into the category of masses of uncertain authorship (Table 4).

Four of the masses (**F2**, **A1**, **Bb1**, and **Bb3**) are preserved in an unusually large number of sources including archives located in Vienna. If the typical distribution patterns for Hofmann's music apply in this instance then we can probably infer from these figures that the four works concerned are authentic, probably pre-date Hofmann's appointment at St. Stephen's and may even have been composed prior to his appointment as *regens chori* at St. Peter's.

A further three masses are preserved in Viennese sources. Two works, **C4** and **D1**, each survive in two copies that can be found in the same two archives. One of these, St. Michael's, is a church with which Hofmann was associated early in his career. They are probably authentic works—certainly there are no stylistic grounds to exclude them—but given the uncertainty of their dating it is every bit as risky to assert that they were composed before 1764 as to claim that they were written after this date.

The remaining works fall into two distinct categories: those that are preserved in multiple sources and those that survive in a single source. Into the first of these categories fall **C9**, **C17**, **C19**, **C20**, and **D9**. Most of the copies of these works are preserved in monastic libraries: Heiligenkreuz (**C9**), Melk (**C9** and **C17**), Kremsmünster (**C19** and **C20**), Lambach (**C19** and **D9**), and Wilhering (**C19** and **C20**). The Wilhering copies, like those of most of their Hofmann works, date from the mid-nineteenth century whereas all of the Lambach copies probably date from the 1770s (Hofmann's identification as "Maestro di Capella a St° Steffano" on the wrapper of Lambach M35 creates a *terminus ante quem* of 1772 for this copy) and may have served as the basis for later copies of the works. Little is known about the Heiligenkreuz, Melk, and Kremsmünster cop-

---

Ducumburg. 1778." This copy of Motet/Offertory **Eb1** *Inimici circumdederunt nos* belonged originally to Herzogenburg Monastery.

Table 4. Masses of uncertain authorship

Work	Sources	Comments
C4	A WMich 23	Professional association
	A WPi 86	
C9	A HE IIc	
	A M I 98	
C11	A Z I/233	Ms. ca. 1780 (RISM)
C15	A SEI D XII 3 e	1773
C17	A M I 94	
	A Wgm Q600	
	A Wn 18717	Identified erroneously as an autograph
	D B Mus.ms.10722/3	
C18	A MS 131	
C19	A KR B 21/397	
	A LA M 26	1773
	A WIL	Late copy (19th Century)
C20	A KR B 15/340	
	SK KRE 83	Ms. ca. 1790 (RISM)
D1	A WMich 28	Professional association
	A WPi 91	
D6	A WS 154	Sti Peregrini
D7	A SEI D XII 3g	1785
D9	A LA M32	
	A LA M35	? After 1772
	AWIL 485	1860
D10	ASEI D XII 3d	1779 (ex Melk?)
d1	A H 463	
F2	18 extant sources	1776 (AGÖ)
A1	25 extant sources	1781
A2	AM I 97	
Bb1	18 sources	1778 (AGÖ)
Bb3	15 sources	1777 (AGÖ)
Bb5	A Ed A-99	
Bb6	CZ Nitra SA HS JP 18	Late copy
QC1	H Bb 47,062	1774
QC2	A KR K48/20	
QC3	CZ Pnm XXXVIII A39	
QC4	H VEs M.1.cl.41	1820
QC5	D Po Hofmann 7	ca. 1768
Qd1	DB Mus.ms.10722/5	ca. 1820
QG1	D Po Hofmann 9	1774
QBb1	A GE I 173	New Bb

ies beyond their inclusion in very important collections of Hofmann's works. **C17** and **C20** are interesting in that they represent the only two works in this particular category that are preserved outside Austria. **C17** is Hofmann's one surviving *a cappella* setting of the mass. The Austrian National Library source purports to be an autograph, the sole authority being Stadler.[24] However, on the evidence offered by the small number of surviving Hofmann music autographs, this score does not appear to be in the composer's hand. All of Hofmann's other *a cappella* settings are associated with St. Stephen's and it is possible that this work too was part of the music collection at one point even if, for unknown reasons, it was not entered into the catalog in 1824. The copy in the Gesellschaft der Musikfreunde was probably made after 1772—the score is headed *Missa / alla Capella / von Herrn Capellmeister Hoffmann*—and may have been copied from a source close to the composer. The Berlin copy, which is dated 1782 on the cover, belongs to the library of the German singer and collector Georg Johann Daniel Poelchau (1773–1836) that was acquired by the Königliche Bibliothek in Berlin in 1842.[25]

The case for accepting **C20** as an authentic work is undermined by a contra-attribution to Georg Reutter.[26] Reutter's authorship is also doubtful and for the moment at least the mass retains its current attribution to Leopold Hofmann.

C20 highlights the problem of works that survive in very small numbers particularly if their sources are far removed from Hofmann's known professional ambit. The remaining masses on our list are preserved in single sources. Once again, certain patterns of acquisition are apparent. Six of the sixteen works—**C11, C15, C18, D10, d1,** and **A2**—are preserved in the libraries of Austrian monasteries and two further works in the archive of St. Martin's Cathedral (formerly the Stadtpfarrkirche) in Eisenstadt. Establishments like Seitenstetten, Herzogenburg, and Melk have many apparently authentic Hofmann works in their archives and the inclusion of these particular masses argues for their au-

---

24. "Nach Stadler" is written next to the identification of the score as an autograph.

25. For information on this collection see Klaus Engler, "Georg Poelchau und seine Musikaliensammlung: Ein Beitrag zur Überlieferung Bachscher Musik in der ersten Hälfte des 19. Jahrhunderts" (PhD diss., Universität Tübingen, 1970).

26. SK KRE 83: "Missa S. Michaelis / a / Canto Alto / Tenore Basso / Conc^{to} / Violino Primo. / Violino Secondo. / Clarino Primo. / Clarino Secondo. / Tympano. / Con / Organo e Violono. / Del Sig. Giorg de Reutern."

thenticity albeit with reservations. The same can be said of the cathedral archive in Passau, which has dated Hofmann copies from the mid-1770s including a Mass in G, possibly the work referred to enthusiastically in a review published in 1843 under the pseudonym "Philokales" (Ferdinand Peter, Graf von Laurencin[27]) in the *Allgemeine Wiener Musik-Zeitung*.[28] In these cases, as in the masses with multiple sources, it is possible that the works were acquired through the offices of the composer or an agent (possibly a copyist) with whom Hofmann was associated. The most problematic works are those like **Bb6, QC1, QC3, QC4,** and **Qd1** that are known only from manuscript copies in collections far removed from Vienna.

If the business of establishing the authenticity and chronology of the masses is problematic enough, it becomes even more challenging with the smaller works beginning with their nomenclature. Whether Hofmann himself considered the terms motet, offertory, and gradual to be interchangeable is not entirely clear. The St. Peter's copies overwhelmingly favor the designation 'motet' but the St. Stephen's catalogs group these works under the rubric, "Gradualien und Motetten." Where these particular works are preserved in multiple sources, the designations are divided equally between motet and offertory with only occasional use of the term gradual. Some copies may retain their cyclical integrity but many other motet and offertory copies omit movements, generally either the recitative and/or the aria, and retain only the closing chorus. It is common for several *contrafacta* to exist for a given work and many copies include sets

---

27. See *Allgemeine Wiener Musik-Zeitung* (1841–1848), RIPM Consortium, 1990.

28. "Kirchenmusik: Am 24 Dezember wurde in der Franciskanerkirche eine Messe in G-Dur von Hoffmann, eine sehr interessante Antiquität, nebst einer gehaltvollen Einlage von Michael Haydn (Graduale) und einer herrlichen Mozart'schen Fuge (Offertorium) mit Präcision gegeben. Da ich mit nächstem beabsichtige, einen größeren Aufsatz über Kirchenmusik namentlich über das Verhältnis der älteren Musica sacra zur neueren für diese Blätter zu schreiben, so denke ich auf diese Hoffmann'sche Messe, eines der bedeutungsvollsten Tonwerke des an sich schon sehr bedeutenden Kirchencomponisten noch zurückzukommen."(Church music: On 24 December a Mass in G—a very interesting antique—by Hofmann, along with an elaborate insertion by Michael Haydn (Graduale) and a wonderful fugue by Mozart (Offertorium) was neatly given at the Franciskanerkirche. Because I plan to write a longer article about church music in the next issue of this journal, namely about the relationship of the older sacred music to the newer, I will return to this Mass by Hofmann—one of the most significant compositions by this quite significant church composer.) *Allgemeine Wiener Musik-Zeitung*, Jahrgang 3 (Vienna, 1843), 658.

of vocal parts with differing texts in order to extend the work's utility. Some *contrafacta* are known from several sources but others are preserved in just one. From what we know of the St. Peter's and St. Stephen's copies, it is likely that Hofmann himself either set multiple texts or, at a later date, sanctioned the use of a *contrafactum* for a specific occasion in the liturgical year. It is not always apparent which text, if any, should be considered of primary importance. Although Hofmann doubtless considered this type of work to be fluid in nature, capable of alteration and adaptation when the need arose, many of the extant motet copies probably represent unsanctioned adaptations for local use. It is possible too that some of the most problematic works—those that are preserved in a single source far removed from Vienna—represent adaptations of authentic works that do not survive.

It seems highly unlikely that a reliable chronology will ever be established for these works. Hofmann's interest in writing motets seems to have peaked in the early 1770s and, on the basis of the current evidence, it seems unlikely that any of these works were composed in the aftermath of the disruptive new regulations governing church music promulgated by Joseph II in 1783.

Litanies

Two categories of sacred work—litanies and psalms—are especially interesting since they are not well represented in Viennese sources, yet, from the number of works known, occupy a significant place in Hofmann's output (see Table 5). Of the two, litanies are the more complex and generally call for larger musical resources. Some of the litany settings have *concertato* vocal parts in addition to Hofmann's usual four-part choir and a number of the works also feature prominent instrumental *obbligati*.[29] The elaborate style of these settings suggests that they were composed for important churches or religious foundations or, perhaps, were commissioned by individuals with substantial musical establishments.

St. Peter's is the only important Viennese source for the twenty-two litanies that are attributed to Hofmann. Six of the seven extant works in the archive

---

29. Litany C2 [Trombone solo in the *Salus*]; Litany C3 [Organo concertato]; Litany C5 [Oboe solo]; Litany C7 [2 Viole concertati]; Litany D1 [2 Viole concertati]; Litany D3 [2 Flauti, 2 Fagotti, 2 Tromboni, 2 Viole, 2 Violoncelli concertati]; Litany Bb2 [Fagotto concertato].

Table 5. Litany sources

Litany	Designation	Sources	Comment
C1	De la Madona	A Ed G114	Esterházy #82 as Pater Joseph
C2	Lauretanae	A GÖ	
		A KR E42/34	
		A TU 199	No. 7 "De Beata"
		CZ KRa A-2095	1778
		CZ LIT 633	Prov. Strobach
		CZ Pkriz XXXV A163	
		CZ Pnm XLIX E 314	
C3	Sanctissimae Trinitate	A Wn F24 St Peter B3	#6 "M.D.C. di Santo Steffano" St.P
C4	Lytaney	A Wn S.m. 2727	No. 4
C5	Sanctissimae Trinitate	A Wn F24 St Peter B4	#8 "M.D.C. di Santo Steffano" St.P
C6	De la Madona	A Ed G113	
		A Wn F4 Baden 208	g6. Prov. Joh. Pernold 1829
		A Wn F5 Mödling 934	#7 Prov. Wieser
		A Wn S.m.2726	Prov. Joh. Winkler
		D PO Hofmann 16	
		SK BRnm MUS VII 83	Esterházy #73
C7	Sanctissimae Trinitate	A Wgm I 70127 P	
		A Wn F24 St Peter B5	#2 "M.D.C. di Santo Steffano" St.P
		A Wn S.m. 0693	Lauretanae
		A WPs 73	1781, Esterházy #72
C8	Lauretanae	CZ KRa A-2094	1774
		CZ OSm A-1954	
		D PO Hofmann 15	ca. 1770
D1	Lauretanae	A MT 9L	
		A MT 29L	
		A Wn F24 St Peter B15	Esterházy #77
D2	Lauretanae	A Wn S.m. 9116	Prov. A.S. de F
D3	Sanctissimae Trinitate	A Wn F24 St Peter B6	"M.D.C. di Santo Steffano"
		CZ Pnm XLIX E315	
F1	Omnium Sanctorum	A Wn HK1299	Processional. Prov. St Stephen's?
G1	Sanctissimae Trinitate	A MT 26L	Prov. Spoth 1852
		A MT 54	
		A Wn F24 St Peter B2	#1 "M.D.C. di Santo Steffano"
		D PO Hofmann 17	1780, Esterházy #81 as Pater Joseph

Table 5 continued

Litany	Designation	Sources	Comment
Bb1	De Beata	CZ LIT 632	Prov. Strobach
Bb2	Sanctissimae Trinitate	A Wn F24 St Peter B7	#4 "M.D.C. di Santo Steffano" St.P
		A WStStephan	lost
Bb3	De la Madona	A Ed G112	Prov. Josephi Richter
		A KN 194	
		A MT 80L	
		SK Mms D II 26	Lauretanae, Esterházy #75
QC1	Litany in C		Esterházy #71
QC2	Litany in C		Esterházy #74
QC3	Litany in C		Esterházy #76
Qd1	Litany in d		Esterházy #79
QG1	Litany in G		Esterházy #78
QBb1	De la Madona?	A Wn F24 St Peter B24	Autogr. Fragment (Virgo prudentissima)

are numbered one to eight: the one work that is preserved without a wrapper may be either Litany No. 6 (**C6**) or No. 7 (**C7**). A possible autograph fragment [**QBb1**], which conveniently brings the total of works to eight, may also belong to this sequence (see Figure 3). All of the extant wrappers identify Hofmann as "Maestro di Capella di Santo Steffano" denoting that they were acquired after 1772; four of the wrappers are marked "St.P" establishing their ownership by St. Peter's. The more usual formula found on the St. Peter's wrappers during this period is "Ad chorum Sancti Petri;" the abbreviated form used on these copies appears to have been added by a new hand and may have served as a reminder that the parts in question needed to be returned to St. Peter's after being used at St. Stephen's.

Although this interpretation is necessarily speculative, it might help to explain why only one Hofmann litany is listed in the St. Stephen's catalogs. The wrappers present us with another conundrum. If these works were composed after 1772 as the wrappers suggest, why did Hofmann not compose them for St. Stephen's or, if he did, why are they not listed in the catalogs? Surely it would have been more prudent for him to write these works for his new employer than for the church he had served so well over the past decade. If only one or two works were involved, it could be argued that the ownership markings were made later and possibly in error as a consequence Hofmann's dual role as *Kapellmeister*

The Sacred Music of Leopold Hofmann

Figure 3. "Virgo prudentissima," a fragment, possibly in Hofmann's hand, from an otherwise unknown setting of the litany. A Wn F24 St Peter B24.

at both churches. But for eight works to be involved, the case for them having been composed for St. Peter's is considerably strengthened. That none of the eight litanies circulated widely may be an indication that they were composed relatively late in Hofmann's career.

The remaining litanies, four of which are preserved in multiple copies with a reasonably wide geographical spread, pose more difficult problems in terms of establishing their origins. On the basis of the usual distribution patterns for Hofmann's sacred music, one would expect to see copies of the litanies in most of the great monastic collections and indeed there are manuscripts at Göttweig (**C2**), Kremsmünster (**C2**), and Klosterneuburg (**Bb3**). But these numbers are small in comparison with those for the composer's masses and none of the monasteries appears to have attempted to acquire multiple settings of Hofmann's litanies. This is unusual enough to lead one to surmise that the monasteries concerned were unaware of the existence of the other works.

The presence of two litanies in the archiepiscopal library at Kroměříž (**C2** and **C8**) is interesting since this collection is a rich source for Hofmann's in-

153

strumental works. It contains the largest single collection of his keyboard concertos and includes a significant number of *unica*. Given the strong interest in Hofmann's music evidenced by this collection, the archiepiscopal court at Kroměříž must be considered a candidate for the role of commissioner of new Hofmann sacred works. The copies in this archive may also have served as the source for other manuscript copies of these works found in Czech collections.

Two of the remaining sources also offer possible evidence of Hofmann's freelance activities: the music archive of St. Martin's Cathedral in Eisenstadt and the sacred music holdings of the Esterházy *Kapelle*. Hofmann is not known to have had any association—either personal or professional—with Eisenstadt or the Esterházy family. Nonetheless, the St. Martin's archive contains an important collection of Hofmann's works and includes within it a number of compositions that are otherwise unknown. Among these works are three litany settings. Two of them (**C6** and **Bb3**) are preserved elsewhere, but **C1** is otherwise known only from an entry in a catalog of the Esterházy music collection made around 1801–1805[30] where it is attributed to Pater Joseph (elsewhere referred to as "Kainz" or "Keinz"). While this casts some doubt on its authenticity, the Esterházy catalog also attributes **G1** to Pater Joseph when Hofmann's authorship is not seriously in doubt. None of these copies can be dated with certainty nor is the acquisition sequence apparent unless it is reflected in the numbering of the works in the Esterházy catalog. The number of sources and their relatively wide distribution may indicate that **C6** is the oldest of the three works.

The most intriguing aspect concerning sources for the Hofmann litanies is the presence of so many of them in the Esterházy catalog, five of which are otherwise unknown. As it stood at the turn of the nineteenth century, this collection included not only the historical holdings of the Esterházy *Kapelle* but also the music that had been acquired or integrated into the collection in more recent times at the instruction of Prince Nicolaus II, who considered that the sacred music holdings had been neglected in recent years.[31] Many of the works added to the collection were presumably acquired in the 1790s, too late, in Hofmann's case, for new works to have been commissioned, but certainly not too late for

---

30. Else Radant, "A Thematic Catalogue of the Esterházy Archives (c.1801–5)," *Haydn Yearbook* 13 (1982): 180–212.

31. For a discussion of Nicolaus II's interest in sacred music see H.C. Robbins Landon, *Haydn: Chronicle and Works*, vol. 4, *Haydn: The Years of The Creation 1796–1800* (London: Thames & Hudson, 1977), 50.

The Sacred Music of Leopold Hofmann

copies of works to be purchased from Hofmann's former copyists or professional associates. The other and more intriguing possibility is that Nicolaus, whose interest in sacred music is well documented, commissioned the works from Hofmann before he succeeded to the title. The duplication of several of the works in the St. Martin's archive might indicate a common origin.

Psalms

With the exception of a single setting of *Confitebor tibi Domine*, which is listed in the St. Stephen's catalogs, no other psalm attributed to Leopold Hofmann is preserved in a Viennese source (Table 6). The absence of copies in any of the other churches with which he is known to have been associated is so startling that it is tempting to surmise that Hofmann composed all of these settings on commission for institutions outside Vienna. The current distribution of the extant copies may provide clues about the origins of these works.

The extant psalm settings fall into three distinct groups. The first of these consists of works that are preserved exclusively in the cathedral archives in Eisenstadt. To these works might be added an additional copy of *Laetatus sum* and an otherwise unknown setting of the *Magnificat* which are listed in the Esterházy catalog. If these works are indeed authentic (and there is little from either a structural or stylistic point of view to challenge the current attribution) then the case for Hofmann having been commissioned to compose them looks plausible given the presence of the litanies in this source and in the Esterházy collection. The second group of works consists of eight settings of the *Miserere*. The present distribution of manuscripts is intriguing. One source, Stift Lambach, has copies of all eight, one of which (**Miserere 8**) is dated 1772. Göttweig also owned a copy of **Miserere 8** (now lost) which was acquired in 1771. Copies of **Miserere 1** (Seitenstetten) and **Miserere 3** (Domarchiv, Passau) are also dated 1772; copies of other settings dating from later in the decade are to be found at Schlierbach and in the Göttweig catalog. Although Lambach owned all eight works and together they might be described as a set, the evidence points to the works having been composed individually over a period of several years. Some of them can be dated to the early 1770s and it is possible that all of the settings were composed around this time. Göttweig's acquisition of **Miserere 4** in 1779 might have little bearing on the actual date of composition. For whom did Hofmann compose these settings of the *Miserere*? If it were not for the 1771 Göttweig copy of **Miserere 8** it would be tempting to assume that they were

Table 6. Psalm sources

Psalm	Source	Comments
Beati omnes/ Confitebor tibi	A Ed G111	
Confitebor tibi	A WStStephan	Lost
De profundis clamavi/ Momento Domine	A Ed G108	
Credidi propter/ Captivitatem Sion/ In convertendo Dominus	A Ed G110	
In exitu Israel No.1	A Ed G107	Esterházy leaping stag watermark
In exitu Israel No.2	A Ed G109	
In te, Domine, speravi	A H 467	No. 6 Graduale. 1802
Laetatus sum/ Nisi Dominus/ Lauda Jerusalem	A Ed G106	Esterházy Catalog #48
Magnificat		Esterházy Catalog #47
Miserere No.1	A LA A MT 11 ½ A SB 808 A SEI E XVI 2 g (III) D PO Hofmann 22	Lambach Catalog RISM 600.251.513 1778 1772 ca. 1770 (RISM)
Miserere No.2	A LA	Lambach Catalog
Miserere No.3	A LA A MT 10 A SB 807 A SEI E XVI 2 g (V) D PO Hofmann 21	Lambach Catalog 1772 ca. 1770
Miserere No.5	A LA	Lambach Catalog
Miserere No.6	A LA	Lambach Catalog
Miserere No.7	A LA	Lambach Catalog
Miserere No.8	A GÖ A KR F 22/23 A LA A SEI E XVI 2 g (II)	1771 (lost) Lambach Catalog 1772
Venite exultemus	A Pfarre Haitzendorf 167	Graduale. Prov. Herzogenburg

The Sacred Music of Leopold Hofmann

written for Lambach and that the copies found at Maria Taferl, Seitenstetten, and elsewhere derive from these manuscripts or a common and as yet unidentified source. The evidence to support this hypothesis is hardly overwhelming but it is not beyond the bounds of possibility. Of one thing, however, we can be quite sure: Hofmann did not compose these settings for use at St. Peter's or St. Stephen's.

Conclusion

The reconstruction of Hofmann's working repertory throws considerable light on his day to day activities both as *Kapellmeister* and as a composer of sacred music but it still leaves many questions unanswered. The proliferation of manuscript copies of his sacred works confirms Hofmann's position as one of the pre-eminent figures in Viennese church music during the middle decades of the eighteenth century. There was a strong demand for his music throughout Austria, Bohemia, Moravia, and, to a lesser extent, Hungary. It seems very likely that he received commissions to compose masses, litanies, and smaller sacred works from "foreign cities" and that some of these works also circulated to a limited extent in Vienna. The bibliographic record is rarely helpful and never conclusive regarding the origins of the works but it does point to the overwhelming majority of Hofmann's sacred works having been composed during the 1760s and 1770s. He was certainly active in the late 1750s and it is likely that his output of sacred music was quite substantial by the time he was appointed *regens chori* at St. Peter's in 1764. That he continued to accept external commissions in the 1770s is implied in Furthmoser's report[32] and confirmed, in all probability, by the large number of works that survive outside the archives of St. Peter's and St. Stephen's.

A few tentative conclusions can be advanced on the basis of known distribution patterns of Hofmann's sacred works:

- multiple sources increase the likelihood that a work is authentic;
- an unknown work preserved in a collection that contains a significant number of "authentic" works is more likely to be authentic than a work which is found in an otherwise unknown source;
- the more copies there are, the older the work is likely to be.

---

32. See note 21.

The last of these points is the most important since it implies that the creation of a rough chronological framework in which to consider Hofmann's career as a composer of sacred music is at least possible. The incompleteness of the bibliographic record means that the internal chronology cannot be considered very reliable but its outer limits probably reflect the reality of Hofmann's professional circumstances.

The bibliographic record suggests that Hofmann's productivity tailed off sharply at the beginning of the 1780s. Some of the works that survive in very small numbers may have been composed towards the end of his career but just how much he wrote during the last decade of his life, considering the radically altered professional environment in which he found himself, is open to debate. Although the post-reform climate would hardly have been conducive to the composition of new works for the cathedral, he might just have felt sufficiently threatened to make amends for his earlier slackness and the fruits of this new-found diligence are to be found in the entries in the St. Stephen's catalogs of otherwise unknown works.

It is possible that Hofmann continued to fulfill external commissions during the last years of his life but it seems more likely that the wealth of additional masses, psalms and litanies were composed during the 1770s when Hofmann was in his pomp. In the 1780s this enigmatic man, who loved solitude, probably spent more and more time at his charming house in Oberdöbling, away from the hustle and bustle of Vienna and its endless musical politics.[33] Although he ceased to be in the public eye, his sacred music continued to be performed in all of the great churches and remained in the public's ear for decades to come.

---

33. "Er war der redlichste Mann von der Welt, liebte ein einsames Leben, und brachte seine lezteren Jahre auf seinem Landhause, unweit der Hauptstadt, auf dem Dorfe Döbling, zu." (He was the most honest man in the world, lived a solitary life, and spent his last years at his country house, not far from the capital, in the village of Döbling.) Meusel, *Neue Miscellaneen*, 47.

Courting the Amorous Muse: The Instrumental Romance in the Music of Antonio Rosetti

STERLING E. MURRAY

Contemporaneous descriptions of Rosetti's music frequently comment upon his special gift for pleasing melody. The Bohemian lexicographer Gottfried Johann Dlabacz claimed that Rosetti's "compositions are especially distinguished by the pleasant, engaging melodies, which predominate,"[1] and Ernst Ludwig Gerber found in his works "a uniquely pleasant, engaging and sweetly-toying tone."[2] Perhaps nowhere in Rosetti's music is this special gift for melody more strongly perceived than in the slow-movement romances that grace many of his chamber and orchestral compositions.

The term "romance" derives from a style of early eighteenth-century French vocal music that Jean-Jacques Rousseau described in his *Dictionnaire de musique* of 1768 as in a "simple, touching style . . . without ornaments, whose melody is both sweet, natural, and rustic."[3] Such unpretentious vocal settings frequently appeared in *opéra comique*,[4] but they also were popularized in settings for voice and keyboard included in the miscellaneous collections that flowed in abundance from the presses of various Parisian publishers beginning in the 1760s and continuing up to the eve of the revolution. This unadorned vocal style gained immense popularity and swept rapidly through the musical salons of the French capital. It was not long before composers of instrumental music adapted the new fashion to their own needs. As early as 1761, Chevardière released a collection of six symphonies by François-Joseph Gossec that included a Symphony in

---

1. "durch angenehme, schmeichelnde Melodien, die in seinen Werken herrschen, besonders aus," Gottfried Johann Dlabacz, ed., *Allgemeines historisches Künstler-Lexikon für Böhmen und zum Theil auch für Mähren und Schlesien* (Prague: G. Hasse, 1816), 2:935 [593].
2. "ein eigener angenehm schmeichelnden und suß-tändelnder Ton," Ernst Ludwig Gerber, *Historisch-biographisches Lexikon der Tonkünstler, welches Nachrichten von dem Leben und Werken musikalischer Schriftsteller, berühmter Componisten, Sänger, usw. . . . enthält* (Leipzig: J. G. I. Breitkopf, 1790–1792), 2:325.
3. "simple, touchant, & d'un goût un peu antique, . . . point d'ornemens, rien de maniéré, une mélodie douce, naturelle, champêtre," Jean-Jacques Rousseau, *Dictionnaire de musique* (Paris, 1768), 427.
4. "Dans ma cabáne obscure" from Rousseau's *Le devin du village* (1752) serves as a good example.

E-flat Major (Op. 5/2) with a second movement entitled "Romanza, Andante."[5] Gossec's experiment was an immediate success, and other composers quickly followed suit with romances soon appearing in symphonies, *simphonies concertantes, quatuors concertants,* and trios by composers like Pierre-Hyacinthe Azaïs (1741–1796), Charles-Ernest Baron de Bagge (1722–1791), Giuseppe Maria Cambini (1746?–1825), Jean-Guillain Cardon (1732–1788), Nicolas-Marie Dalayrac (1753–1809), Papavoine (1720–1790), Giovanni Giornovichi (1747–1804), Étienne Ozi (1754–1813), and Giovanni Punto (1746–1803). Among the German composers resident in the French capital at this time, Carl Stamitz (1745–1801) seems to have entertained a particular affinity for the instrumental romance, which he employed in the slow movements of several of his string and wind quartets, concertos, and *simphonies concertantes.* Although unquestionably Stamitz's attraction to the romance was stimulated by his residence in Paris, he continued to cultivate such pieces even after his departure from the city.

By the early 1770s, the instrumental romance began to make its appearance in the aristocratic courts of Germany and Vienna.[6] Its new-found cultivation in the Hapsburg Empire reflected the strongly French artistic taste of many of the German nobility. This new style was embraced with special enthusiasm at the small south German court of Kraft Ernst, Prince von Oettingen-Wallerstein.[7] Indeed, it seems to have been the Wallerstein *music-intendant* Franz Ignaz von Beecke (1733–1803) who first introduced the instrumental romance in Germany in his keyboard "Duetto pastoral" composed in 1772 and dedicated to the Countess Batthyány.[8] Beecke was a frequent visitor to Paris, where in

---

5. This year also marks the beginning of a period in Gossec's life in which he was heavily involved in the composition of a number of stage works, including several *opéra comique* pieces for the private theaters of the princes of Conti and Condé.

6. Roger Hickman has suggested that the instrumental romance was first cultivated in the imperial city of Vienna by Carl Ditters von Dittersdorf, who included a slow-movement romance in his Symphony in E-flat Major, published in 1773 as op. 7/1.

7. In her study of the instrumental romance in Germany, Heidi Gülow focuses upon the south German *Hofkapellen* of Karl, Count von Bentheim-Steinfurt and his son Ludwig von Bentheim-Steinfurt, Karl Alexander, Prince von Thurn und Taxis, and Kraft Ernst. See Heidi Gülow, *Studien zur instrumentalen Romance in Deutschland vor 1810* (Frankfurt am Main: Peter Lang, 1987), 126–142.

8. D-Au, III 4½ 4° 399: Duetto pastoral: fait pour Madame la / Comtesse de Batiani p[ar]:Capitanio de Becke. The date is established by a receipt for copying the work signed by Johann Sebastian Albrecht Link (d. 1795). See also Gülow, *Studien zur intrumentalen Romance,* 129 (and various other places). Another contender for this honor is a composer

Courting the Amorous Muse

all probability he first encountered the fashion for the romance. Rosetti, who joined the Wallerstein *Hofkapelle* in 1773, must certainly have known Beecke's keyboard romance, and he may well have discussed this new fashion with his older colleague. It was not long after this that Rosetti began incorporating romances in some of his own compositions. In all, Rosetti composed fifty-five slow-movement romances (see Table 1).

In addition, there are a few pieces whose slow movements conform to the romance style, but bear no specific designation. Some of Rosetti's romances appeared in works that today unfortunately are lost and known to us only through catalog references. One or two romances appear in multiple settings. Thus, the charming *Adagio non tanto* of the Oboe Concerto in F Major (C34) also serves as the second movement of the Keyboard Concerto in G Major (C2) and the Clarinet Concerto in E-flat Major (C63). Likewise, the romance from a second concerto for clarinet in E-flat major (C62) resurfaces as part of a Flute Concerto in G Major, where it is linked to the first movement by an inserted recitative.[9] Lastly, this same work is also found in the Wallerstein collection as a Romance in B-flat Major for Oboe and Orchestra.[10]

The majority of these works are multi-movement compositions in which the designation romance is included as part of the tempo marking for the slow movement. This includes concertos, wind partitas, symphonies, and various types of chamber music, although it is in the concertos—especially those for one or two horns—that the romance finds its most secure home in Rosetti's oeuvre.[11] In addition, there are ten independent Romances for solo keyboard (E27–36).[12] These pieces, which require only the most modest keyboard profi-

---

named Buschman, about whom almost nothing is known. A wind partita in the music library of the Thurn und Taxis court in Regensburg attributed to Buschman includes a second movement marked "Romance Andantino." The manuscript is not dated, but has received a catalog date of ca. 1760. Since this date is suspiciously early and has not been verified, and there have been numerous questions about the authorship of certain instrumental pieces in this collection, this work is not being considered here.

9. D-BFb, [MÜu]: R-os 9. This collection is especially rich in romances.

10. D-Au, III 2½ 4° 438.

11. In his *Versuch einer Anleitung zur Composition*, Heinrich Christoph Koch points out that in "modern concertos" a romance is sometimes used to replace the customary adagio.

12. Identification numbers for Rosetti's compositions are derived from Sterling E. Murray, *The Music of Antonio Rosetti (Anton Rösler) ca. 1750–1792: A Thematic Catalog* (Warren, MI: Harmonie Park Press, 1996).

161

Table 1. Romances in the instrumental music of Rosetti

No.	Title	Key	No.	Mvt key	Meter	Tempo
1	Symphony	C	A7	G	6/8	Andante
2	Symphony	C	A9	G	2/4	Andante grazioso
3	Symphony	D	A20	A	¢	Adagio non tanto
4	Partita	D	B5	G	¢	Adagio non tanto
5	Partita	E♭	B7	E♭	¢	Adagio
6	Partita	E♭	B11	E♭	3/4	Andante
7	Quartetto*	E♭	B17	E♭	¢	Andante poco adagio
8	Notturno	D	B24	A	¢	Adagio
9	Notturno	E♭	B27	B♭	¢	Andantino
10	Keyboard Concerto	G	C2	C	¢	Adagio non tanto
11	Flute Concerto	G	C25	C	3/4	Larghetto
12	Flute Concerto†	G	C27	G	2/4	Adagio
13	Oboe Concerto	F	C34‡	C	¢	Adagio non tanto
14	Horn Concerto	d	C38	F	C	Adagio
15	Horn Concerto	d	C39	F	¢	Adagio agitato
16	Horn Concerto	E♭	C43	B♭	¢	Adagio non tanto
17	Horn Concerto	E♭	C48	B♭	¢	Adagio non tanto
18	Horn Concerto	E♭	C49	B♭	C	Adagio ma non tanto
19	Horn Concerto	E	C50	B	C	Adagio
20	Horn Concerto	E	C52	e	3/4	Andantino
21	Horn Concerto	F	C53	f	3/4	Adagio non tanto
22	Horn Concerto	E♭	C54Q	A♭	¢	Andante
23	2-Horn Concerto	E♭	C56	e♭	¢	Adagio
24	2-Horn Concerto	E♭	C57	A♭	¢	Andantino
25	2-Horn Concerto	E	C58	e	¢	Adagio non tanto
26	2-Horn Concerto§	E	C59L	?	?	Adagio non tanto
27	2-Horn Concerto	F	C60	f	C	Andante
28	2-Horn Concerto	F	C61	f	¢	Andante
29	Clarinet Concerto‖	E♭	C62	B♭	¢	Un poco adagio

Table 1 continued

30	Clarinet Concerto	E♭	C63	B♭	C	Adagio non tanto
31	Clarinet Concerto§	E♭	C65L	?	?	Romance
32	Bassoon Concerto	B♭	C74	E♭	₵	Adagio
33	Quartet	A	D9	A	₵	Larghetto
34	Quartet	E♭	D10	E♭	C	Adagio
35	Accom. Sonata	F	D19	d	₵	Adagio
36	Accom. Sonata	E♭	D20	B♭	₵	Adagio non tanto
37	Accom. Sonata	B♭	D21	E♭	3/8	Andantino
38	Accom. Sonata	B♭	D23	E♭	₵	Larghetto
39	Accom. Sonata	C	D24	F	₵	Andantino
40	Keyboard Trio	G	D26	D	C	Adagio
41	Keyboard Trio	F	D27	C	C	Adagio non tanto
42	Keyboard Trio	C	D29	G	C	Adagio non tanto
43	Keyboard Trio	D	D31	D	C	Larghetto
44	Keyboard Trio*	B♭	D36	B♭	₵	Adagio non tanto
45	Keyboard Sonata	G	E2	G	₵	Larghetto
46	Romance	E♭	E27	n/a	₵	Adagio
47	Romance	A	E28	n/a	₵	Andante
48	Romance	E♭	E29	n/a	3/4	Adagio non tanto
49	Romance	A	E30	n/a	₵	Andante
50	Romance	B♭	E31	n/a	₵	Andantino
51	Romance	A	E32	n/a	₵	Andante con espressione
52	Romance	B♭	E33	n/a	6/8	[Andante]
53	Romance	G	E34	n/a	₵	Andantino
54	Romance	B♭	E35	n/a	3/4	Andante grazioso
55	Romance	B♭	E36	n/a	₵	Andante molto

* Romance found as first movement
† also for clarinet or bassoon
‡ = C63
§ lost
|| also for flute or oboe

ciency, are preserved in various keyboard collections designed specifically for a dilettante market. Most were published between 1782 and 1787 in Heinrich Bossler's popular collection of songs and keyboard pieces entitled *Blumenlese für Klavierliebhaber*. Some were included in *Musikalischer Blumenkranz*, also published by Bossler between 1782 and 1786, Franz Anton Hoffmeister's *Collection de Rondeau et Romances* (Leipzig, ca. 1784), and Bernhard Schott's *Recueil des 12. Pièces pour le Clavecin* (Mainz, 1785).[13]

Precise dating poses a daunting problem with eighteenth-century music. In this regard, Rosetti research has been especially fortunate. It has been possible to establish trustworthy dates for a greater portion of Rosetti's output than most of his contemporaries, but a precise chronology for his total oeuvre still eludes modern scholarship. However, based on both internal and external evidence, it seems likely that Rosetti's earliest romances are three divertimento-like pieces composed between his hire in 1773 and about 1776. Included in this group are two wind partitas (B11 and B17) and an orchestral Notturno (B27), preserved today in an *unicum* copy in the Thurn und Taxis music collection in Regensburg. The partitas are likely to be the earliest of the group. B17, set for two clarinets and two horns, is entitled "Quartetto" in its sole source in the Benedictine monastery of Einsiedeln, Switzerland.[14] The term "Romance" appears as part of the first-movement tempo marking, *Andante poco adagio*. The Partita in E-flat Major for wind octet (B11) is a three-movement composition, in which the second movement is cast in 3/4 and marked *Romance Andante*. This work was also known in an arrangement as a symphony (A26) through a set of partbooks in the library of the Jasna Góra monastery at Czestochowa, Poland, and an entry in a thematic index of the Prince-Bishop of Freising's music library.[15] B11, which was published by Pleyel in Paris after the composer's death, has the distinction of being the only one of Rosetti's wind partitas to appear in print.

---

13. Roger Hickman's claim that Daniel Gottlob Türk's *Kleine Handstücke für angehende Klavierspieler* (1792–1795) and Johann Friedrich Reichardt's *Kleine Klavier- und Singstücke* (1783) contain the earliest romances for solo keyboard overlooks the publication of Bossler's *Blumenlese für Klavierliebhaber*.

14. CH-E, Th 71,45 (Ms. 2334). The words "con/Fagotto" at one time appeared on the title page, but were later crossed out.

15. "Themata von allen vorhandenen Kirchen und Kammer Musicalien welche in der den 1. Setpber [sic] 1796 neu verfassten Designation enthalten sind," Munich, Kreisarchiv.

Courting the Amorous Muse

In March 1776, musical activities at the Oettingen-Wallerstein court came to an abrupt halt following the tragic death of Kraft Ernst's young bride, Maria Theresa, Princess von Oettingen-Wallerstein, as the result of complications following the birth of her daughter. The prince was devastated by the loss of his young wife and imposed on the court a period of mourning that lasted for several years. With the suspension of regular court concerts, court musicians found themselves with little to occupy their time and talents. Some, like the oboist Joseph Fiala, sought greener pastures elsewhere, while others, including the cellist Joseph Reicha and the violinist Anton Janitsch, undertook concert tours. Rosetti chose neither of these options. Instead, he remained at Wallerstein and used the opportunity allowed by this lull in his court duties to devote additional time to composition. By 1779–1780, the long period of mourning came to an end and the prince undertook a reorganization of his *Kapelle*. Several of the compositions that Rosetti produced in this period of rejuvenation feature slow romance movements. Included in this group is a horn concerto "pour Monsieur Dürrschmied" (C49) completed in July 1779 and a group of keyboard trios (D26, 27, 29), which probably date from the spring or summer of 1781. In that same year, Rosetti requested and was granted a leave of absence to travel to Paris.

No other eighteenth-century cities could match the musical brilliance of the French capital, which overflowed with excellent performers and composers as well as an admiring aristocratic audience willing and able to support their passion for the arts. Paris was also a center for music publishing not to be rivaled by any other city of the day. It was truly a land of opportunity for someone wishing to establish or further his reputation as a composer or performer. Rosetti started out on his long journey in the last days of October. By late November early December, he had arrived in the French capital, where he would remain for the next six months. During this period of time, Rosetti made every effort to absorb as much as possible of the music the city had to offer. He enthusiastically reported his impressions of musical life there in a series of letters to Prince Kraft Ernst, *intendant* von Beecke, and *Hofrat* Philipp Chamot. Rosetti was not a mere observer, however. During his sojourn in Paris, he composed a number of new pieces.

The active musical life of Paris provided Rosetti with ample occasion to experience a rich array of new music by composers both French and foreign. In January 1782, he wrote to his patron that he had already acquainted himself with a "great variety of local music." Rosetti must have reasoned that if he captured in his own compositions the taste of Parisian audiences, his music might receive greater approbation in local performances and perhaps even attract the interest of music publishers. All of this could translate into financial success for him and greater honor for his prince. The special affection of Parisian audiences for the romance could not have escaped his attention, and, thus, it is hardly surprising that several of the works that Rosetti composed in Paris include romance movements. Notable in this group is the sweet and melancholy *Adagio non tanto* of his *La Chasse* Symphony in D Major (A22), designed specifically for the *Concert spirituel*,[16] and later published in 1786 by Jean-Georges Sieber. Also dating from this period is a Symphony in C Major (C7) whose romance is in 6/8 and assumes a character somewhat different from the other Parisian romances. During his tenure in Paris, Rosetti also composed four clarinet concertos, which Sieber published as a set in 1782.[17] These works probably were influenced by the playing of Michel Yost (1754–1786), a frequent performer at the *Concert spirituel*, and may even have been composed specifically for him. Yost included romances in four of his own clarinet concertos (scored by Johann Christoph Vogel, 1756–1788). This penchant was imitated and continued in the clarinet concertos of Yost's student, Jean Xavier Lefèvre (1763–1829), as well as those by Mathieu-Frédéric Blasius (1758–1829), professor of violin and clarinet at the conservatoire.[18]

The style of the haunting slow-movement romance of the Keyboard Concerto in G Major (C2) suggests that it might also have been composed or revised during his stay in Paris.[19] Romances also appear in several other compositions from the early 1780s whose dating is not precise enough to propose that they were actually composed during Rosetti's tenure in Paris.

---

16. This is undoubtedly the "powerful symphony" (eine starke Sinfonie) that Rosetti mentions in his letter to Prince Kraft Ernst of 28 January 1782.

17. Only two have survived (C62 and C63).

18. Apparently, the solo clarinet was considered an especially appropriate instrument for the lyric character of the romance. In addition to those mentioned here, slow-movement romances also are included in the clarinet concertos of Henri-Jacques de Croes, Baron Theodor von Schacht, and Franz Tausch, as well as a Concerto for Two Clarinets by Rosetti's Wallerstein colleague Paul Wineberger.

19. Sieber advertised his edition of this concerto in 1782. Haueisen in Frankfurt-am-Main republished Sieber's edition as Op. 3. Breitkopf listed Haueisen's edition in their 1782–1784 thematic catalog, and a review of the concerto dated 25 August 1783 appeared in the *Magazin der Musik*. The following year, Hummel republished the same work as his Op. 2.

Courting the Amorous Muse

By this point, the romance had assumed a firm foothold in Rosetti's musical language, and he continued to cultivate it in his concertos and chamber music in the years after his return to Wallerstein in May 1782. He was certainly not alone in his fondness for this genre. Examples abound in the works of composers active during the second half of the eighteenth century. Mozart included romances in his Gran Partita (K. 361), two horn concertos in E-flat Major (K. 447 and K. 495), the Piano Concerto in D minor (K. 466), and *Eine kleine Nachtmusik* (K. 525). Haydn's involvement was more limited, although the romance from his Symphony in B-flat Major (Hob. I:85), popularly known as "La Reine," is an excellent example of the type and may well have served as a model for several of his contemporaries. Others working in musical centers throughout Europe who also contributed to this repertory include (in addition to those already mentioned): Karl F. Abel (1723–1787), Friedrich Graf (1727–1795), Ignaz Fränzl (1736–1811), Gaetano Brunetti (1744–1798), Leopold Kozeluch (1747–1818), Johann Sperger (1750–1812), Johann Franz Xaver Sterkel (1750–1817), Christian Carl Hartmann (1750–1804), Franz Anton Pfeiffer (1752–1787), Paul Wranitzky (1756–1808), Franz Krommer (1759–1831), Franz Neubauer (1760–1795), Anton Wranitzky (1761–1820), and Johann Friederich Eck (1767–ca. 1838).[20] Prince Kraft Ernst's *Hofkapelle* at Wallerstein appears to have been a German center for the cultivation of the instrumental romance. Every composer attached at one time or other to the prince's service contributed to the repertory of the instrumental romance (see Table 2).

Although not all of this music coincides with Rosetti's tenure at Wallerstein between 1773 and 1789, the presence of romances in the works of so many composers certainly must be recognized as a musical proclivity of the Wallerstein *Hofkapelle* which itself is significant in accounting for Rosetti's fascination with the genre.

Rosetti clearly found the romance well suited to his musical language. His commitment to this special topos persisted throughout his career and found expression in various genres, both orchestral and chamber. But what did the term "romance" actually signify for Rosetti? How did a slow movement by Rosetti marked "romance" differ from any other slow movement? Were there significant conventions of form and style that Rosetti drew upon when composing

---

20. Gülow provides a list in *Studien zur instrumentalen Romance*, 183–412.

Table 2. Romances in compositions by Wallerstein composers

Composition	Key	Mvt key	Meter	Tempo
Franz Ignaz von Beecke (1733–1803)				
Partita	E♭	E♭	3/4	un poco largo
String Quartet	A	A	2/4	Larghetto
Serenade	D	D	₵	Un poco larghetto
Symphony	C	G	₵	Adagio un poco
Symphony	F	B♭	2/4	Larghetto
Duetto pastoral	C	C	2/4	un poco allegretto
Keyboard Sonata	c	c	6/8	Larghetto
Keyboard sonata	C	c	2/4	Andante
Joseph Fiala (1748–1816)*				
Symphony†	C	F	₵	Andante poco Allegretto
Oboe Concerto	C	c	₵	Andante
Simphonie concertante‡	F	C	2/4	poco Andante
Anton Hutti (1751/52–1785)				
Violin Concerto	A	D	3/4	Romance adagio
Joseph Reicha (1752–1795)				
Cello Concerto	E♭	c	₵	Romance cantabile
Concertante§	D	A	₵	Andante
Cello Concerto	C	G	3/4	Romance cantabile
Cello Concerto	f	A♭	₵	Adagio
2-Horn Concerto	E	e	₵	Romanze Cantabile
Duet for violin and cello	G	G	₵	Romance
Georg Feldmayr (1756–after 1831)				
2-Horn Concerto	F	f	3/4	Romance adagio cantabile
2-Horn Concerto	F	B♭	2/4	Romance Adagio

Table 2 continued

Oboe Concerto	C	F	¢	Andante sostenuto
Oboe Concerto	C	F	¢	Romance adagio
Partita	D	B♭	¢	Romance come adagio
Partita	D	B♭	¢	Romance come adagio
Partita	F	B♭	3/8	Andante non tanto
Partita	F	B♭	6/8	Andante un poco vivace
Serenade	D	G	¢	Romance Andantino
Serenade	D	G	¢	Andantino
Simphonie concertant‖	C	F	3/4	Andante sostenuto

Paul Wineberger (1758–1821)

2-Horn Concerto	E♭	A♭	¢	Romance
Oboe Concerto	C	G	¢	Adagio

Johann Nepomuk Hiebsch (1766–1820)

2-Horn Concerto	E♭	E♭	3/8	Romance Andantino
2-Horn Concerto	E♭	E♭	¢	Romance un poco adagio
Partita	D	A	6/8	Romance grazioso
Partita	D	A	2/4	Romance
Partita	F	B♭	2/4	Romance

Friedrich Witt (1770–1836)

Partita	E♭	E♭	3/4	Romance adagio
Partita	E♭	B♭	6/8	Romance Andante
Partita	F	B♭	2/4	Allegretto scherzando

* Additional examples may be Fiala's String Quartet and Bassoon Quartet in F Major that both contain slow movements identified as "Andante Romana [sic]."

† The romance of Fiala's Symphony in C Major (Garland C1) may be the first use of this genre in a symphony in Germany.

‡ for 2 oboes

§ for 2 violins

‖ for oboe and bassoon

a romance, and, if so, what were they? To what degree did Rosetti adhere in his romance movements to a conventional musical language? What significant expressions of originality are found within this repertory? In addition to such mechanical considerations, one might also ponder the more interesting questions of the significance of Rosetti's continued commitment to this style type. In adopting the term "romance" was Rosetti merely paying homage to a popular vogue or did the presence of such a movement denote some additional aesthetic significance? If so, what did this convey to the composer's audience? In order to respond to these questions and achieve a deeper understanding of Rosetti's employment of the romance, let us begin by singling out features of form and style that are applied consistently enough in his oeuvre that they may help us define a norm. Then, with this general description in place, it will be possible to consider the significance of those situations that conform less clearly to that norm.

The prototypical romance movement by Rosetti is set in a duple meter—most often common or *alla breve*—with a tempo marking of *Adagio non tanto* or simply *Adagio*.[21] In multi-movement contexts, romances offer the sole tonal contrast within the cycle. Rosetti actually exercises some variety in creating this contrast. Not surprisingly, the dominant and subdominant are the most common choices, but there are also examples of the parallel or relative minor, and in a dozen pieces—mostly chamber music—the tonic is retained. For the two horn concertos in D minor (C38 and C39), the relative major is selected as the contrasting tonality.

Almost all conform to a three-part structural design, based on statement, contrast, and reprise (ABA) with or without a concluding coda. In point of fact, however, Rosetti's choice of ternary design is at variance with the accounts of Koch and others, who claim the rondo is the preferred form for an instrumental romance. Gülow's study of the instrumental romance in Germany supports this contention. A full third of the examples that she considered (thirty-three and a third percent) are in rondo form, either with or without tonal contrast. That number increases to over half when one considers those rondos that incorporate elements of variation. On the other hand, according to Gülow only a little

---

21. There are a few examples in 2/4 or 3/4 but these are exceptions. The slow movement of the Symphony in C Major (A7) is the only example in 6/8, and 3/8 appears only in the Accompanied Keyboard Sonata in B-flat Major (D21). Adagio occasionally is replaced by a more moderate Andante or Andantino. With the exception of the Flute Concerto in G Major (C25), Larghetto is used only in chamber music.

over twenty-one percent of her population conforms to a straight-forward ABA form.[22] The only romance by Rosetti to adopt the rondo form is the *Adagio* from the Flute Concerto in G Major (C27), which follows a five-part design with coda.[23] The only other work not to employ a ternary design is the Horn Concerto in E Major (C52). In the *Romance Andantino* (E minor) of this work, the contrasting B section (in the parallel major and played by the tutti) unexpectedly reappears after the conclusion of the repeated A unit, now reassigned to the soloist and in E minor. After only about a dozen measures, the movement concludes in a hushed whisper.

The first section of the ternary form is the meat of the movement, and it is in this opening passage that the essence of the romance must effectively be conveyed. The romance's defining element is its commitment to a melodic disposition that the German theorist Daniel Gottlob Türk, paraphrasing Rousseau, described as "simple, pleasing, and unassuming [naive]."[24] But how is the musical expression of these general attributes to be understood in this period? Given the popularity of the romance as a stylistic topos, one might expect that it bore certain conventions of form and style that easily could be singled out and evaluated from one work to the next. Such an assumption might well lead us to seek clarification from contemporary theorists, but, unfortunately, these sources offer little assistance. Like Türk, the other German theorists who commented on the subject all paid homage to Rousseau's definition, but provided no concrete elucidation of just how this commitment to simplicity was to be achieved or measured. In his *Versuch einer Anleitung zur Composition* of 1787, Koch asserted that romance movements have a definite character, but neglected to define that character. Instead, he referred his readers to Johann Georg Sulzer's description of the poetic romance in his encyclopedia, *Allgemeine Theorie der schönen Künste*, which, in turn, simply led one back to Rousseau. According to Sulzer, while the content of a romance may be passionate, tragic, amorous, or even merely entertaining, its "ideas and expression must be of the utmost simplicity and very

---

22. Gülow, *Studien zur instrumentalen Romance*, 164.
23. This concerto is also found in versions for bassoon (C69) and clarinet (listed in Breitkopf's supplement of 1785–1787, both without extant example).
24. "simple, gefällige, naive," Daniel Gottlob Türk, *Clavierschule oder Anweisung zum Klavierspielen für Lehrer und Lernende, mit kritischen Anmerkungen* (Leipzig and Halle, 1789), reprinted in *Documenta Musicologica, Erste Reihe: Druckschriften-Faksimiles* XXIII (Basel, 1962), 398.

naïve."[25] Türk cautioned performers that the desired effect of the romance is best accomplished through expression rather than elaborate ornamentation and embellishment.[26] Implicit in his admonition is the notion that all manner of unseemly display should be avoided.

Thus, we are left with the view that romances were identifiable to eighteenth-century audiences primarily through their commitment to agreeable melodies placed in uncomplicated settings. Intricate harmony, texture, phrasing, and structure should be rejected in favor of natural expression and unaffected sentiment. In order to maintain his romances within the established aesthetic associated with its type, Rosetti had to design music that was both simplistic and attractive. Moreover, this had to be accomplished within a sensuous context capable of eliciting an expressive and emotional response, without, however, overstepping the bounds of taste and succumbing to overt sentimentality.

The following examples drawn from different genres and time periods are good examples of the sort of opening theme one is likely to find in Rosetti's romances (see Examples 1a–d).

Any one of them could meet the expectation for simple melodic expression recognized as a defining element of the romance. Indeed, the agreeable charm of these melodies quickly fixes them in one's memory where they tend to remain after the auditory experience has passed. Although their ingratiating tunefulness may appear almost effortless, Rosetti actually has made a number of calculated compositional choices in order to achieve this effect. Some of these are instantly apparent, while others are more subliminal and perceptible only upon closer consideration. For many, it is the nature and shape of the melody that makes the most immediate impact. Its basic diatonic pitch content not only is effective in its own right, but it also enhances the sparring deployment of chromatic pitches that occasionally interrupt to color and enrich cadences. Scalar construction and limited *ambitus* (moving within an octave and often focusing on the range of only a fifth) allow melodic lines to unfold in an undulating fashion within a narrow pitch span. These elements, in combination with an underlying harmonic

---

25. "Gedanken und Ausdruk müssen in der höchsten Einfalt und sehr naiv seyn," Johann Georg Sulzer, *Allgemeine Theorie der schönen Künste* (Leipzig, 1794) 4:544.

26. "Der Spieler hat sich dabey vor allen Manieren und Zusätzen sorgfältig zu hüten; denn die simple Melodie wird blos durch zunehmenden Ausdruck, nicht durch Verzierungen oder Zusätze, veredelt und eindringender gemacht," Türk, *Clavierschule*, reprint, 398.

Courting the Amorous Muse

Example 1a. Keyboard Concerto in G Major (C2) II: Romance, mm. 1–8

language that seldom deviates from fundamental triads, conspire to project an ingenuous quality reminiscent of folk music. Textures are kept quite thin. In some concerto movements this often involves little more than the first violin doubling the soloist supported by slowly changing chords in a reduced string accompaniment. In his keyboard textures, Rosetti frequently draws upon the saccharine sound of parallel thirds or sixths, as in the Keyboard Romance in A Major and Concerto in G Major (see Examples 1d and 1a). Ornamentation is employed sparingly and always applied with caution.

A crucial attribute of Rosetti's romance themes is their dependence on pitch and rhythmic patterning. Quasi-declamatory repeated notes, motives of

Example 1b. Two-Horn Concerto in E♭ Major (C57) II: Romance, mm. 1–8

descending thirds repeated in sequential groupings, and cadential appoggiaturas are all within the arsenal of expressive gestures Rosetti calls forth to instill his melodies with an appropriate combination of emotional affect and tender charm. Rhythm and meter also play their part. Any hint of rhythmic or metric nuance is judiciously avoided. Rhythmic patterns are kept square and repetitive, designed to coincide effortlessly with metric stress so that the listener is easily lulled into the regularly of two-pulse measures. This effect often is enhanced by a basso part whose prime responsibility is to mark the implied pulse on strong

Example 1c. Symphony in D Major, "La chasse" (A20), II: Romance, mm. 1–8

beats. Changes of texture, chord, and figuration are also calculated to support this macro-rhythm.

A common feature within this repertory is the application of standard rhythms in the opening theme. In particular, two different clichéd rhythmic patterns are encountered frequently. One begins on the beat with a half note following by either two quarter notes or four eighth notes. A variant in which a

Example 1d. Romance for Keyboard in A Major (E28), mm. 1–8

dotted quarter–eighth pattern is substituted for the half note is also encountered (see Figure 1a). The same rhythmic options make up the second clichéd pattern although here the metric pulse has been misplaced to produce an anacrusis (see Figure 1b).[27] Of course, any one of these can be further embellished with slides and turns.

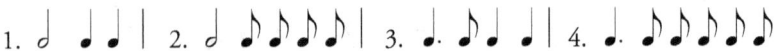

Figure 1a. Clichéd rhythmic beginnings, type 1

Figure 1b. Clichéd rhythmic beginnings, type 2

Although all of the factors just enumerated are significant in creating the romance's desired effect, the simplicity inherent in these melodies derives less from immediate issues of melodic style than factors of structural stability. Phrasing and balance are perhaps less apparent to the listener on a cognitive level, but it is these devices—perceptible on both broad and detailed levels—

---

27. The anacrusis pattern lends to the melodies in which it is applied a rhythmic-metric effect reminiscent of the gavotte.

that most effectively contribute to an impression of solid simplicity. Partitioning these melodies into an overall ternary design whose last section recalls fully or in part the first reinforces the priority of order and balance at the broadest level. Typically, the ternary format of the movement as a whole is echoed at the phrase level within the A sections. Most conform to a simple a + b + a (or a + b + a¹) pattern, although this can be expanded to a + a + b + a (or a + a + b + a¹) or truncated to encompass only a single melodic idea, a + a (or a + a¹). In the romances of two wind partitas (B7 and B27), Rosetti designs both the A and B sections as full rounded-binary forms, a pattern commonly encountered in minuet and trio movements:

a + a + b + a + b + a (or a + a + b + a¹ + b + a¹)

Indeed, in both examples, the B section is termed a "trio," and in B7 this section also assumes a standard convention of such dance forms in featuring paired solo instruments. The *Adagio non tanto* from Rosetti's Concerto for Two Horns in E Major (C58) poses a unique situation. In this movement's A section, the first phrase (a) fails to return at the end of the section, leaving the design open rather than closed. Moreover, the scope of "b" is greater than the norm, with a tutti-solo-tutti exchange apportioned over its three melodic fragments:

a		b		
x	y	x	y	z
		tutti	solo	tutti

Typically, the structure of the first theme (a of A) is laid out as an eight-measure phrase, constructed from two four-measure units that are either contrasting (x + y) or complementary (x + x). Having presented the primary theme, Rosetti's normal procedure at this juncture is to shift the tonality to either the dominant or the relative minor and introduce a new idea (b).[28] This "b" unit generally is less developed than the opening phrase and in some instances has the effect of being a transition between statements of the principal melody. In the concerto literature, Rosetti often takes advantage of this passage to turn the stage over to the ensemble, providing both textural contrast and a much needed

---

28. The Adagio of the Bassoon Concerto in B-flat Major (C74) is the only example among the romances in which there is no contrasting idea within the A section.

opportunity for wind soloists to breathe. A sections tend to conclude in a full or partial repetition of the opening phrase and a strong cadence in the tonic.

Contrast is the primary musical function of the mid section (B) of the design. This point is conveyed in several examples by the abrupt *forte* appearance of a new theme in minor. What then follows has an integrity of its own. While the general lyricism established in A seldom is totally abandoned, the character of the contrasting area often is less simplistic and tuneful than the movement's beginning. Instead, the themes of this passage assume an aura of greater intensity and expressivity. Unlike the neat and balanced melodies of A, here one is more likely to encounter increased flexibility in melodic design and phrasing as well as an increased range of expression. The quasi-declamatory style of the opening gives way to melodies of increased breadth incorporating expressive leaps, chromatic inflection, additional dynamic nuance, variability in phrase structure, and a richer harmonic palette (see Example 2).[29]

In the concerto repertory, the soloist is allowed in these passages a greater degree of technical display—seldom approaching that of the fast movements, but still offering significant contrast within the romance. The tonal stability associated with the opening also becomes compromised in this mid section. In the Keyboard Concerto in G Major (C2), for example, the listener is taken on a rapid tonal excursion that leads through several keys patterned in thirds, until ultimately reaching a cadence on the dominant that prepares the return of the principal theme in the tonic.

A comparison of the opening of the A and B sections in the *Adagio* of the Notturno in D Major (B24) illustrates the contrast in moods frequently found between these parts of the form (see Examples 3a–b). The general melodic type and phrase structure of A matches our earlier description, with the only surprise being the three-measure cadential extension. Instantly, the opening measures of the B section replace this mood of sweet innocence with one of more intense emotion. The somber tones of the cello proclaim a brooding and passionate plea quite divorced from the aesthetic of the opening.

The framing recall of A often is prepared by a short retransition, normally no more than a cadential fragment repeated sequentially as it works its way back

---

29. The stylistic deviation found in the mid sections of Rosetti's romances seldom reach the same degree of contrast heard in the slow-movement romance from Mozart's Piano Concerto in D Minor, K. 466.

Courting the Amorous Muse

Example 2. Two-Horn Concerto in E Major (C58) II: Romanza, mm. 22–35

Example 3a. Notturno in D Major (B24) II: Romance, mm. 1–8

to the tonic and the by-now anticipated reprise of the opening theme. In several works, the repeat of A is exact, mimicking a da capo design, occasionally with a cadenza worked into the final structural unit. In other examples, however, while the parallelism between the framing sections of the design is clear enough, the return of A deviates in some significant manner from its first appearance. In the Larghetto romances of Keyboard Sonata in G Major (E2) and the Keyboard Trio in D Major (D31) the return of A is very brief and instead of coming to a cadential conclusion, links directly with the following movement. More typically, the reprise of A involves a truncating of the internal structure of this section by eliminating one or more of its final phrases. In the Flute Concerto C25 only the final repetition of the opening unit is left out:

Courting the Amorous Muse

```
A                B          A¹         Coda
a     b     a               a    b
```

whereas the cuts in B27 are more extensive:

```
A                         B          A¹         Coda
a     codetta   b    a               a
x     x              x    x          x    x
```

Example 3b. Notturno in D Major (B24) II: Romance, mm. 31–39

Only a few of Rosetti's romances are set in a triple meter, and judging from this group, the adoption of this meter called forth a slightly different interpretation of the genre. Each of these examples begins with themes that—while undeniably lyric and tuneful—are much less straightforward than the melodies associated with common and *alla breve* meters. With some, such as the poignant F-minor romance of the Horn Concerto in F Major (C53), there is a passionate undertone that is decidedly foreign to the usual sweetness of Rosetti's romances (see Example 4).

Example 4: Horn Concerto in F Major (C53) II: Romance, mm. 1–12.

In others, a lighter mood prevails. Such is the case in the *Larghetto* of the Flute Concerto in G Major (C35) and the keyboard Romances in E-flat and B-flat Major (E29 and E35). Both, however, have themes which appear to incorporate greater artifice and imagination than what is commonly encountered in other romances.

The preceding discussion concerns primarily romances that form substantial movements within larger compositions. There are, however a number that are more diminutive in scope. Included among these are the independent keyboard pieces labeled Romance as well as others found in multi-movement chamber works. Much of what has been said also applies to this group, albeit on a more limited scale. Excellent examples of Rosetti's deployment of the romance type within a diminutive compass are found in his two romances for string quartet (D9 and D10). Both movements conform to an ABA structural design, but in these instances the last part of the design includes only the briefest reference to the primary theme. As if to compensate, however, Rosetti appends to both movements an unorthodox cadential passage that contributes increased vigor to the final portion of the design by briefly placing in doubt the integrity of the tonic.

Even such a cursory review as the present demonstrates that Rosetti considered the romance a distinctive musical type and approached the composition of such works with certain preconceived notions of form and style. However, even while working within such a body of conventional gestures, Rosetti was able to instill his own unique fingerprint on many of these compositions, a fact especially apparent in the pieces composed after 1784. For the most part, these personalized stylistic gestures are most perceptible in small details. They are not unique to Rosetti's treatment of the romance, but rather occur in varying degrees of consistency throughout his mature works. For example, Rosetti's tendency to conclude movements or sections of movements with decreasing dynamic levels, sometimes marked *perdendosi*, which occurs time and again in his symphonies of the 1780s, is also encountered in the romance repertory. Likewise, his fondness for inserting within a particular design passages in which the wind instruments are extracted from the full ensemble to function as an independent color group (*Harmonie*) also finds expression in the romances. The use of a pizzicato string accompaniment in both Paris symphonies containing Romance movements (A7 and A20) may well have been intended as an imitation of a mandolin or guitar, which in turn suggests a lover's serenade, itself well within the milieu of the romance.

This brings us to one special remaining example: the *Romanze* from the Symphony in C Major (A9) of 1784. Without question, this is one of Rosetti's most original excursions into the romance topos. It illustrates rather graphically that although committed to the conventional musical language of the romance, Rosetti refused to allow this expectation to restrict his creative powers. Ignoring the established norm, Rosetti has selected a meter of 2/4. The tempo indication, *Andante grazioso* (unique among his orchestral romances), hints at the possibility of a more playful mood than is generally associated with a romance. Although it is cast in the conventional ternary design, the intricacy of construction and subtlety of expression found in this movement set it apart from most of this repertory. The opening melody lacks the anticipated straightforward and simplistic elements. Instead, Rosetti begins with a gracious and courtly theme laid out as a conversation between the violin and cello, leaving the rest of the ensemble to supply the necessary harmonic backdrop. This witty repartee is initiated by the muted violin to which the cello responds in imitation by reversing its pitch direction (see Example 5).

Example 5: Symphony in C major (A9) II: Romanze, mm. 1–8

A shift to minor announces a contrast that creates the mid section in what the listener will soon realize is a tripartite theme. An overriding sense of cohesion is maintained by drawing upon the motive of the first phrase as a building block for the secondary idea. Indeed, Rosetti continues to call upon this somewhat innocuous figure throughout the movement. The formal clarity often encountered in Rosetti's romances is not the case here. Those expecting the A section to be closed and marked off by a firm and conclusive cadence in the tonic will be surprised when A fails to achieves a definitive conclusion, allowing the contrasting material to simply develop out of its remnants. Moreover, the B area has more of the flavor of a development than a contrasting section. In it, Rosetti continues to pursue his preoccupation with the distinctive motive, sounding it repeatedly in a *fortissimo* climactic passage quite out of keeping with the usual tone of a romance. The contrapuntal passage for *Harmonie* that follows is equally difficult to reconcile with the notion of Rosetti's previous romance movements. Although the opening theme returns to initiate the requisite reprise, this last portion of the movement turns out to be a mere shadow of A. Instead of a faithful recall, Rosetti has added more work for the wind instruments and a rather dark aside in the subdominant. The movement is then allowed to conclude with one last wispy *pianissimo* reminder of the opening motive.

There is little in this movement that meshes well with our evolving description of Rosetti's treatment of this genre. To be sure, in the face of the previous discussion, one might well question just what aspect of this movement could have led the composer to label it a romance. Even at the very beginning, the decidedly coquettish quality of the opening theme is clearly at variance with the natural simplicity that defines the romance. Moreover, although the formal structure employed here conforms in its broadest dimensions to what is expected, as it unfolds its clarity is compromised by conflicting thematic and tonal gestures. The lack of conformity to the standardized conventions of form and style in this movement are paralleled in the final movement of the same symphony, which Rosetti labels "Capriccio: Allegro molto." A9 is one of five symphonies from the 1780s to conclude with movements identified with the term "capriccio." The exact meaning of the term in these circumstances remains unclear, but each of these movements is distinguished by an exceptional approach to both form and style.[30] A number of unorthodox structural occurrences in A9 pose exceptions to established convention. While on the surface, the movement appears to conform to a rondo design as custom might dictate in the final movement of a symphony from this time, such a comfortable interpretation is challenged when odd turns of direction and decidedly mixed signals introduce ambiguous gestures into an otherwise predictable context. The appearance within the cycle

---

30. See Sterling E. Murray, "Capriccio Finales in the Symphonies of Antonio Rosetti: Meaning and Significance," in *Genre in Eighteenth-Century Music*, ed. Anthony R. DelDonna (Ann Arbor, MI: Steglein Publishing, 2008), 160–186.

of this non-conventional finale places the anomalies of the preceding romance in a different light. While recognizing this may help justify the irregular procedures uncovered in A9's romance, we are still left begging the question as to why Rosetti would have made these particular decisions. The challenges to anticipated musical conventions observed in both of these movements may simply have been a way for Rosetti to bring greater personal expression to what might have become commonplace musical experiences.

Rosetti's commitment to the romance was exceptional for his day. He probably first encountered the genre in Beecke's music, but its absorption into his own working methods was undeniably solidified through his personal exposure to Parisian musical circles in 1781–1782. But why did his fascination with what could truthfully be dismissed as a popular fad continue to dominate his artistic muse? Although Rosetti is silent on this matter and it is thus impossible for us at our historical perspective to pose any sort of authoritative answer to such a question, certain possible explanations do suggest themselves. The conditions of his employment offer one possibility. As a court composer, Rosetti was obliged to write music to suite the taste of his patron. Prince Kraft Ernst had a deep love for music and a keen interest in French culture. Moreover, Beecke, his chief musical advisor, was equally enamored with the French style and saw to it that the court repertory included music popular in the French capital. Although Rosetti's desire to please his patron may offer a plausible and convenient explanation for his attachment to the romance, perhaps the explanation for his fascination with this topos has a much more practical origin. As a composer with a decided gift for melodic creation, Rosetti may simply have appreciated the slow-movement romance as a natural venue for his innate lyric expression. Moreover, the presence at Wallerstein after 1780 of the Bohemian horn virtuosos Joseph Nagel (1751/52–1802) and Franz Zwierzina (1751–1825) provided Rosetti with opportunity to write concerted music for *Waldhorn*, which perhaps more than any other instrument possessed a timbre uniquely suited to the sort of lyric expression that was the particular domain of the romance. Indeed, the majority of Rosetti's romances are found in his concertos for horn or two horns and orchestra. Part of Rosetti's fondness for the instrumental romance may have been generated by nothing more than his desire to match the mellow and lush quality of the *Waldhorn* with an appropriate vehicle for expression.

Perhaps, however, his intent was less obvious than any of these possibilities. Rosetti's fondness for inserting tuneful and unpretentious movements fashioned as romances within extended orchestral or chamber compositions might be perceived as an expression of bourgeois values within an otherwise aristocratic context—the intertwining and mingling of folk-like naïveté with refined accomplishment. The adulation of that which is natural and ordinary—although viewed from a safe distance—was a basic tenet of eighteenth-century aesthetics. Perhaps the popularity of the instrumental romance rested in part upon its sentimental glorification of that which is ordinary and unaffected.

Mozart's Quintet for Horn and Strings in E-flat Major, K. 407 (386c), in Two Arrangements for *Harmoniemusik* by Joseph Heidenreich

PETER HECKL

The origins of Mozart's Quintet for Horn and Strings, presumably composed in Vienna in 1781 or 1782[1] for the horn player Joseph Ignaz Leutgeb (1732–1811), appear rather complicated, primarily because the autograph was not present among Mozart's estate holdings and by 1847 at the latest had disappeared completely.[2] From the outset, early publications of the piece presented widely differing versions.

Table 1 gives an overview of the early sources of the original instrumentation of the work in chronological order. The Leipzig first edition from

Table 1. Early sources of Mozart's Horn Quintet, K. 386c, original instrumentation

QUINTETTO pour COR VIOLON DEUX ALTO ET BASSE composé par W. A. MOZART, parts. Leipzig: Schmiedt & Rau 1796/1797, pl. nr. 18. (RISM [M 6029)
1st movement: 135 mm., 2nd movement: 113 mm., 3rd movement: 188 mm.

Quintetto von W. A. Mozart, manuscript score, before 1802. Offenbach, André publishing archives (D-OF, M 12523)
1st movement: 120 mm., 2nd movement: 113 mm., 3rd movement: 136 mm.

QUINTETTO pour le Cor Violon, deux Violes et Violoncelle composé par W. A. Mozart, parts. Offenbach: J. André 1802, pl. nr. 1631. (RISM [M 6032)
1st movement: 120 mm., 2nd movement: 113 mm., 3rd movement: 136 mm.

---

1. Ernst Fritz Schmid presumes, as does Alfred Einstein, that the work originates from the last months of 1782; see Ernst Fritz Schmid, Preface to *Wolfgang Amadeus Mozart, Neue Ausgabe sämtlicher Werke* VIII/19/2, ed. Ernst Fritz Schmid (Kassel: Bärenreiter, 1958), vii–xiii, esp. viii. Henrik Wiese and Norbert Müllemann maintain that it is more likely the work originated during 1781 because of the musical parallels to the Rondo for Horn and Orchestra in E-flat major, K. 371, and to the first act of *The Abduction from the Seraglio*, K. 384, both from 1781; see Henrik Wiese and Norbert Müllemann, eds., *Wolfgang Amadeus Mozart, Hornquintett Es-Dur KV 407 (386c): Study Score* (Munich: Henle, 2010), ii–iii (hereafter Wiese and Müllemann, *Mozart Hornquintet*).

2. See E. F. Schmid, Preface, viii, and Manfred Hermann Schmid, *Kritischer Bericht* in *Wolfgang Amadeus Mozart, Neue Ausgabe sämtlicher Werke: Kritische Berichte* VIII/19/2, ed. Manfred Hermann Schmid (Kassel: Bärenreiter, 2007), 9–57, esp. 11.

Harmoniemusik Arrangements of K. 407 by Heidenreich

1796/1797[3] served as the main source for the *Neue Mozart Ausgabe* and of the recently issued *Urtext* Edition.[4] It offers the most extensive notational material compared to the André edition, which, in the first movement, contains fifteen fewer bars and in the third movement all of fifty-two fewer bars. The *Neue Mozart Ausgabe* sticks to the André printing only with regard to the articulation of the theme in the third movement. A few bars of the second movement diverging from the melodic line or from the rhythm found in the first edition are acknowledged and given a footnote in the *Neue Mozart Ausgabe*. The manuscript score from the André publishing archives is the template for the printed parts from 1802. Manfred Hermann Schmid proposes that this score originates from a transcript of the work that Constanze Mozart had ordered up from Leutgeb's copy. Henrik Wiese and Norbert Müllemann maintain the improbability of this supposition, based on the cuts in the music.[5]

Constanze does indeed mention the Horn Quintet several times in her correspondence with the publisher Johann Anton André. On 31 May 1800 she reports of Joseph Leutgeb being in possession of a copy of the work, whose original Constanze at the time wrongly supposes to be in André's hands.[6] In a letter to André dated 26 November 1800 she offers "to send a transcript copy of the utmost authenticity, just like Leutgeb's own copy, which he gave to me. . . . An authentic copy of the Quintet, the one you enquired about, given to me by Leutgeb in his own copy, who himself got it from Mozart."[7] The copy was indeed sent off on 26 January 1801[8] and on 4 March 1801 Constanze notes that

---

3. Manfred Hermann Schmid dates the print from Schmiedt & Rau to approximately 1796; see M. H. Schmid, *Kritischer Bericht*, 11. In fact, the publication was first advertised in June 1797; see Gertraut Haberkamp, *Die Erstdrucke der Werke von Wolfgang Amadeus Mozart: Bibliographie, Textband* (Tutzing: Hans Schneider, 1986), 194.

4. Wiese and Müllemann, *Mozart Hornquintet*.

5. See M. H. Schmid, *Kritischer Bericht*, 13, and Wiese and Müllemann, *Mozart Hornquintet*, 16–25, esp. 16 and 21.

6. See Wilhelm A. Bauer and Otto Erich Deutsch, eds., *Mozart: Briefe und Aufzeichnungen* IV (Kassel: Bärenreiter, 1963), 358.

7. "eine höchstauthentische Abschrift zu senden, so wie Leitgeb mir sie in seinem eignen Exemplar gegeben hat. . . . Authentische Copie vom Quintett, wornach [sic] Sie fragen, so wie ich sie von Leitgeb in seinem eignen Exemplar bekommen habe, der sie von Mozart hatte," Bauer and Deutsch, *Mozart* IV, 388–389.

8. See Bauer and Deutsch, *Mozart* IV, 395.

André already had the Horn Quintet in his possession.[9] On 3 April 1802 she thanks the publisher for sending the printed edition but asks why it lacked an endorsement note stating "that it was taken from the manuscript."[10]

If Constanze Mozart's information is correct, then she provided André with a transcript of Joseph Leutgeb's copy, which derived directly from the Mozart autograph. The result was a printed edition that, compared to the Leipzig first edition and all arrangements to be examined here, was also the most significantly abridged. Assuming therefore that the André edition is not "of the utmost authenticity," the question is where, along the way between Leutgeb, Constanze Mozart and André, did the Horn Quintet lose these bars? Or is it perhaps possible that the template from the André publishing archives was not actually based on the transcript from Leutgeb's copy that Constanze sent? The lack of a reference stating "from the manuscript" can, at any rate, be an indication that André was aware of the modifications.

Mozart's Horn Quintet was in circulation not only in its original instrumentation, but also in transcriptions for other instrumental ensembles from very early on. Two arrangements for string quintet are to be mentioned, beginning with an anonymous arrangement for violin, two violas, and two cellos that appeared in Vienna in 1799 or 1800 from Artaria & Co.[11] The horn part in it is given to the first cello; the first movement is five bars shorter than the first edition of the original instrumentation and what was originally a three-movement work is now expanded to four with the addition of an arrangement of the second minuet from the Wind Serenade in E-flat major, K. 375. Franz Anton Hoffmeister's version—for two violins, two violas, and cello, published in Vienna and in Leipzig in 1801 or 1802[12]—retains the original three-movement plan, but drops two bars from the finale movement. The horn part, in many instances varied and ornamented, is distributed throughout the first violin, first viola and cello parts.

The work was also arranged for two different *Harmoniemusik* instrumentations. The 1804 publication of an anonymous version for two clarinets, two

---

9. Ibid., 401.

10. "daß es nach dem Manuscript ist," Ibid., 416.

11. M. H. Schmid, *Kritischer Bericht*, 9, gives the date as 1800; Wiese and Müllemann, *Mozart Hornquintet*, 16 and 21, give the date as 1799.

12. M. H. Schmid, *Kritischer Bericht*, 9, gives the date as 1802; Wiese and Müllemann, *Mozart Hornquintet*, 16 and 21, give the date as 1801.

horns, and two bassoons from Breitkopf & Härtel in Leipzig[13] (Figure 1) shortens the first movement by six bars and for the third movement inserts an arrangement of the second minuet from the String Trio in E-flat major, K. 563. A manuscript copy of this arrangement is found in the archives of the Benedictine monastery Rajhrad in Moravia, Czech Republic (CZ-R), whereby the third movement in this case is once again the second minuet of the Serenade in E-flat major, K. 375, this time in a rearranged version (Figure 2). In addition there is a version for two oboes, two clarinets, two horns, and two bassoons that is found in the Princely Music Archives Esterházy in Eisenstadt (A-Ee), which also bears the name of the arranger: Giuseppe, that is to say, Joseph Heidenreich (Figure 3). And just like the sextet versions, this arrangement, too, is missing six bars from the first movement; and for the third movement the minuet from the Serenade, K. 375, reappears, this time in a rearranged version.

Joseph Heidenreich customarily advertised his compositions and arrangements in the newspaper *Wiener Zeitung*. On 30 April 1794, for example, under the headline "New Pieces of Music" one could "order brand new from Joseph Heidenreich: ... a quintet from Mozart, set as six- and eight-part *Harmoniemusik*."[14] Taking into consideration the current state of knowledge, this description can refer only to Mozart's Horn Quintet; in any case no *Harmoniemusik* arrangement from Heidenreich's pen of any other Mozart quintet is extant. The identity of the eight-part version can be traced to the Parthia, in Eisenstadt, but where is the six-part version to be found?

A comparison of Heidenreich's octet version with the two anonymous adaptations for six winds reveals one melodic detail, found only in m. 109 of the first movement (m. 114 in the original), that significantly differentiates the sextet versions (not, however, the octet version) from all other early sources. On the other hand, there are about twenty instances where both *Harmoniemusik* arrangements diverge identically from the other sources, namely with regard to melodic line, harmony, rhythm, cut measures, tempo markings, and repeti-

---

13. The publication was first advertised in the *Allgemeine musikalische Zeitung, Intelligenzblatt Nr. IV* (December 1804); see Gertraut Haberkamp, "Anzeigen und Rezensionen von Mozart-Drucken in Zeitungen und Zeitschriften I," in *Mozart Studien* 1, ed. Manfred Hermann Schmid (Tutzing: Schneider 1992), 195–256, esp. 226.

14. "Neue Musikalien. Bey Joseph Heidenreich . . . sind ganz neu zu bestellen: . . . Ein Quintett von Mozard [sic], in 6= und 8stimmige Harmonie gesetzt," *Wiener Zeitung* (30 April 1794), 1295.

tions of particular segments. An examination of a few of these divergences and the possible inferences drawn from them follows. But even by this point we can confidently assume a Heidenreich authorship of the six-wind version as well. Moreover, Heidenreich's arrangement must have provided the basis for the Breitkopf & Härtel publication, at the least.

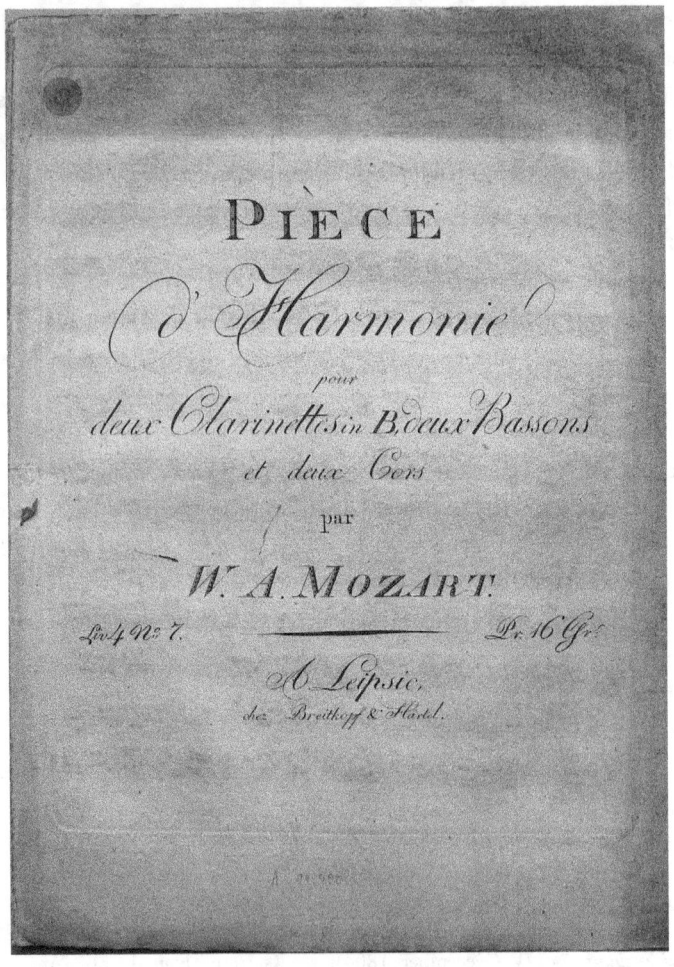

Figure 1. W. A. Mozart, Horn Quintet, K. 386c,
arrangement for six-part *Harmoniemusik*, Breitkopf & Härtel printing,
frontispiece (Brno, Czech Republic, Moravské zemské muzeum,
oddelení dejin hudby; shelfmark: A. 19.490)

Harmoniemusik Arrangements of K. 407 by Heidenreich

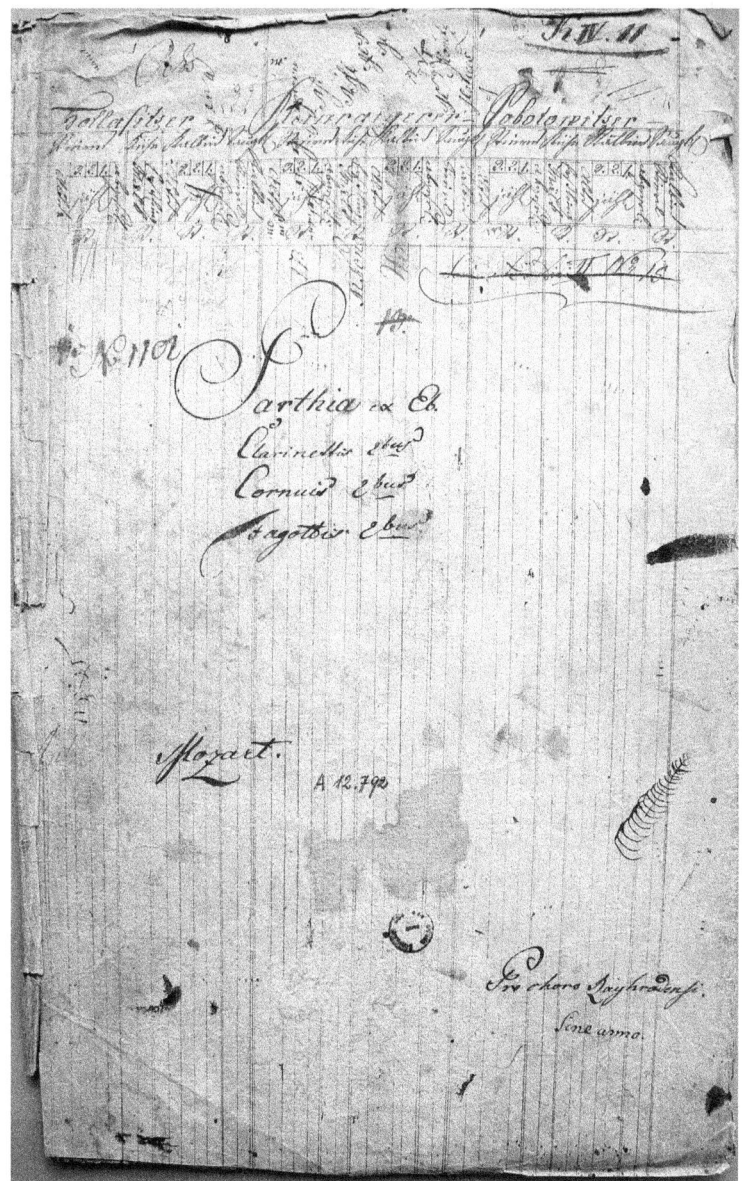

Figure 2. W. A. Mozart, Horn Quintet, K. 386c, arrangement for six-part *Harmoniemusik*, anonymous manuscript, front jacket (Brno, Czech Republic, Moravské zemské muzeum, oddelení dejin hudby; shelfmark: A. 12.792)

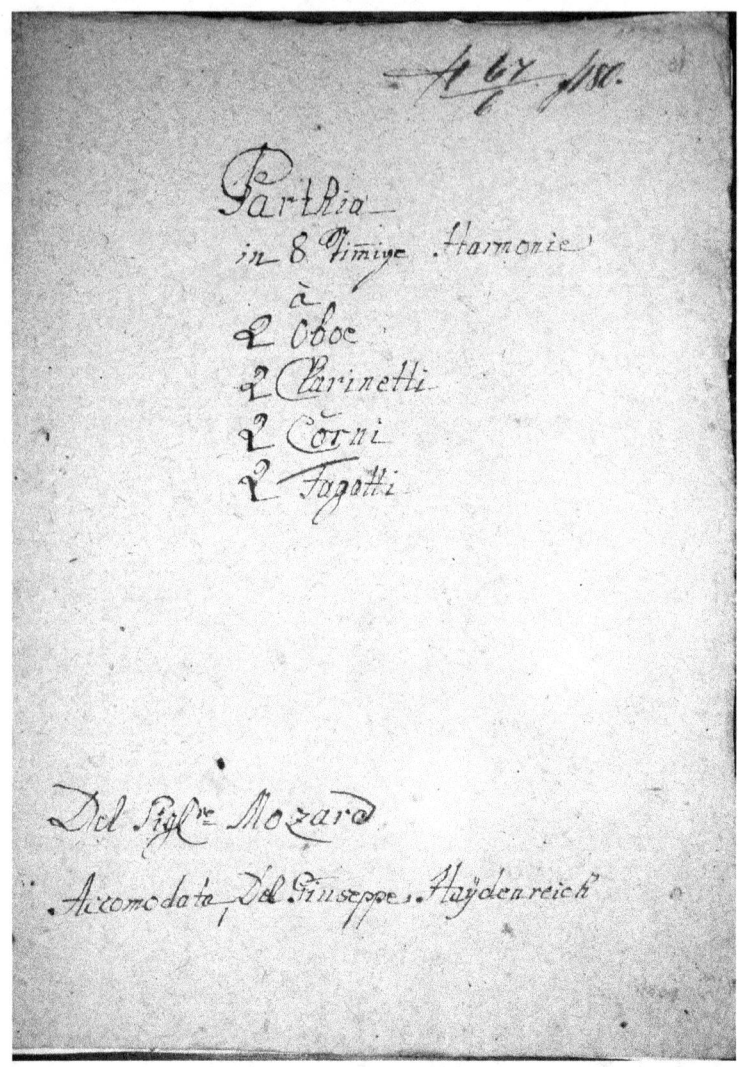

Figure 3. W. A. Mozart, Horn Quintet, K. 386c, arrangement for eight-part *Harmoniemusik* by Joseph Heidenreich, manuscript, front jacket (Eisenstadt, Fürstlich Esterházysches Musikarchiv; shelfmark: Mus. 1133)

But why would two different minuets need to be inserted into the wind versions, when there are so many corresponding points already established between them? The Serenade, K. 375, from which the minuet for the eight-part

Harmoniemusik Arrangements of K. 407 by Heidenreich

version is derived, was, after all, initially written by Mozart himself for pairs of clarinets, horns, and bassoons and then later expanded to an octet with the addition of two oboes. Therefore, a minuet from this work, even in its original guise, could have been used in both of the *Harmoniemusik* treatments. Heidenreich probably did indeed insert the K. 375 minuet into his sextet arrangement, but Breitkopf & Härtel published the Serenade, K. 375, in precisely this six-wind version only a few months before bringing out the arrangement of the Horn Quintet—at any rate in 1804 as well.[15] Corralling the same minuet into a second composition, and right on the heels of the first, would have meant testing the customers' good will, to say the least, and so the minuet in question was passed over in favor of a transcription of a minuet from the String Trio, K. 563. The clearly inferior quality of this arrangement, however, argues against any involvement on Heidenreich's part.

The manuscript from Rajhrad corresponds in its first, second, and fourth movements so closely to the Breitkopf & Härtel edition that it can be considered a copy—but the K. 375 minuet is once again pressed into service. Perhaps the parts for this minuet were not available at the time and the transcriber had to resort to reconstructing the movement from memory. This would explain not only the numerous structural and harmonic differences from the original minuet but also, and above all, the erroneous use of the dominant key in the Trio (B-flat major), instead of Mozart's choice, the subdominant A-flat major, which consequently forces a complete change in instrumentation.

We can therefore assume that Joseph Heidenreich brought out the Mozart Horn Quintet in two *Harmoniemusik* arrangements as early as 1794. These arrangements are therefore the oldest surviving and hitherto completely disregarded sources for this work. Consequently these arrangements have been entered into the list of early arrangements of Mozart's Horn Quintet, shown in Table 2.

The almost complete scarcity of recent literary references to Joseph Heidenreich is relieved only by Otto Erich Deutsch, who describes him as a "composer of modest skills and a prolific arranger of operas for Harmoniemusik."[16]

---

15. *Pièce d'Harmonie pour deux Clarinettes in B, deux Bassons et deux Cors par W.A. Mozart. Liv. 3, No. 6*, parts (Leipzig: Breitkopf & Härtel, 1804), pl. nr. 202. (RISM M5892).

16. "ein bescheidener Komponist und fruchtbarer Arrangeur von Opern für Harmonie-Musik," Otto Erich Deutsch, *Mozart: Die Dokumente seines Lebens, Wolfgang Amadeus Mozart, Neue Ausgabe sämtlicher Werke* X/34 (Kassel: Bärenreiter, 1961), 278.

Table 2. Early sources of Mozart's Horn Quintet, K. 386c, arrangements

Parthia in 8stimmige Harmonie à 2 Oboe 2 Clarinetti 2 Corni 2 Fagotti Del Sigre Mozard Accomodata Del Giuseppe Haydenreich, manuscript parts, Vienna 1794. Eisenstadt, Princely Music Archives Esterházy (A-Ee: Mus. 1133). A rearranged version of the 2nd minuet from the Serenade in E-flat major, K. 375, is inserted as the 3rd movement. 1st movement: 129 mm., 2nd movement: 113 mm., 4th movement: 188 mm.

Grand QUINTETTO per due Violini due Viole e Violoncello [recte: per Violino due Viole e due Violoncelli] del SIG. MOZART No 8, parts. Vienna: Artaria & Co. 1799/1800, pl. nr. 852. (RISM [M 6030 and 6073). An arrangement of the 2nd minuet from the Serenade in E-flat major, K. 375, is inserted as the 3rd movement. 1st movement: 130 mm., 2nd movement: 113 mm., 4th movement: 188 mm.

QUINTETTO Pour Deux Violons, 2 Alto et Violoncelle composé PAR W. A. MOZART. Arrangé par F. A. Hoffmeister d'un Quintetto pour Cor, Violon, 2 Alto et Violoncelle. No 1, parts. Vienna: Hoffmeister & Co. and Leipzig: Bureau de Musique 1801/1802, pl. nr. 7. (RISM [M 6076). 1st movement: 135 mm., 2nd movement: 113 mm., 3rd movement: 186 mm.

PIÈCE d'Harmonie pour deux Clarinettes in B, deux Bassons et deux Cors par W. A. Mozart. Liv. 4 No 7, parts. Leipzig: Breitkopf & Härtel 1804, pl. nr. 285. (RISM [M 6079). An arrangement of the 2nd minuet from the String Trio in E-flat major, K. 563, is inserted as the 3rd movement. 1st movement: 129 mm., 2nd movement: 113 mm., 4th movement: 188 mm. This publication was based on Heidenreich's 1794 arrangement.

Parthia ex Eb. Clarinettis 2bus Cornuis 2bus Fagottis 2bus. Mozart. Pro choro Rayhradensi. Sine anno, manuscript parts, undated. Archives of the Benedictine monastery Rajhrad in Moravia, Czech Republic (CZ-R: A.12.792). A rearranged version of the 2nd minuet from the Serenade in E-flat major, K. 375, is inserted as the 3rd movement. 1st movement: 129 mm., 2nd movement: 113 mm., 4th movement: 188 mm. 1st, 2nd and 4th movements: transcripts of the Breitkopf & Härtel edition.

Heidenreich's most well-known *Harmoniemusik* arrangement is, after all, his setting of Mozart's *Die Zauberflöte*. Deutsch lists his dates as 1753–1821.[17] Heidenreich was in fact born between 1751 and 1753 in Austrian Silesia, a region that is now part of the Czech Republic, located near the Polish border. The

---

17. See Deutsch, *Mozart*, 383.

Harmoniemusik Arrangements of K. 407 by Heidenreich

information on his birth year differs among the documents made available to me, and unfortunately, research still yields no evidence of his birth certificate.[18] When Heidenreich offered his music for sale in the *Wiener Zeitung* he always listed his home address in the advertisements so that prospective customers could contact him directly. Based on this information, Heidenreich lived from 1788 at the latest until the end of his life in Leopoldstadt, one of the outer districts of Vienna. This certainly had to do with his main profession: he was a violist in the Leopoldstadt Theater orchestra.

Johann Ferdinand von Schönfeld's *Music Yearbook for Vienna and Prague from 1796* (Figure 4) lists Heidenreich's name among the orchestra members of this theater,[19] which had a repertory composed of plays (especially popular was the Punch-like character "Kasperl"), productions of fairy-tale pieces with song, musical comedies or *Singspiele*, and operas, for example those by Florian Leopold Gassmann, Antonio Salieri, Carl Ditters von Dittersdorf, Giovanni Paisiello, Vicente Martín y Soler, Giuseppe Sarti, and Christoph Willibald Gluck.[20] A "Mr. Heidenreich" is named as a second flutist in this orchestra in 1814.[21] This is probably a reference to Joseph's son Georg; if not, then perhaps Joseph Heidenreich had later managed to switch from viola to flute. Figure 5 shows an interior view of the Leopoldstadt Theater from the 1780s, around the time Joseph Heidenreich began working in its orchestra pit located in the lower left-hand edge of the engraving. Figure 6 presents an exterior view of the theater from 1820, from around the time of his death.

According to the 1793 *Lexicon of Viennese Artists and Writers*, Heidenreich is "highly notable for his settings of larger works of other masters—operas, ora-

---

18. According to the coroner's report on 2 January 1821 (*Wiener Stadt- und Landesarchiv*: Vol. 148 *Todtenprotokoll* 1821 A-H, letter H, p. 1r) Heidenreich was born in Weidenau, today's Vidnava, Czech Republic, and was sixty-eight at the time of his death, which results in a birth year of either 1752 or 1753. Heidenreich's conscription papers from 1805 (*Wiener Stadt- und Landesarchiv*: 1.1.8.A102/1—*Konskriptionsbogen Leopoldstadt* | 1805–1856 Nr. 466, p. 466/1) list the birth year as 1751.

19. See Johann Ferdinand von Schönfeld, *Jahrbuch der Tonkunst von Wien und Prag* (Vienna: Von Schönfeldischer Verlag, 1796; facsimile reprint, Munich and Salzburg: Katzbichler, 1976), 95.

20. See Rudolph Angermüller, *Wenzel Müller und "sein" Leopoldstädter Theater: Mit besonderer Berücksichtigung der Tagebücher Wenzel Müllers* (Vienna: 2009), passim.

21. See *Theatralisches Taschenbuch zur geselligen Unterhaltung vom K.K. priv. Theater in der Leopoldstadt* (Vienna: [1814]), 8.

XIII.

Orchester, bei marinellischen Theater, in der Leopoldstadt.

Kapellmeister: Hr. Müller.
Direktor bei der Violin: Hr. Kauer.

Violin 1mo.
Hr. Franz Kleschnitzky.
— Franz Blumberger.
— Bas. Bosdanovich.

Violin 2do.
Hr. Johann Benschka.
— Leopold Segner.
— Franz Zierer.

Bratschen.
Hr. Georg Schreiner.
— Jos. Haidenreich.

Violoncello.
Hr. Joseph Michler.

Violon.
Hr. Michael Perschel.
— Georg Böck.

Oboe.
Hr. Alois Spoibelle.
— Andreas Martin.

Fagott.
Hr. Christoph Sartori.
— Joseph Münzberg.

Horn.
Hr. Joseph Schubert.
— Johann Hollreder.

Klarinett.
Hr. Ignaz Bräuer.
— Friedrich Scholl.

Flaute.
Hr. Niklas Ruprecht.
— Karl Scholl.

Trompete,
Hr. Paul Zimmermann.
— Weidinger.

Paucker.
Hr. Ignaz Kicker.

Figure 4. Johann Ferdinand von Schönfeld, *Jahrbuch der Tonkunst von Wien und Prag*, Vienna, 1796 (facsimile reprint, Munich and Salzburg, 1976), p. 95

Harmoniemusik Arrangements of K. 407 by Heidenreich

Figure 5. Leopoldstadt Theater, longitudinal interior view, after 1781 (Austrian National Library, Bildarchiv; shelfmark: NB 606.324 B)

torios, and so on—in *Harmonie* and a quatro."[22] Heidenreich's occupation as arranger for wind as well as for string ensembles is confirmed by his advertisements in the *Wiener Zeitung* and by works of his preserved in the Music Collection of the Austrian National Library (A-Wn). Original compositions are also found in this collection; they consist mainly of dances for orchestra and for piano. His Mass in B-flat major survives in the music archives of the St. Leopold parish church in Vienna.

Heidenreich also composed for the theater and for the concert hall: his ballet/comic pantomime, *Die eifersüchtige Ehefrau*, or *La moglia* (sic) *gelosa* (The Jealous Wife) was performed in 1795 in the Josefstadt Theater[23] and in 1813 in

---

22. "Er machte sich vorzüglich dadurch bekannt, daß er grössere Werke anderer Meister, als: Opern, Oratorien u.s.f. sehr glücklich auf Harmonie und a Quatro übersetzet," *Wiener Schriftsteller und Künstler Lexikon oder alphabetisches Verzeichniß aller gegenwärtig in Wien lebender Schriftsteller, Künstler und Künstlerinnen mit der Angabe ihrer Namen, Stände und Werke: Gesammelt und herausgegeben von einer Gesellschaft ihrer Freunde* (Vienna: Franz Joseph von Reillyscher Verlag, 1793), 55.

23. See Peter Tomek, "Die Musik an den Wiener Vorstadttheatern 1776–1825: Theatermusik und Zeitgeist. Eine Bestandsaufnahme" (PhD diss., University of Vienna, 1989), 207 and 434.

Figure 6. Leopoldstadt Theater, frontal view, engraving by Cohn, ca. 1820 (Austrian National Library, Bildarchiv; shelfmark: LW 74.919-C)

the Leopoldstadt Theater.[24] On 8 September 1798, in the Leopoldstadt Theater, Heidenreich gave "a grand musical academy with more than seventy musicians" entitled *Das Kriegslager, oder die Schlacht* (The Encampment, or the Battle). This concert had been already previously performed "with acclaim before the most high imperial court."[25]

Heidenreich advertised not only his compositions and arrangements in the *Wiener Zeitung*, but his services as a teacher as well. In fact, the name of one of his pupils is known: Gottlob Leopold Immanuel Schefer (1784–1862), a writer and composer from Muskau in Saxony, paternally related to a family from Silesia, who studied composition with Antonio Salieri and Joseph Heidenreich in 1816.[26]

---

24. See Franz Hadamowsky, *Das Theater in der Wiener Leopoldstadt 1781–1860: Bibliotheks- und Archivbestände in der Theatersammlung der Nationalbibliothek* (Vienna, 1934), 124.

25. "eine grosse musikalische Akademie von mehr als 70 Tonkünstlern ... vor dem allerhöchsten Hofe mit Beyfall," concert announcement in the *Wiener Zeitung* (25 August 1798), 2593.

26. See Helmut Scheunchen, "Schefer, Gottlob Leopold Immanuel," in *Schlesisches Musiklexikon*, ed. Lothar Hoffmann-Erbrecht (Augsburg: Wißner, 2001), 654.

Harmoniemusik Arrangements of K. 407 by Heidenreich

On 2 January 1821, a nearly destitute Heidenreich died of gangrene in the Barmherzigen Brüder hospital in Leopoldstadt. His meager belongings were auctioned off and those proceeds just barely covered hospital and burial costs. His music was sent to his son Georg, a piano teacher (Klaviermeister) in Rzeszów, at that time in the Habsburg-Austrian kingdom of Galicia, in today's Poland.[27] A search for a Heidenreich estate is therefore unfortunately not very promising.

Even if Deutsch assigns Heidenreich to the also-rans among Vienna's musicians and composers, there is nevertheless no denying that he cuts a solid figure as a multi-talented old hand. His arrangements are not only the oldest surviving sources of Mozart's Horn Quintet, they are, like the original, "made in Vienna" and it can be presumed that Heidenreich would have used authentic copies for these arrangements.

As pointed out above, both of the *Harmoniemusik* versions of Mozart's Horn Quintet correspond very well in their musical substance. Significant differences emerge in Heidenreich's manner of distributing the solo horn part throughout the instruments of the ensembles. In the sextet version the solo part remains primarily in both of the horns, alternating on the solo. The first clarinet and the first bassoon do also take part, but in comparatively few solo passages.

Example 1 shows the original horn part in the exposition of the first movement. The solo passages played by the clarinet in the sextet arrangement are underlined; the remaining material is divided between the two horns. In the original instrumentation the natural horn, with its tonal limitations—and sophisticated and virtuosic hand-stopping techniques notwithstanding—is up against four stringed instruments having an entire chromatic range at their disposal. In a wind sextet only the agile woodwinds could maneuver around the demands of idiomatic string-writing, and Heidenreich would have consequently transferred the string work to them and left the solo part in the horns in his arrangement. The result is a sextet version that still gives the impression of being a composition for solo horn.

The hierarchy changes in the octet arrangement: oboes now join the clarinets as a further descant pair of instruments and the number of chromatic woodwind instruments expands to six. If six woodwinds had stuck to the four

---

27. See Heidenreich's estate protocol (*Wiener Stadt- und Landesarchiv*: 1.2.3.2.A2 – *Faszikel 2 – Verlassenschaftsabhandlungen* | 1783–1850 2469/1821).

Example 1. W. A. Mozart, Horn Quintet, K. 386c, 1st mvt, exposition. Distribution of the original horn part in the six-part *Harmoniemusik* version

Harmoniemusik Arrangements of K. 407 by Heidenreich

original string parts, the players would have been downright underemployed. Heidenreich therefore logically lets them join in on the solo part to an accordingly greater degree. In Example 2, which shows how the horn part has been partitioned in the exposition of first movement of the octet arrangement, the oboe part is marked by a dotted underline, the bassoon part by a wavy underline. The clarinet part remains marked by a single underline. It is clear that the major part of the original horn solo has wandered to the woodwind instruments, chiefly to the clarinets. This is made possible by transferring parts of the clarinet work in the sextet version—mostly the violin and high viola writing—to the oboes. The octet arrangement therefore no longer maintains the character of a piece for concert horn, but rather that of *Harmoniemusik*: an ensemble piece.

To what extent are Heidenreich's arrangements helpful in the reconstruction of the original Mozart Horn Quintet? For this purpose Examples 3 through 5 present three passages from the slow movement, each submitted in four versions: in the first printing of the original instrumentation, which corresponds to the *Neue Mozart Ausgabe* text; in the printing of Johann André; in the anonymous arrangement for string quintet from Artaria, with the original horn part in the first cello; and in the version for six winds from the Breitkopf & Härtel edition, where Heidenreich's arrangement is presumably found. For reasons of space, the octet version has been left out, but it conforms to the sextet version with regard to the details in question.

Example 3 shows how the rhythm in the horn, first viola, and bass parts in mm. 25–27 differs in the first printing from the other versions. The relevant measures are enclosed in boxes. The fact that the downward scale begins on the third beat of the measure in the *Harmoniemusik* arrangements, the André printing, and the string quintet version, would argue against the version in the first printing. In the print template of the André edition the first viola and cello parts in mm. 26 and 27 were, by the way, originally rhythmically annotated like the corresponding spots in the arrangements; the third beat of the measure was corrected in both cases to four thirty-second notes just before going to print. Does the first printing in fact stick to Mozart's intention—on the one hand adhering rhythmically to the numerous parallel passages in the second movement, but allowing, on the other hand, the harsh dissonance of f' (first viola) against e' (second viola) on the third beat of m. 26—or did Mozart himself smooth out this dissonance by altering the rhythm? This first-edition writing appears highly questionable in light of the *Harmoniemusik* versions. The version in the André

SECM in Brooklyn 2010

Example 2. W. A. Mozart, Horn Quintet, K. 386c, 1st mvt, exposition.
Distribution of the original horn part in the eight-part *Harmoniemusik* version

Harmoniemusik Arrangements of K. 407 by Heidenreich

Example 3. W. A. Mozart, Horn Quintet, K. 386c, 2nd mvt, mm. 23–28

Schmiedt & Rau

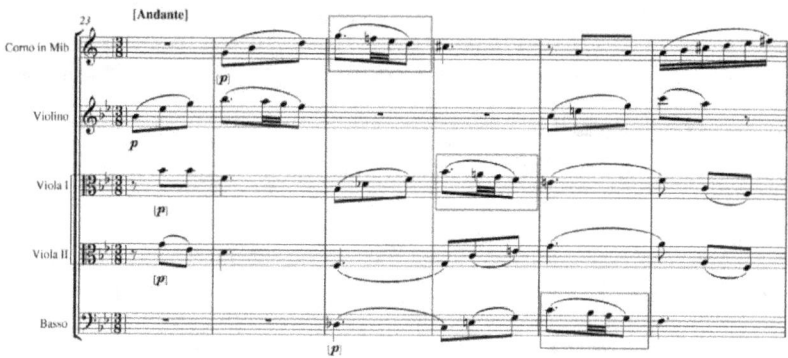

André

String Quintet, Artaria & Co.

Example 3 continued

Harmoniemusik à 6, Heidenreich

printing receives a footnote in the *Neue Mozart Ausgabe*; however the version in the print template and in the arrangements with thirty-second-note triplets seems to stay closer to the Mozart original.

Less convincing, however, are the wind versions when it comes to a voice-leading segment, presented in Example 4. In the passage enclosed in boxes in m. 38, the violin part in the first printing passes from d" down to c" in m. 39 by way of d-flat". In the André edition the pitches in m. 38 are switched: the direction is d-flat"-d"-c". The dissonance created by the d-flat" against the d in the second viola is worth noting. It finally resolves on the third beat of the bar with the d" in the violin. The string quintet arrangement matches the version in the first printing; the *Harmoniemusik* arrangements correspond to that of the André printing, without, however, the dissonance: m. 39 begins clearly in B-flat minor. The passage enclosed in boxes in m. 39 varies rhythmically in the wind versions from the original horn part, but this is most likely due to an error on the part of the arranger because the dominant C7 is followed by an unsatisfactory and fleeting III chord on the third beat, instead of making a solid perfect cadence to F-major, as it does in all other versions.

Harmoniemusik Arrangements of K. 407 by Heidenreich

Example 4. W. A. Mozart, Horn Quintet, K. 386c, 2nd mvt, mm. 36–41

Schmiedt & Rau

André

String Quintet, Artaria & Co.

Example 4 continued

Harmoniemusik à 6, Heidenreich

Example 5 concerns the horn-writing in mm. 60–63, enclosed in the larger boxes. In contrast to the first printing, where the upward jump reaches only the written c"—a sounding e-flat'—the melody in all of the other versions leaps an octave higher, to the sounding e-flat". The *Harmoniemusik* settings therefore argue clearly in favor of this high e-flat. That said, a comparison of the thirty-second-note passage in m. 61 to the sixteenth-note movement found in all other versions probably should not be treated with undue significance. Even if it is impossible to pigeonhole these jumps in mm. 61 and 62 (is it first an octave, then two; or is it the other way around?) then the wind-arrangement writing straight from mm. 60 and 61 would argue in favor of the version from the André printing.[28] On the other hand, mm. 64–66 of the Heidenreich arrangements contain harmonic variations (enclosed in smaller boxes) that do not exactly bear the seal of authenticity: first of all, the melodic alterations in mm. 64 and 65, found in all other versions, are missing; and secondly, Heidenreich reaches F major already in m. 66, at which point the other versions are still in F minor, landing

---

28. Henrik Wiese and Norbert Müllemann arrive at the same conclusion but for different reasons and with no knowledge of Heidenreich's arrangements: they consider the version in the first printing a simplification and therefore presumably not authentic. See Wiese and Müllemann, *Mozart Hornquintet*, 19 and 23.

Harmoniemusik Arrangements of K. 407 by Heidenreich

Example 5. W. A. Mozart, Horn Quintet, K. 386c, 2nd mvt, mm. 60–67

Schmiedt & Rau

André

String Quintet, Artaria & Co.

Example 5 continued

Harmoniemusik à 6, Heidenreich

then in F major in m. 67 by way of an augmented sixth chord over a pedal point F on the third beat of m. 66.

In conclusion, more detailed research and comparisons are necessary in order to make any assertions on correlations between the various sources and to thereby hopefully be better able to assess their origins, paths, and authenticity.[29] But the significance of Joseph Heidenreich's arrangements goes beyond their value as sources for Mozart's original composition: they deserve to be heard and to be perceived in their respective instrumentation and conception as convincing pieces of *Harmoniemusik*. They invite the supposition that turning to wind arrangements as sources generally merits closer scrutiny than has been the practice up to now, and that even in other cases interesting light can be shed on an original work from the vantage-point of a *Harmoniemusik* arrangement.

(TRANSLATION: TIM PURCELL)

---

29. In this context we will have to take notice of a further arrangement for string quartet, found in the Music Collection of the Austrian National Library (A-Wn: Mus. Hs. 11475 Mus), which I only recently examined. These hand-written parts, originally from the private collection of Emperor Franz II (I), lack any attribution of an arranger's name but do bear the initials "NH" on the title page (those of the arranger or the copyist?) as well as the year 1794. The arrangement draws several parallels to Heidenreich's wind versions.

Musical Landskips: Scottish Songbooks in English Drawing Rooms

Paul F. Moulton

During the eighteenth century British songbooks proliferated, and Scottish songbooks were central to this phenomenon. Of particular interest is the puzzling English attraction to Scottish songs, especially considering the history of conflict between both nations. To expose this paradox I will provide a quantitative overview of the output of Scottish songbooks. Then I will address the English attraction and illuminate the function of this domestic music, in the process shedding some light on the way music creates a sonic representation of place.

Songbook Production

The first books containing Scottish songs appeared in the latter half of the seventeenth century, published not in Scotland but in England.[1] John Playford included Scottish tunes in his English Dancing Master (1650) and several subsequent publications. Other English musicians, including Henry Playford and Henry Purcell, soon produced their own books containing "Scotch songs."[2] Scottish musicians and entrepreneurs eventually began publishing their own collections, although many continued to market their books to the English. Over the course of the eighteenth century the output of Scottish songbooks would increase. (See Figure 1, which graphs the initial printings of books).

Songbook production was fairly minimal during the first decades of the eighteenth century, but beginning in the 1730s the number of publications increased from an average of two books per decade to a peak of seventeen books in the 1780s. It dropped to thirteen during the last decade of the century, and by the middle of the nineteenth century had tapered back considerably. A review of the books also reveals a fairly equal distribution of publications in and out of Scotland. This balanced production shifted after the turn of the nineteenth

---

1. Roger Fiske observed that the English were so intrigued with Scottish, Irish, and Italian songs that their own native songs were neglected. See Fiske, *Scotland in Music: A European Enthusiasm* (Cambridge: Cambridge University Press, 1983), 79.
2. For a complete list of songbooks, see Paul F. Moulton, "Imagining Scotland in Music: Place, Audience, and Attraction" (PhD diss., Florida State University, 2008), appendix A.

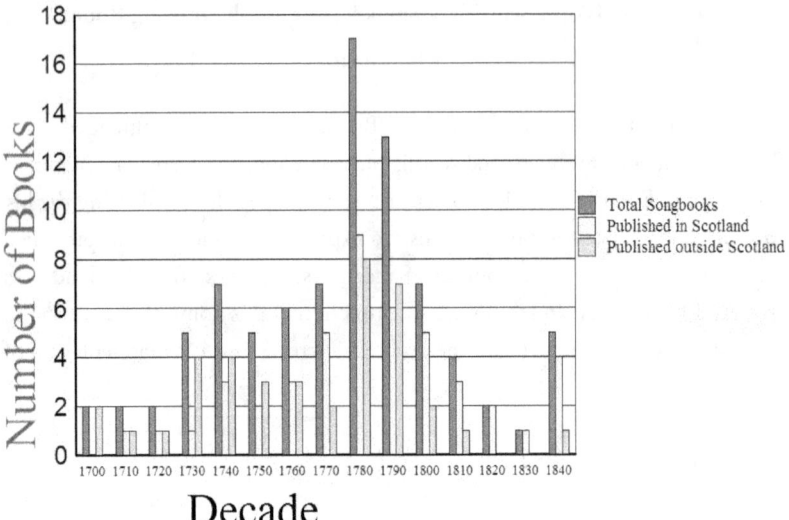

Figure 1. Scottish songbook production, 1700–1850

century; Scotland's interest in its own music understandably remained fairly steady, while the English penchant for native Scottish music declined. To better understand this eighteenth-century phenomenon let me highlight four particularly influential songbooks.

Allan Ramsay's (1684–1758) highly influential *The Tea-Table Miscellany* appeared in Edinburgh in 1724 and in London soon thereafter.[3] Without regard for the historical accuracy of the songs, and with great success, Ramsay and a few peers composed new texts for old tunes.[4] *The Miscellany* eventually comprised four volumes and went through no fewer than fifteen official editions. Many pirated editions also appeared. I have identified a remarkable total of thirty-seven editions.[5] By the 1740s Ramsay's work had become the standard source book

---

3. Allan Ramsay was a wig maker and professed little musical ability, but he was a very active patron and promoter of the visual, literary, and dramatic arts. See Martin Burns, *Allan Ramsay, A Study of His Life and Works* (Cambridge: Harvard University Press, 1931).

4. David Johnson, *Music and Society in Lowland Scotland in the Eighteenth Century* (London: Oxford University Press, 1972), 134, 143.

5. For a list of these editions see Moulton, "Scotland in Music," appendix B.

Musical Landskips

for Scottish songs. It was regularly plundered by other editors who were creating their own songbooks, and it also filtered into theater and literary works, with John Gay's *The Beggar's Opera* being one of the best examples.[6]

Like many songbooks printed during the century, the *Tea-Table Miscellany* initially contained only the words of the songs. Music was not provided, although Ramsay did indicate the name of the tune to which each song should be sung. The texts largely conform to the pastoral genre, with stock pastoral names appearing throughout, such as Chloe, Phoebus, Lydia, and Cynthia, often located in fields, in meadows, and at brooksides. But Ramsay laced the poetry with Scottish words, and swains and nymphs named Jean, Jenny, Jockey, and so forth, sitting not by the stream but by the burn or on the brae. Ramsay recast Scotland as Arcadia.[7]

Ramsay's work was soon competing with William Thomson's newly published and successful *Orpheus Caledonius*, printed with music in London in 1725 and marketed to Britain's elite. Ramsay was outdone by Thomson's printing of music, and he responded the following year with an addendum to his book that included music with harmonizations by Alexander Stuart.[8] He was particularly incensed by Thomson's unacknowledged borrowing of many of the *Miscellany's* texts. However, Ramsay's work still maintained its popularity, and he gently reproached Thomson in the preface to his ninth edition (1733), saying he "ought to have acquainted his illustrious list of subscribers, that most of the songs were mine, the music abstracted."[9] It is a sign of Ramsay's generosity that he is included in the list of subscribers to Thomson's second edition, printed in London in 1733.

A native of Scotland, William Thomson (ca. 1684–ca. 1760) moved to London and became a court musician known for his singing of Scottish songs.[10]

---

6. For a literary example see Walter Scott's reference to the work in his famous 1814 novel *Waverly: Or, 'Tis Sixty Years Since'* (New York: Signet Classics, 1964), 114.

7. Matthew Benjamin Gelbart, "Scotland and the Emergence of 'Folk Music' and 'Art Music' in Europe, 1720–1850" (PhD diss., University of California, Berkeley, 2002), 95.

8. *Musick for Allan Ramsay's Collection of Scots Songs* is now an extremely rare publication, and it does not seem to have had much success. See Johnson, *Lowland Scotland*, 251.

9. *Tea-Table Miscellany*, 9th ed. (London, 1733), 7.

10. Little is known about William Thomson's life, although Henry George Farmer has written about him and his songbook in *A History of Music in Scotland* (London: Hinrichsen, 1947) and in his foreword to a reprint of the second edition of William

213

Partially due to his court position, *Orpheus Caledonius* was popular among English aristocrats. Before it was printed, Thomson had a large list of subscribers who pre-purchased 292 copies. For the second edition (1733) this number more than doubled to 598 subscribers, who purchased a total of 693 books before printing.[11] The collection was issued in two handsome volumes, with the first dedicated to Queen Caroline and the second to the Duchess of Hamilton. Thomson held the attention—and money—of Britain's elite, even securing a royal license from the king to hold the rights to the publication for fourteen years (including the rights to the songs by Ramsay).

Several decades later at the peak of the century's songbook production, the Scottish engraver James Johnson (1750–1811) began publishing his multi-volume *The Scots Musical Museum* (1787–1803). The publication is one of the most famous, in large part because the famous Scottish poet Robert Burns was a major contributor to the work. Burns joined in the venture when the first volume was being published, and he became the primary editor, compiler, and writer for what would amount to a six-volume work containing some 600 songs.[12] In meeting the aims proclaimed in the title—to collect and present a museum—Burns was primarily concerned with collecting Scottish songs and not with selling them to the English aristocracy. He seemed more driven by patriotism, and he continually insisted that he not be paid for his work, even when he needed financial support. In a letter to another editor, George Thomson, Burns refused payment, saying it would be "downright sodomy of the soul!"[13] The publication included melodies set to simple, figured accompaniments by Stephen Clarke.[14] Yet despite its simplicity, or perhaps because of it, each volume sold out and was reprinted several different times and in multiple locations, including Edinburgh, London, and Glasgow.[15]

Thomson, *Orpheus Caledonius: A Collection of Scots Songs* (1733; reprint, Hatboro, PA: Folklore Associates, 1962).

11. Farmer, foreword to *Orpheus*, iii, v.

12. Farmer, *History*, 255.

13. J. Cuthbert Hadden, *George Thomson, The Friend of Burns: His Life and Correspondence* (London: John C. Nimmo, 1898), 141.

14. Farmer, *History*, 255.

15. George Henry Farmer explains that "obscurities . . . have clouded the Museum from the birth. . . . God forbid that anyone should devote a lifetime—it could not be done in less—in attempting to collect and collate a complete corpus of every issue of the Museum"; in the foreword to James Johnson, ed., *The Scots Musical Museum*, ed. William Stenhouse (Hatboro, PA: Folklore Associates, 1962), xxiii.

The texts are far more Scottish than those in the *Miscellany* or *Orpheus Caledonius*. Arcadian places and people have almost completely disappeared, having been replaced by Scottish places populated with various lads and lassies, although an occasional nymph or swain wanders onto the scene. The themes are similar to those found in pastoral poetry, but they have a rough candor about them that distinguishes them from the idyllic Mediterranean genre. Burns, like his predecessors, continued to use the Scottish vocabulary, intermingled with English. But in his masterful poetic style Burns crafted lyrics that seem strikingly sincere in comparison with his predecessors' often trite, pastoral poetry.

Burns was also the primary contributor to George Thomson's (1757–1851) *A Select Collection of Original Scottish Airs*, which also eventually comprised six volumes (1793–1841). Thomson's work is most well known today because of the celebrities whom he assembled to assist as arrangers, such as Pleyel, Kozeluch, Hummel, Haydn, and Beethoven. In addition to Burns, he also turned to the well-known poets Scott, Hogg, and Byron to assist with the lyrics. As an amateur musician, he hoped to elevate Scottish music to a higher artistic standard.[16] Thomson worked on the *Collection* in his spare time and financed the project primarily with his own money. Yet this government clerk had no difficulty critiquing his esteemed contributors. He was conscious of the general lack of musical proficiency among his potential patrons, and in many of his letters to arrangers he requested that the composers simplify their accompaniments to suit the amateur British musicians. The issue became a particularly contentious and recurring one with Beethoven.[17]

In general Thomson tried to preserve the original lyrics of the songs, but he also felt compelled to sanitize any pieces that were too bawdy or ribald. In adding "improved" accompaniments and lyrics, Thomson hoped to outdo his competitors. Concerning other songbooks he remarked that "there were no symphonies to introduce and close the airs, and the accompaniments (for the piano or harpsichord only) were meagre and commonplace, while the words were in a great many cases such as could not be tolerated or sung in good society."[18] He

---

16. Thomson's primary biographer is J. Cuthbert Hadden (see note 13).
17. Hadden, *George Thomson*, 234–25, 344; Barry Cooper, *Beethoven* (Oxford: Oxford University Press, 2008), 300; see also Barry Cooper, *Beethoven's Folksong Settings: Chronology, Sources, Style* (Oxford: Clarendon, 1994).
18. Hadden, *George Thomson*, 23.

was particularly critical, and likely envious, of Johnson and his *Musical Museum*, which was dull-looking and less expensive, but which sold better.

Many contextual factors influenced the production of these and the many other songbooks during the eighteenth century. The English interest was bolstered by Britain's increased wealth in the century and the changing English-Scottish political climate. This English attraction was not without some irony, however, since significant tension had existed between the two nations for centuries. Although intended to reconcile bad blood, the 1707 union of England and Scotland was perceived by many in Scotland as a forced marriage, precipitating two military conflicts in 1715 and 1745. But as the century wore on, Scotland gradually became a generally congenial partner, so that by the 1780s (and with the concurrent spike in songbook production) the two earlier revolts were generally regarded as romantic memories instead of signs of imminent violence. However, tensions still remained high for some. The Scot James Boswell's journal contains a vivid account of English disdain for the Scottish people as late as 1762:

> At night I went to Covent Garden and saw . . . a new comic opera, for the first night. . . . Just before the overture began to be played, two Highland officers came in. The mob in the upper gallery roared out, "No Scots! No Scots! Out with them!," hissed and pelted them with apples. My heart warmed to my countrymen, my Scotch blood boiled with indignation. I jumped up on the benches, roared out, "Damn you, you rascals!," hissed and was in the greatest rage. . . . I hated the English; I wished from my soul that the Union was broke and that we might give them another battle of Bannockburn.[19]

The love-hate relationship between nations underscores the complex, paradoxical English interest in Scottish songbooks.

Audience attraction

Turning to native music served different functions for the two contrasting nations. For the English, these simple songs appealed to their growing interest in romanticizing other places and the past; for the Scottish, who were experiencing a national identity crisis, looking to music of the past shored up their

---

19. *Boswell's London Journal, 1762–1763*, 2nd ed., edited by Frederick A. Pottle (New Haven: Yale University Press, 2004), 71–72.

independent history and cultural identity. It was during the 1760s that James Macpherson first published his influential *Poems of Ossian*. The work can be seen as an attempt to establish a Celtic identity for Scotland that distanced it from its Anglo-Saxon neighbors, but for many in and out of Scotland, the *Poems of Ossian* were an artistic and historic phenomenon that incited interest in folk tales and folk music.[20] Claire Nelson has convincingly argued that *Ossian* led to a flood of Scottish songs.[21]

One particularly pronounced reason for the English attraction was the strong contemporary interest in primitivism, which the Scottish people, particularly the Highlanders, were thought to exemplify. Theories about the advancement of humans from a primitive to a refined state became especially prominent during this time. Interestingly, Scottish Enlightenment figures such as Adam Smith, Adam Ferguson, John Millar, and William Robertson were foremost in the development of these social evolution theories.[22] All societies, it was believed, progressed through these "stages of mankind." For "civilized" European societies, "primitive" cultures were viewed as fossils of the past living in the present, and Scotland provided an observation deck.[23]

The Highlands experienced an increase in tourism at the end of the eighteenth century as a partial result of this popular interest in primitivism. At this time, John Lane Buchanan, a missionary for the Church of Scotland, wrote about his experiences living on the Isle of Harris in the Outer Hebrides of Scotland. His account reads like an ethnography of a foreign people. He describes the customs and daily life of these primitive British citizens who lived in wood and mud huts that he and others thought worse than the living conditions of the American Indians.[24] Another traveler, Charles Burney, also viewed

---

20. Gelbart, "Scotland," 110–118; Murray G. H. Pittock, *The Invention of Scotland: The Stuart Myth and the Scottish Identity, 1638 to the Present* (New York: Routledge, 1991); Paul F. Moulton, "Of Bards and Harps: The Influence of Ossian on Musical Style" (MM thesis, Florida State University, 2005).

21. Claire Nelson, "Tea-Table Miscellanies: The Development of Scotland's Song Culture, 1720–1800," *Early Music* 28, no. 4 (2000): 602–603.

22. See Harro M. Höpf, "From Savage to Scotsman: Conjectural History in the Scottish Enlightenment," *The Journal of British Studies* 17, no. 2 (1978): 19–40; and Alan Swingewood, "Origins of Sociology: The Case of the Scottish Enlightenment," *The British Journal of Sociology* 21, no. 2 (1970): 164–180.

23. Gelbart, "Scotland," 104, 109, 110.

24. John Lane Buchanan, *Travels in the Western Hebrides, from 1782–1790*, introduction by Alasdair Maclean (1793; reprint, Waternish, Scotland: Maclean, 1997).

Scotland in primitivist terms, while making puzzling comparisons of Scottish music with ancient Greek and Chinese music.[25]

Evidence of the primitiveness of Scottish music was often found in its artlessness. Social "evolution" was actually seen by some as devolution, as European philosophers believed that the artifice of advanced societies was shallow and corrupt and that primitive simplicity and gracefulness expressed something emotionally more pure. William Tytler commented in his "Dissertation" of 1783 that the music of Scotland was unburdened with the degenerative artifice of society and its philosophies, claiming that "from their artless simplicity, it is evident, that the Scottish melodies are derived from very remote antiquity."[26] He later bragged that "As the Scottish songs are the flights of genius, devoid of art, they bid defiance to artificial graces and affected cadences."[27]

William Thomson, in the prefatory poem of his *Orpheus Caledonius*, seemed to be selling attractive primitivism to his aristocratic patrons. Thomson gently extols the virtues of these songs to young English lovers:

> You Beaus and Belles so fine and fair,
> Here learn to love, and be sincere; . . .
> You falsly vow, and whine, and sigh,
> And make no Conscience of a Lye;
> Oh! How can Beaus fair Belles deceive?
> Or why will Belles fine Beaus believe?
> Love's brightest Flames warm Scottish Lads,
> Tho' cooly clad in High-land Plads . . .[28]

---

25. Charles Burney, *A General History of Music: From the Earliest Ages to the Present Period*, 2 vols. (1789; reprint, New York: Harcourt, Brace, 1935), 1:45–46; William Tytler makes a similar connection between Scottish music and Greek music in his "Dissertation on Scottish Music," in *Poetical Remains of James the First, King of Scotland* (Edinburgh: J. and E. Balfour, 1783), 233.

26. Tytler, "Dissertation," 196.

27. Tytler, "Dissertation," 237. See also Lois Whitney, *Primitivism and the Idea of Progress in English Popular Literature of the Eighteenth Century* (Baltimore: Johns Hopkins Press, 1934); and Joseph Ritson, "A Historical Essay on Scottish Song," a preface to *Scotish* [sic] *Songs*, 2 vols. (London: J. Johnson and J. Egerton, 1794), lxxxiii.

28. William Thomson, *Orpheus Caledonius or a Collection of the best Scotch Songs set to Musick by William Thomson* (London: printed for the author at his house in Leicester Fields, 1726), 1.

He preaches that the English gentry can learn something about love from the simple Scottish people, who express love more purely, even passionately, than their "fine and fair" English brothers and sisters.

Images of lower-class flirtations must have amused the social elite with their portrayal of vulgar love. Some of Thomson's songs present amusing ways to seduce a lover in the cold weather of Scotland. In "Come Hap Me with Thy Petticoat," we find a literal skirt-chasing song. The male narrator says that he is "starving cold, while thou art warm," and he pleads for her to have pity on him and wrap him in that "charming petticoat of thine." In a reversal of genders, a female narrator in "The Highland Laddie" makes a similar request of her male lover. In the verses of this song she praises the masculine qualities of the Highland laddie over his Lowland counterparts and pines, "When I was sick and like to die, He row'ed [rolled] me in his Highland Plaidy [cloak]." The sexual innuendo is obvious, and likely delighted the English gentlefolk.

Ramsay similarly seemed attuned to the primitive—via bawdiness. Dedicating his *Tea-Table Miscellany* "To ilka [each] lovely British lass," he promises in the dedication that singing the songs may "ward you frae the sowr, and gayley vacant minutes pass" (ward you from the sour, and gaily vacant minutes pass). Sexual images abound in the song texts, surely helping him to fulfill his promised entertainment. In "The Lass of Peaty's Mill," for example, he describes a bonny lass. Such a poem would definitely amuse and drive away the "sowr" emotions of an uneventful and idle day.

> Her Arms, white, round and smooth,
> Breasts rising in their dawn,
> To age it would give youth,
> To press 'em with his hand.
> Thro' all my spirits ran
> An extasy of bliss,
> When I such sweetness sand [sic]
> Wrapt in a balmy kiss.[29]

---

29. The preface quotation and the song text come from Ramsay, *Tea-Table Miscellany*, 9th ed. (London, 1733).

Seeking a more sanitized path several decades later, George Thomson sought to edit out the sexual innuendos and present a work that would be acceptable to a more virtuous audience. In the Preface he says that he "has been scrupulously careful to remove those doggerel rhymes only by which the music has been debased; giving place to none inconsistent with that delicacy of the sex, which in too many publications of this sort has been shamefully disregarded."[30] Despite his high aim, he still included a few songs, similar to those in William Thomson's work, that might incite blushed giggling, such as "Come Under my Plaidy,"[31] which describes a sixty-two-year-old man successfully wooing a woman half his age. But the song is not explicit and thus maintains some modesty. Fifty years earlier, William Thomson had included similar songs, although more in number. Although intended for the same elite class, George Thomson's more sterilized publications show that he was not aware of the sexual interests of the upper class. His lackluster sales may partially be the result of this decision, coupled with his desire to make Scottish music more artful and less primitive.

However, George Thomson's volumes do contain other aspects that extol primitivism. Each volume includes one or two interesting engravings that depict various Scottish images. The frontispiece of volume 2, for example, depicts an elderly couple in their cottage (see Figure 2).[32] It is a humble home with a set of bagpipes on a corner shelf, an oversized cat, and a kettle on the fire. The engraving, by Thomson's brother Paten Thomson, is inspired by the song "John Anderson, My Jo [joy],"[33] which describes an old married couple, with the wife doting over her husband and reminiscing about the past.

The engraving at the end of volume 2 portrays a related theme but different setting. Subtitled "The "Birks [birch] of Ivermay," it depicts lovers seated beneath a birch tree (see Figure 3). She is reclined against his lap and looks dreamily towards the picturesque landscape to which he gestures. The landscape is not drawn with great detail, but the area is hilly and dotted with sheep. Clearly the scene is pastoral; however, the figures are not dressed like shepherds and nymphs

---

30. George Thomson, *A Select Collection of Original Scottish Airs, for the Voice. With Introductory and Concluding Symphonies and Accompaniments for the Piano Forte, Violin & Violincello by Pleyel Kozeluch & Haydn.* . . . (London: T. Preston, 1814).

31. The song is found in volume 4 of the *Select Collection*, 1814 edition, 171.

32. The images in figures 2 and 3 come from the *Select Collection*, 1814 edition.

33. The song's text is by Burns and the accompaniment is by Kozeluch, 1:51.

Musical Landskips

Figure 2. Frontispiece engraving of volume 2 of George Thomson's *Select Collection*

Figure 3. End engraving of volume 2 of Thomson's *Select Collection*

but in eighteenth-century clothing, within a Scottish setting. The dandy's gesture towards the sheep-dotted hills mirrors the beckoning of the songbooks, which similarly invite the English to look to the wildness of Scotland.

Related to the interest in primitivism was a fascination with the past. The songbooks from the first half of the eighteenth century simply purport to be collections of "Scots Tunes," but reference to "curious," "old," "ancient," and "original," become increasingly common during the last half of the century, with several claiming to contain songs "some of which [have] never before [been] printed."[34]

Johnson's *Scots Musical Museum* was concerned with musical artifacts. It was intended for the antiquarians of Scotland, but it tickled the fancy of a much wider audience in both Scotland and England. Reacting to embellished and ornamented contemporary works by publishers like Thomson, Johnson proudly declared the authenticity of the book's content on the cover page: "In this publication the original simplicity of our Ancient National Airs is retained unencumbered with useless Accompaniments & graces depriving the hearers of the sweet simplicity of their native melodies."[35]

The drive to collect and publish songs during the century was partially motivated by the fear that native songs would soon be lost.[36] John Hawkins, in his *History*, noted his belief that the Scottish songs must have been originally written down, but had been lost and thus transmitted by oral tradition. He believed, however, that "they seem not to have been corrupted."[37] Hawkins's logic may be faulty, but his belief in the purity of the Scottish songs was likely shared by his contemporaries. Although many songbook editors freely altered the texts, ultimately it was the old Scottish tunes that were more valued for their historical purity, and the song texts were, as Burns said, only a "vehicle to the music."[38]

Recognizing one's connection to the past provides a psychological grounding for members of any culture. The Scottish song collections represented for

---

34. See Moulton, "Scotland in Music," appendix A.
35. Johnson, *The Scots Musical Museum*, xviii.
36. Susan Stewart, "Scandals of the Ballad," *Representations* 32 (Autumn 1990): 135.
37. John Hawkins, *A General History of the Science and Practice of Music*, 2 vols. (J. Alfred Novello, 1853; reprint, New York: Dover, 1963), 563.
38. Quoted in Mary Ellen B. Lewis, "'The joy of my heart': Robert Burns as Folklorist," *Scottish Studies* 20 (1976): 48.

the Scots a personal link to something enduring. English citizens could also participate in singing Scottish songs and enjoy a shared kinship with their new British co-citizens.[39] Songbooks were of particular value because they presented authentic artifacts from history that could be recreated through performance. They shored up one's personal connection to the past and the primitive through active performance, rather than passive reading.

Songbooks in the Drawing Room

To further understand the English attraction to these songbooks, I now turn to the way they functioned within drawing rooms of wealthy patrons. The Scottish songs would likely have been performed in the separated space of the drawing room—an elegant room used for withdrawing from everyday life. It was common in drawing rooms to have artwork displayed, and by the middle of the eighteenth century landscape paintings, called landskips at the time,[40] were often part of the decor. In the fifteenth century landscape artists had begun to provide more detail in their paintings, although at that time they functioned primarily as backdrops.[41] Eighteenth-century landskips increasingly focused on natural scenery, although people and buildings were also frequently part of the setting.

Landskips were sometimes painted on canvas, but they were often painted directly onto walls and furniture. The most common place for landskips was above the fireplace mantle. Other preferred spots were door panels, walls, harpsichord interiors, and chimney boards.[42] A landskip served as a decoration that brought the outdoors inside and introduced nature to the urban dwelling. In describing the landskip as a form of interior decoration, Edward Casey wrote,

---

39. Most authors on the subject focus on the way the Scottish songbooks contributed to a national identity (see Johnson, *Lowland Scotland*, 188), but none, to my knowledge, have adequately addressed the reasons that the English were also interested in the songs.

40. See "Landscape," *Oxford English Dictionary*, 2nd ed. (Oxford: Clarendon, 1989), 8:628.

41. For example, Giotto's and Simone Martini's fourteenth-century paintings depict very little landscape. When painters added perspective to their paintings landscapes became more detailed, as seen in the works of fifteenth-century painters like Jan van Eyck, Hieronymus Bosch, and Leonardo da Vinci.

42. Edward S. Casey, *Representing Place: Landscape Painting and Maps* (Minneapolis: University of Minnesota Press, 2002), 4, 12; see also Nina Fletcher Little, *American Decorative Wall Paintings, 1700–1850* (New York: E. P. Dutton, 1972).

"Landscape is not just let in by the back door or by the side windows, it is allowed to flourish in the midst of daily living."[43]

In our efforts to understand the use of songbooks, it is helpful to compare them with landskip paintings. They proliferated at the same time, inhabited the same space, and seem to have functioned in similar ways. The landskip's "reemplacement" of nature indoors, to borrow a phrase from Casey,[44] parallels Scottish songbooks and the way they brought Scotland inside. As the figures and place-names of Scotland were evoked in music, the image of Scotland was recreated, or reemplaced, within the drawing room.

Scottish songbooks served in part as visual decorations. The handsome publications and engravings of George Thomson, for example, contained music intended for performance, but the books themselves were also meant to be seen. Merely displaying the books, without performing the songs in them, was a way of bringing Scotland indoors. Musical performances could also function as aural decorations. Just as the owners of drawing rooms decorated and furnished the rooms according to their own tastes, they could also use music to construct an aural environment to their liking. Performing songs such as the popular "The Highland Laddie" was akin to having a temporary landskip painting of the Scottish Highlands hanging above the fireplace.

Also helpful in understanding the function of Scottish songbooks is the Claude glass. Painters and tourists in the late eighteenth and early nineteenth centuries regularly carried this device, which contained a small mirror named for the seventeenth-century painter Claude Lorrain. To use it, the viewer turned his back to the object and held up the mirror slightly to his side.[45] Painters used the glass to imitate Lorrain's picturesque landscape paintings.

The mirror thus framed the subject, blocking out the less impressive landscape and objects that might ruin the view. Often the mirrors were oval and the lens convex, so that the image was circumscribed by a graceful line and given a painterly perspective. The mirrors were often overlaid with colored lenses in gray, blue, yellow, or hoar-frost, creating an image that was tinted with a subdued and

---

43. Casey, *Representing Place*, 13.
44. Ibid., xv, 19.
45. My ideas about the Claude glass are influenced by Malcolm Andrews's discussion about tourism in Britain; see *The Search for the Picturesque: Landscape Aesthetics and Tourism in Britain, 1760–1800* (Aldershot: Scolar, 1989).

unifying hue. Tourists would turn their back on nature and consider the framed and tinted images in the glass more picturesque than the actual place itself.

Scottish songbooks operated in a similar manner. Drawing-room audiences were not actually listening to the authentic music of Scotland, but to a framed and tinted version of it. The aural reproduction of Scottish folksongs was visually tinted through music notation, which appeared within the framed shape of the page.

The songs within the books were inevitably altered to make them more picturesque for the listeners. As mentioned above, changes were abundant in all the works, with George Thomson being the most zealous editor of bawdy texts. All of the editors also applied various musical lenses to make the music conform to the expectations of the patrons. These subtle filters can be discerned and brought into view by comparing multiple edited versions. "The Highland Laddie" appears in all four books, first in Ramsay's *Miscellany* with the text likely by Ramsay himself. A close look at this song's musical settings (excluding Ramsay's, since the *Miscellany* contained only text) reveals the Claude-glass-like lenses that color the music.

The melody of "The Highland Laddie" is clearly based on a pentatonic scale. Scottish melodies often emphasize the interval of a minor third, and most scholars of Scottish music refer to the "gapped" pentatonic scale as one of the central features of the style.[46] In William Thomson's setting, the melody is based upon the pentatonic scale of G A B D E, and accordingly the tune regularly skips the "missing" C and F of the melody. Only two exceptions occur, when C is treated as a passing tone (see mm. 2 and 6 in Figure 4). The ornamental nature of these two exceptions may indicate that the notes were added by William Thomson in preparing the music for his English audience.

Thomson's bass line confirms that he was comfortable altering the pentatonic quality of the tune. Although simple, the bass line completely changes the harmonic make-up of the melody. Thomson sets the melody in G major, and thus regularly employs the missing C in the bass line, which functions as either the root of the subdominant chord or the first inversion of the supertonic.

---

46. David Johnson addresses the challenge songbook composers have had in trying to harmonize gapped scales, double-tonic sequences, and endings on notes other than tonic; see Johnson, *Lowland Scotland*, 150.

Figure 4. "The Highland Laddie," in Thomson's *Orpheus Caledonius*

Consequently the pentatonic tune is framed as a diatonic one, and the added harmonies obscure the melody's Scottish characteristics.

The same piece in Johnson's *Scots Musical Museum* shows additional alterations.[47] One immediately discernable difference is that Johnson's setting is longer, containing both a verse and a chorus, whereas Thomson's version contained only the humorous chorus. The chorus melody of both songs is the same, although here the pentatonic melody is transposed down a fifth (based on C D E G A). Johnson's arranger, Stephen Clarke, managed to avoid F and B in the verse, but in the chorus he inserted some pronounced Fs (see mm. 10 and 14 in Figure 5). Interestingly, Clarke filled in the gaps in different places than Thomson did.

Clarke's awkward harmonic setting in the key of C major also obscures the pentatonic nature of the melody. He included a simple but rather crude figured bass for the accompaniment. In the bass line a foreign F appears regularly, although not as a likely subdominant; it often acts more like an upper neighbor tone for the bass line (see mm. 4 and 7 in Figure 5). Near the beginning of the chorus Clarke clumsily treats the out-of-place F in the melody as the seventh of a dominant G chord, which then resolves to the tonic at the beginning of the next phrase (see mm. 10–11 in Figure 5). This rather dramatic cadence here seems out of place. Clarke used the chord to emphasize the highest part of the melody, but instead of dramatizing the melodic peak the mis-harmonization undermines the intended effect. The awkward harmonization, however, produces an unintentionally primitive-sounding result.

In contrast, George Thomson's setting completely transforms the song into a more sophisticated work.[48] The text largely parallels Ramsay's original, with a few alterations made for virtue's sake. Thomson also changed the title to conform to the first line of the text, "The Lawland lads think they are fine."

Thomson asked Pleyel to write the accompaniment for the "The Highland Laddie," with opening and closing "symphonies," which were short but elaborate introductions and codas (see Figure 6). Although the songbook indicates that the text is set to the tune "The Highland Laddie," Pleyel set it to an entirely different tune and proceeded to write a vocal duet with extravagant piano accompaniment. Melodically the tune has pentatonic qualities, with the leading tone regularly skipped (see the treble voice in Figure 6). But Pleyel's Austro-

---

47. "The Highland Laddie" appears in the first volume of the *Museum*, 22.
48. The song appears in volume 2, 78.

Figure 5. Johnson's "The Highland Laddie," arranged by Stephen Clarke

German sensibilities required the regular inclusion of the leading tone to create effective harmonization. Perhaps compensating for the Continental sound, he tried to infuse it with a Scottish sound by adding the cliché of the Scottish snap (see m. 4 in Figure 6). Neither of the versions by the native Scots includes the snap, however. Pleyel's setting is lively, inventive, and harmonically lush. Of all

Figure 6. Excerpt from Pleyel's setting of "The Highland Laddie" in *Select Collection*

three settings this is the most inauthentic but also the best crafted piece musically speaking.

In terms of authenticity, all versions under discussion here might be considered equally credible. The differences reveal the transformation a piece undergoes when it is written down; folk-song scholars often describe and lament the "freezing" process that results from an aural song's being transfixed in notation.[49] But my tracking of this song in songbooks over the course of a century shows that the text and the music continued to undergo alteration despite being notated and published. The music changed as a result of the editor's and his patrons' personal preferences in a way that is similar to a folk performer who adapts his singing to correspond to the events and audience that surround him. Notated music can undergo some of the same changes often solely associated with aural practice, and the songbooks themselves may be seen as part of a fluid tradition.

In adapting and arranging the songs for what were often aristocratic and foreign audiences, the arrangers and publishers fundamentally transformed the music. Much like a landskip painting that took scenery out of its context, songbooks reframed musical depictions of place. In the process of recontextualizing the song, the music itself was framed and tinted, as if through a Claude glass, to make it more fitting as parlor music.

Taming the Scots

Let me provide one example of music performed in the drawing room, focusing on Queen Caroline (1683–1737), the dedicatee of William Thomson's *Orpheus Caledonius*. This queen hosted frequent evening entertainments in her drawing room, at which Thomson, himself a singer at the court, may have performed. Kensington Palace was the preferred residence of Queen Caroline and George II, each of whom had their own drawing rooms, which were lavishly decorated with paintings. Keyboards were included among the furnishings.

Caroline was known for her education and thoughtfulness; Voltaire described her as "a delightful philosopher on the throne."[50] She was also interested in gardening, and particularly in the characteristic English style of making the

---

49. See the summary of the difference between folk and classical music in Johnson, *Lowland Scotland*, 15.

50. Stephen Taylor, "Caroline (1683–1737)," *Oxford Dictionary of National Biography* (Oxford: Oxford University Press, 2004), http://www.oxforddnb.com/view/article/4720 (accessed 2 July 2007).

landscape more natural. In her gardening endeavors she commented that her desire was in "helping nature, not losing it in art."[51] Undoubtedly the Scots vocabulary in the songs was challenging to this native German queen, but if her interest in music mirrored her interest in gardening, she would have preferred the coarse and primitive naturalness of the Scots.

In the course of an evening's activities, Queen Caroline and her guests might have withdrawn into her Kensington Palace drawing room. The notion of a "withdrawing room" describes the area's function as a place where a small group disengaged from their daily routines and distracted themselves from their cares. Cloistered within the luxuriously decorated room, in a palace that was in turn surrounded by acres of gardens, Queen Caroline and her guests inhabited a space that was made quasi-sacred by its separation from the outer world.

It was in the separate space of the drawing room that the Scottish songs would have been performed and the figures and place-names of Scotland "re-emplaced." For patrons in their drawing rooms the songbooks not only framed Scotland's music and made it more picturesque, like a landskip painting or a Claude glass, but they also kept the land's wildness at a distance. Performing or listening to Scotland's music in a drawing room was akin to a brief tourist experience within one's own home.

These drawing-room tourists were attracted to the historic, primitive, scenic nature of Scotland, but most lacked either the time, money, or perhaps desire to observe the real thing and actually encounter the natives. When they wanted to be entertained with the place of Scotland, they would withdraw to a separate place, perform Scottish songs, and momentarily imagine the people and places of Scotland. Kenneth McNeil described a parallel process for visitors to the Highlands: "Travelers to the Highlands from the eighteenth century onward constructed themselves as outsiders to the Highlands who must . . . journey into the Highlands from someplace else and eventually journey out."[52] Writing about his journey to the Highlands and western islands of Scotland, Samuel Johnson wrote, "We were now to leave the Hebrides, where we have spent some weeks with sufficient amusement, and where we had amplified our thoughts

---

51. Ibid.
52. Kenneth Michael McNeil, "Inside and Outside the Nation: Highland Identity in Nineteenth Century Britain" (PhD diss., The Ohio State University, 1998), 201.

with new scenes of nature, and new modes of life."[53] Within the drawing room the English songbook audiences could likewise journey into the books. After they had spent time imagining Scotland and being amused with the "new scenes of nature, and new modes of life," they could close the book and leave the place of Scotland.

The deluge of Scottish songbooks in the eighteenth century appeased the Scottish sense of nationalism, but the English responded differently. The paradoxical English attraction to the music of their disgruntled neighbor can be viewed neither as pure adoration nor as political assimilation. In actuality, the songbooks simultaneously enamored the English to Scotland, while also keeping the Scots at a safe distance. The songbooks tamed both the "wildness" of the tunes, and, in the minds of the patrons, the place and people of Scotland.

---

53. Samuel Johnson, *A Journey to the Western Islands of Scotland*, introduction and notes by J. D. Fleeman (Oxford: Clarendon Press, 1985), 130.

Censoring the Censor: Karl Glossy's Selective Transcription (1897) of Karl Hägelin's Directive on Viennese Theatrical Censorship (1795)

LISA DE ALWIS

The disastrous 1927 fire at the Viennese *Justizpalast* destroyed, among other things, a large number of original documents regarding theatrical and musical censorship from the late eighteenth and early nineteenth centuries. In Vienna today, scholars joke that the advantage of this is that they can simply blame the blaze when they are unable to locate a certain document. While this may indeed be convenient, it is not always accurate. There are still a number of surviving manuscripts, such as the one about censorship I shall discuss here, that will add to our knowledge of cultural life in eighteenth-century Austria.

In the years following the outbreak of the French revolution, Austrian writers who had enjoyed a period of relative freedom under Joseph II were subjected to severe censorship. Francis II, famously concerned that a similar uprising could occur on Austrian soil, curtailed the activities of publishers and restricted public gatherings throughout the empire. Practically the only place that people were allowed to come together was at the theater, and it was therefore in the government's interest to closely control what material was allowed onto the stage. The censorship of theatrical works was entrusted to Franz Karl Hägelin who, by 1795 when he wrote the document under consideration here, had been carrying out his duties for twenty-five years. In order to form an accurate picture of eighteenth- and nineteenth-century theatrical and musical works in Vienna, we need to familiarize ourselves with methods of censorship and the criteria according to which censors passed their judgments. The relative decline in the quality of Viennese theatrical pieces after Mozart's time is inextricably related to censorship, but even Mozart's works and those of his contemporaries were affected; after all, Hägelin's career began in 1770 under Empress Maria Theresia. In the *Hof- und Staats-Schematismen*, Hägelin's name can be found in the list of censors, where he is placed together with all of the book censors. This catalog of Habsburg employees does not mention that he was the only censor responsible for theatrical works.[1] Hägelin's name can also be found on copies

---

1. Hägelin is listed as a *nieder-österreichischer Regierungsrath* (lower Austrian senior civil servant), an honorary title that was conferred on men who had served Austria by working in their fields for a long time. Felix Czeike, *Historisches Lexikon Wien* (Vienna: Kremayr und Scheriau, 1994), s.v. "Hägelin."

of various plays and librettos, where he sometimes commented extensively and added many suggestions and even corrections to the texts. He was active in his work from 1770 until 1805, witnessing the profound political upheavals that rocked the Empire and participating in the formation of the increasingly restrictive system of government that defines the Biedermeier period.

This essay is really a tale of two men and a document. We know Hägelin's writings largely because of the efforts of the late-nineteenth-century scholar Karl Glossy, an important figure in Viennese life during this period (see Figure 1). His publications of manuscripts that were later destroyed form the basis of what is known about theatrical censorship in Vienna. Glossy's work is widely cited and so it is common knowledge, for example, that theatrical censorship needed to be stricter than other types of censorship and that lovers in a play or opera could not kiss on stage or exit it together.

Glossy was born in the turbulent year of 1848 and a considerable amount of his work is devoted to studying various aspects of the cultural ramifications of that year's revolution, particularly in the area of censorship. In 1889, he became the director of the Stadt und Landesbibliothek, today the Wienbibliothek, and when the library moved to its current location at the Rathaus, Glossy gave the inauguration speech. Under his stewardship the library's holdings increased from 16,700 to 40,300 items. Glossy also acquired important Schubert, Beethoven, and Johann Strauss manuscripts that form the foundation of the library's music collection.

In 1889 Glossy helped found the Grillparzer Gesellschaft, and he also served as the editor of its yearbook until his death in 1937. He was appointed *Zensurbeirath*, or censorship advisor, in 1902. The irony of this honor can hardly have escaped him since he was an outspoken critic of censorship, at least of how it was practiced in the nineteenth century. Official censorship in some form continued almost uninterrupted in Austria until well after the Second World War. Glossy's great interest in the history of theatrical censorship is evident from the number of his publications that deal with it. As a scholar, he is known to have been somewhat generalizing in his approach, preferring to summarize rather than delve deeply into his subjects. Several scholars have also pointed out his inaccuracies and one dissertation devotes a chapter to the positive and negative aspects of his research.[2]

---

2. Helga Herberg-Solbrig "Carl Glossy" (PhD diss., University of Vienna, 1971).

One of Glossy's most important contributions to scholarship is his transcription of Hägelin's guidelines for censors in Hungary from 1795. The document was published in the seventh yearbook of the Grillparzer Gesellschaft, which appeared in 1897. A *Sonderabdruck* edition of the document incorrectly lists the original publication date as 1896. The wealth of information that Hägelin provides in the document is clear from Glossy's publication. The censor systematically proceeds through the main types of potentially objectionable material, which consist of offenses against the state, religion, and good morals. Using these categories, Hägelin further distinguishes between offensive subject matter in general and specific transgressions within the dialogue, his main point being that dialogue is easier to clean up than thematic material.

A quick glance at Glossy's publication makes it clear that he omits some material from Hägelin's memo. There are many passages where he includes ellipses, sometimes in the middle of a sentence. The natural assumption, of course, is that these omissions were made because the original document was somehow damaged or otherwise illegible. I was fortunate to discover a manuscript version of this document in the Haus-, Hof- und Staatsarchiv in Vienna.[3] I am quite sure that this is not Hägelin's original document: neither the paper nor the ink appears to be of eighteenth-century origin. Glossy hired a large number of copyists who wrote out the historical manuscripts that were of interest to him. There was even a special room in the Rathaus where they worked copying the documents, in strict *Kurrentschrift* rather than in the hybridized script that was common in the late nineteenth and early twentieth centuries (and that is more legible to readers today). I believe that this document, and the one I found subsequently in the Austrian National Library,[4] are products of Glossy's team of copyists. It is immediately clear upon comparing these manuscripts with Glossy's work that Glossy omitted single words, sentences, and entire paragraphs of Hägelin's text in his publication.

But Glossy actually believed that the faithful transcription of documents was important and even criticized a fellow scholar for not adhering to an original document in a transcription. Regarding the work from 1839 of I. E. Schlager, Glossy writes, "These contributions, although they do not always correspond textually to the original, have been repeatedly used in historical works about

---

3. Vienna, Haus-, Hof- und Staatsarchiv (hereafter HHStA) Gen. Int. 2.
4. Vienna, Österreichische Nationalbibliothek (hereafter ÖNB) HSS Ser. n. 4012.

theater of the past."⁵ The possible reasons for this sort of hypocrisy on the part of a scholar and the social and political circumstances that affected his work would provide enough material for a different study. Suffice it to say that we should be cautious in accepting at face value the work of even the most prominent Austrian scholars from this period.

The manuscripts seemed unremarkable at first since I knew their contents had already been published. The first several pages are identical to Glossy's publication and it is clear to me now why the omissions were not found earlier: why would anyone bother reading through pages of *Kurrentschrift* if there is no apparent reason to do so? Glossy's ellipses begin on the seventh page of his publication, which corresponds to the eighth page of the manuscript. From here on, one can see just by the number of ellipses used that a fair amount of Hägelin's text was omitted. Showing a few of these omitted examples (in bold in the excerpts below) will help to illustrate the significance of Glossy's distortions and the importance of eventually making Hägelin's full text available to scholars.

One immediately noticeable trend in the passages Glossy chose to omit is that he is generally more conservative than his object of study from over a hundred years earlier. For example, Glossy tries to go beyond Hägelin in trying to protect the reputations of emperors and members of the nobility:

Excerpt 1

Auch sind solche Stücke nicht zu passieren, worin die Regenten, besonders aber die vaterländischen in nachtheiligen oder herabwürdigenden Characteren geschildert werden; wie z.B. im Stücke Baumkircher von dem Kalchberg, **worin der Kaiser Friedrich III. als wahrer Lapp erscheint** so in dem Stücke von nemlichen Autor, betitelt: die Grafen von Cilly, worin die Kaiserin Barbara Gemahlin Kaisers Sigmund als ein **geiles und**	Also, such pieces in which regents, especially those of the fatherland, are represented in a disadvantageous or demeaning manner are not to be passed [by the censor]; as for example the piece *Baumkirchner* by Kalchberg, **where Emperor Frederick III appears as a real idiot** and similarly, in the piece by the same author entitled *Die Grafen von Cilly*, in which Empress Barbara, wife of Emperor Sigmund is portrayed as a **horny and** vengeful

---

5. "Diese Beiträge sind, obwohl sie textlich nicht immer dem Originale genau entsprechen, zu geschichtlichen Arbeiten über das Theater vergangener Zeiten wiederholt benützt worden"; Karl Glossy, Foreword to *Jahrbuch der Grillparzer Gesellschaft* 25 (Vienna: Carl Konegen, 1915).

Excerpt 1 continued

rachsüchtiges Weib geschildert wird, und wo der Character durch das ganze Stück verwebt ist.	woman and the character is woven into the whole piece.

Clearly it was important to Glossy to protect the reputation of a long-dead emperor, and while it was acceptable for him that an empress be portrayed as vengeful, any reference to sexual matters was taboo. In fact, most of the portions of Hägelin's text that Glossy left out concern sexuality and women in particular.

Concerning the topic of pregnancy, Glossy is especially sensitive: Hägelin often tries to instruct his fellow censors by first describing something that is generally offensive and then proceeding to give a specific example, usually out of the theatrical or operatic repertoire. In the following passage, as in numerous others, Glossy publishes Hägelin's general description but eliminates the example. "When the material or moral of a piece is against religion, the constitution or good manners, i.e. fundamentally flawed, then it cannot be condoned for performance and must be discarded." After this, Glossy proceeds to the next general description, and omits Hägelin's example of a fundamentally flawed piece in its entirety.

Excerpt 2

z. B. in der Sonnenjungfrau von Kotzebue waren zwei Hauptfehler, der erste, daß Cora oder die Sonnenjungfrau eine Art von Vestalien von ihrem Liebhaber schwanger war; und zweitens daß der König das Gelübde der Keuschheit durch den Unfall der Cora und andere Umstände bewogen, ganz aufhob, mithin sich die Moral daraus ergab, daß das Gelübde verwerflich ist, welches in einem katholischen Staate auf dem Theater nicht gelehrt werden kann. Als man es in Wien aufführen wollte, so musste der Theater Dichter Jünger das Stück beinahe neuschmelzen, die Schwangerschaft der Cora	For instance in *Die Sonnenjungfrau* by Kotzebue, there were two main mistakes: the first, that Cora, or the sun maiden, a type of vestal virgin, was pregnant by her lover; and secondly, that the king, moved by Cora's accident and other circumstances, fully annulled the vow of chastity. The consequent moral that arises is that the vow is objectionable; this cannot be taught in the theaters of a Catholic state. When they wanted to perform it in Vienna, theater poet Jünger practically had to recast the piece by eliminating Cora's pregnancy and the annulment of the statutory vow, in the case of the latter, rather

Excerpt 2 continued

und die Aufhebung des gesetzlichen Gelübdes wegschaffen, welches letztere dadurch geschah, dass statt der Aufhebung des Gesetzes in diesem besonderen Falle daran nur dispensirt wurden.	than doing away with the law, in this special case, they dispensed with it.

Another omitted passage indicates that Glossy may have felt some squeamishness with regard to the subject of pregnant women.

Excerpt 3

Charactere von **schwangeren geschwächten Frauenzimmern**, Ehebrecherinnen können eben so wenig auf das Theater gebracht werden. Es existirt ein einziges französisches Stück, wo eine geschwächte Person vorkömmt, es heißt „Eugenin" und ist unter der höchst seligen Kaiserin Königin ohne Anstoß aufgeführt worden; allein ihr Zustand ist so schonend, und delikat darin behandelt, daß er von hundertsten Zuschauer nicht wahrgenommen wird.	Characters of **pregnant, debilitated women**, adulteresses may also not be brought onto the stage. There exists one lone French piece named "Eugenin," in which a debilitated person appears, that was performed without offense during the reign of the blessed Empress Queen [Maria Theresia]; **but her condition** [that of the pregnant woman] **is handled so protectively and delicately therein, that it would not be noticed by one hundredth of the audience.**

The subject of sex was obviously of great concern to Glossy and he assiduously removed entire passages of Hägelin's text that refer to it. Interestingly, the passages Glossy removed were often an attempt on Hägelin's part to offer tamer alternatives to commonly understood sexual content, in terms of both theme and vocabulary. The following passage presents pregnancy, again described as a disease, within a list of sexual vices.

Excerpt 4

Die Ausdrücke: Hörner tragen, aufsetzen etc. sind nicht zu dulden, es heißt dafür: den Mann betrügen, die Treue verletzen, **anstatt Schwager kann Hausfreund Hausfreundschaft gedul-**	The expressions: wearing horns, putting on horns etc. are not to be tolerated, and are to be replaced by betraying the man, injuring faithfulness, **instead of brother-in-law**, *Hausfreund*, **or**

Excerpt 4 continued

det werden. Wollust, Wollüstling, Weichling sind Ausdrücke welche durch Üppigkeit ersezt werden können, auch von einer gewissen heimlichen Krankheit, von entnervten geschwächten Menschen u dergleichen kann nie die Rede sein, außer die Sache wird durch gelindere Ausdrücke bezeichnet. Begierlichkeit, Geilheit, geile Begierden sind Wörter, die im reinen Dialog nie statt haben, man kann unedle sträfliche Wünsche und Absichten nach Umständen setzen.

Hausfreundschaft can be tolerated. Lust, voluptuary, milksop, are expressions that can be replaced with lusciousness; also, there may never be talk of a certain, secret illness, of enervated, debilitated people and the like, unless the matter is described with milder expressions. Desirability, horniness, lascivious desires are words that may never occur in pure dialogue; one can set ignoble wishes and intentions according to the circumstances.

It is also interesting to note Hägelin's distaste for (and Glossy's elimination of) the common vocabulary for surgically altered male anatomy. Castratos were no longer popular on the stage during this period but even mentioning them by name was considered unacceptable.

Excerpt 5

Castrat kann durch Sopranist, Verschnittener durch Haremswächter gegeben werden. Die Wörter Freudenmädchen, Nachtnimpfen sollen auch nicht erscheinen, sie können durch Dirnen Creaturen ersezt werden. Anstatt Kuppler und Kupplerin kann Zubringer und Zubringerin oder auch Mäckler oder Unterhändler nach Umständen gesezt werden. Doch sind manchmal gedachte Wörter nicht auffallend, wenn sie nur Jemanden angedichtet wer[den,] weil die gehässigen Charactern von dieser Art wenn es auf Verführung ankömmt, wie obengesagt worden, nie erscheinen.

Castrato can be replaced with soprano and eunuch by harem guard. The words prostitute and night nymph should also not appear and can be replaced by wench [-like] creatures. Instead of pimp, provider, broker or mediator can be used according to the circumstances. Yet sometimes words that are thought are not noticeable if they are just imputed to someone, because the malicious characters of this sort (when it has to do with seduction, as mentioned above), never actually appear.

Censoring the Censor

One of the most famous and frequently quoted passages from Glossy's publication is the warning that lovers should not depart the stage together. The implication of what the lovers' departure will lead to is obvious even in Glossy's edited version of the passage, but the uncensored sentence takes on a new meaning. There are many examples in Viennese theatrical works of lovers departing the stage together that leave scholars wondering how they passed the censor. But lovers leaving the stage in order to enter a private, enclosed area is actually the conduct that Hägelin deemed problematic. Indeed of the manuscripts that he censored, he diligently crossed out these specific incidents every time they occurred.

Excerpt 6

| Die Censur hat auch darauf zu sehen, daß nie zwei verliebte Personen miteinander allein vom Theater abtreten **um sich in ein Kabinet oder Haus hineinzubegeben wodurch der Zuschauer bewogen wird, arges zu vermuthen.** | The censorship office must see to it that two lovers are never allowed to leave the theater alone **in order to betake themselves into a cabinet or house, whereby the audience member would be encouraged to suspect the worst.** |

The following excerpt is particularly important because it is a rare reference to the censoring of actual music. As in other portions of the text, Glossy preserved the general idea but removed Hägelin's specific example. The first sentence, which Glossy does include, reads as follows: "Even given that one had purified the dialogue by crossing out all ambiguities, there can nevertheless be multiple *doubles entendres* made through improvised additions, tone of voice, and emphasized speeches or pauses." Hägelin's example illustrates the point:

Excerpt 7

| z.B. in der schönen Schusterin hieß es: sie ist so vermessen, und lässt sich die Schuhe anmessen. In der Musik wurden die Worte, und läßt sich und läßt sich—wiederholt und erst nach einer Pause folgten die Worte: die Schuhe anmessen. Das Repetiren und die Pause machten also den Text zweideutig. | For instance in *Die schöne Schusterin* it reads: she is so brazen and she lets her shoes be measured. In the music the words "and she lets" "and she lets" are repeated and only after a pause, do the words "her shoes be measured" follow. The repetition and the pause therefore make the text suggestive. |

The relevant excerpt from the score of Umlauf's piece does not include a repetition or a rest in the place that Hägelin is complaining about. But there is a rather cheeky sixteenth-note figure that repeats on both the words "vermessen" (brazen) and "anmessen" (measured), which is followed by a rest (see Figure 2). This musical moment may be the reason Hägelin remembers a repetition here, but there may also have been some improvisation by the performers that he found objectionable. The appoggiatura does not occur anywhere else in the aria, and this is by far the most musically interesting phrase of the piece. The composer further emphasized the two "unsavory" places with a *fortepiano* marking, which cannot have improved Hägelin's opinion of the passage. The censors were evidently paying close attention to the music as well as to the text. Certainly, most of them would not have had the necessary knowledge or time to read a score, but they were required to attend rehearsals of operas and at least one performance, usually the first.

Of course it is difficult to ascertain the degree, if any, to which Umlauf intended to emphasize the objectionable aspects of the passage, if indeed that was his intent. The complex game of cat and mouse played between performers, librettists, and composers on the one hand and censors on the other resulted in many veiled references and inside jokes. The enjoyment that audiences derived from this game no doubt encouraged even greater creativity. Theater directors were placed squarely in the middle of these conflicts, since they surely understood and perhaps even appreciated the jokes but nevertheless needed to get new pieces past the censors in a timely manner. To this end, they sometimes engaged in forms of self-censorship, where they crossed out possibly offensive sections and thereby relieved the censors of some of their work.

These newly found passages of Hägelin's text are crucial to our understanding of theatrical and musical culture in Habsburg Austria. The sorts of slang used on stage, the kinds of situations that were deemed objectionable, the taboo of pregnancy, and the offensive potential of improvisation and musical phrasing are all issues that would not have been addressed by Hägelin had they not played a significant role in Viennese performances of his time. Commonly cited works like Glossy's and many others from nineteenth- and early twentieth-century sources are often in need of re-evaluation. The social pressures and customs that perhaps burdened Glossy and caused him to leave out relevant parts of Hägelin's text are themselves worthy of study, and the fact that an eighteenth-century censor was able to write more freely about controversial subjects than an early-twentieth-century scholar should give us pause and make us consider our own scholarly constraints and limitations.

Figure 1. Karl Glossy, photo, Wienbibliothek im Rathaus, ZPH 602, 3.5.2

Figure 2. Excerpt from Umlauf's *Die schöne Schusterin*, A-Wn, Mus. Hs. 16481

www.ingramcontent.com/pod-product-compliance
Lightning Source LLC
Chambersburg PA
CBHW050439240426
43661CB00055B/2441